Ritual, Resistance and Liberation

Ritual, Resistance and Liberation

A Global Intersectional Perspective

Edited by Jin Young Choi

Series Editor: Graham McGeoch

© the Editor and Contributors 2025

Published in 2025 by SCM Press

Editorial office
3rd Floor, Invicta House,
110 Golden Lane,
London EC1Y 0TG, UK

www.scmpress.co.uk

SCM Press is an imprint of Hymns Ancient & Modern Ltd
(a registered charity)

Hymns Ancient & Modern® is a registered trademark of
Hymns Ancient & Modern Ltd
13A Hellesdon Park Road, Norwich,
Norfolk NR6 5DR, UK

All rights reserved. No part of this publication may be reproduced,
stored in a retrieval system, or transmitted,
in any form or by any means, electronic, mechanical,
photocopying or otherwise, without the prior permission of
the publisher, SCM Press.

The Author has asserted his/her/their right under the Copyright, Designs
and Patents Act 1988 to be identified as the Author of this Work

British Library Cataloguing in Publication data

A catalogue record for this book is available
from the British Library

ISBN: 978-0-334-06635-4

EU GPSR Authorised Representative
LOGOS EUROPE, 9 rue Nicolas Poussin, 17000, LA ROCHELLE, France
E-mail: Contact@logoseurope.eu

Typeset by Regent Typesetting

Contents

Contributors vii
Foreword xi
Acknowledgements xiii

  1 Ritual Knowledge and Performance from the Margins   1
     Jin Young Choi

Part 1 Gender Oppression and Ritual

  2 The Impact of Religious Rituals and Ceremonies on Gender   21
     Gifta Angline Kumar

  3 Cultural Crossroads: Women's Ritual Participation in
     Northeast India and the Mainland   39
     Ajungla Jamir

Part 2 Colonialism and Indigenous Spiritualities of Liberation

  4 African Spiritualities and the Normalization of Ancestral
     Rituals in Brussels Afro-diasporic Contexts   59
     Christel Zogning Meli

  5 'The Absurdity of Joy': Reclaiming *Pinkster* (Pentecostal)
     Rituals as Decolonial Indigenous Expressions of Existence,
     Resistance and Solidarity   80
     Johnathan Jodamus

6 Dancing, Drinking and Feasting: Rarámuri Worship During
   Holy Week Creates an Ecclesial Third Space   95
   Ángel F. Méndez Montoya

Part 3 Trauma, Spectrality and Ritual

7 Rituals of the (Para)normal: Spectrality, Trauma and
   Liberation in Latin America   115
   Miguel M. Algranti

8 Conjure Freedom: A Womanist Perspective on Ritual   135
   Teresa L. Smallwood

Part 4 Ritual as a Site of Struggle and Transgression

9 Liberating Liturgy: Liturgy as a (Biblical) Site of Struggle   153
   Gerald O. West

10 Defiance and Democracy: Protests as Rites for Rights
   in Singapore   170
   Lynnette Xiangling Li

Part 5 Rituals of Healing and Planetary Thriving

11 Bearing Grief and Breathing Liberation: Rituals after the
   Anthropocene   187
   Cláudio Carvalhaes

12 Release from the Tyranny of the Small Self: A Modern
   Subject's Initiation into the Power of Indigenous Ritual   205
   S. Lily Mendoza

Index of Names and Subjects   223

Contributors

Miguel M. Algranti is a social anthropologist (University of Buenos Aires, 2009; PhD Universidad Nacional de las Artes, 2016). He is a founding member of the *Laboratorio de Antropología Decolonial* (LAD), Associate Professor at the Universidad Nacional de las Artes (UNA), and researcher at the Centro Argentino de Etnología Americana (CAEA-CONICET). His current research focuses on esoterism in Argentina, where he is working on topics of religious diversity, technology, memory and media.

Cláudio Carvalhaes, from Brazil, is a theologian, liturgist and artist. He is Associate Professor of worship at Union Theological Seminary in New York City.

Jin Young Choi is a US-based transnational feminist scholar from South Korea. She is Professor of New Testament and Christian Origins and the Baptist Missionary Training School Professorial Chair in Biblical Studies at Colgate Rochester Crozer Divinity School (NY), located on land sacred to the Seneca Nation.

Ajungla Jamir is an Indian theological educator specializing in Christian Ethics particularly concerning the lived experiences of Northeast tribal women in India's diaspora. She earned her Doctorate in Theology from United Theological College, Bangalore, where her research addressed Christian ethics for tribal women of India. Jamir serves as an Associate Professor at Gossner Theological College and has contributed to various theological publications, notably on gender, racism and peace ethics, reflecting her dedication to theological scholarship and education.

Johnathan Jodamus is Associate Professor at the University of the Western Cape (UWC), Cape Town, South Africa, teaching in the Department of Religion and Theology. He engages students in biblical texts, which continue to regulate norms for daily living. His primary research and teaching interests intersect the disciplines of biblical studies, gender studies and critical race studies. Theoretical insights plus political commitments (gender studies and race studies) and textual analysis (biblical studies) come together in his work as an interdisciplinary scholar.

Gifta Angline Kumar is Assistant Professor in the Department of Religions and Philosophy at Bishop's College, Kolkata, West Bengal, India, and holds a PhD in Theology. As an active member of the Church of North India, she is actively engaged in ministry. Her scholarly contributions to various Indian journals focus on women's empowerment, gender justice, interfaith dialogue and ecology.

Lynnette Xiangling Li is a doctoral student at the University of Denver – ILIFF School of Theology's joint PhD programme. Her academic interests include postcolonial studies, environmental ethics, Ecodharma and liberative theologies. She has published interdisciplinary work in the geosciences around environmental vulnerability and hazardous mitigation. She is a doctoral fellow with the Louisville Institute and an academic fellow with the Council for World Mission.

Ángel F. Mendez-Montoya was born in Mexicali, BC, Mexico. He was a professional dancer and co-founder of the company U.X. Onodanza (Mexico City) and earned his PhD in Philosophical Theology from the University of Virginia. He is currently a full-time professor and researcher at the Department of Religious Studies at the Universidad Iberoamericana in Mexico City. He has published in various anthologies and in national and international journals.

Christel Zogning Meli is a lecturer of Practical Theology and Liturgy at the University Faculty of Protestant Theology in Brussels (FUTP). She is a PhD candidate in Theology, after having studied international economics. She is also a founding member of CARES (Centre for Afropean and Religious Studies) and currently works as a catechetical officer in the EPUB (United Protestant Church of Belgium). Her research focuses on the forms of Afro-militancy and the dynamics of cultural and religious transmission within the Afro-European population of Brussels, based on ethnographic fieldwork and the intercultural approach and its challenges in Christian pastoral work in the age of globalization.

CONTRIBUTORS

S. Lily Mendoza is Professor of Culture and Communication at Oakland University in Rochester, Michigan, USA and Executive Director of the Center for Babaylan Studies, a non-profit organization committed to decolonization and indigenization among diasporic Filipinos on Turtle Island. She hails originally from the Philippines in the traditional homeland of the Ayta and other indigenous peoples.

Teresa L. Smallwood earned a BA from the University of North Carolina at Chapel Hill, a Juris Doctor from North Carolina Central University School of Law, a Master of Divinity at Howard University School of Divinity and a PhD at Chicago Theological Seminary. She holds the James Franklin Kelly and Hope Eyster Kelly Chair as Associate Professor of Public Theology at United Lutheran Seminary in Gettysburg, PA. She also serves as Vice-President and Dean of Academic Affairs at United Lutheran Seminary. She is licensed and ordained to public ministry and serves on the ministerial staff of St. John African Methodist Episcopal Church, Nashville, Tennessee.

Gerald O. West is Professor Emeritus in the School of Religion, Philosophy and Classics at the University of KwaZulu-Natal, South Africa. He has worked extensively with the Ujamaa Centre for Community Development and Research for the past 30 years, a project in which socially engaged biblical scholars and ordinary African readers of the Bible from poor, working-class and marginalized communities collaborate for social transformation. He has used the Ujamaa Centre's Contextual Bible Study praxis in a variety of collaborative projects with the Anglican Communion.

Foreword

This book is the fruit of the work of the Council for World Mission (CWM). From its very beginning, the mission of CWM has extended beyond the confines of worship and faith communities into public arenas where services relating to education, health, welfare and ecology are provided, assessed and re-envisioned. Since the 1970s, CWM has wrestled with how to decolonize mission globally and locally – its praxis, pedagogy and theory – and how to proclaim fullness of life at a time when all of life is threatened.

CWM is committed to radical discipleship and prophetic spirituality. Through the Discernment and Radical Engagement (DARE) Programme, CWM conveys its prophetic role in the present socio-political, economic, ecological and global landscapes. DARE is inspired by liberation theologies that have emerged from the diverse context of struggles, its praxis, pedagogies and theories; and it explores, shares, transforms and tries to make sense of divinities, scriptures, traditions, responsibilities, destinies, practices, experiences and biases. DARE is open to the signs of the times and committed to the mission from the margins. Engagement with the margins is the first step for mission, theology and the ecumenical movement to manifest their radical, liberating, decolonizing spirits.

DARE and liberation theologies are radically interdisciplinary, interreligious and intersectional in their approach. This accompanies the shifts in academic trends, but transcends those trends to root DARE in praxis, pedagogies and theories of struggles for liberation, decolonization and counter-imperial testimonies. As DARE is one of the key priorities of CWM's missiological discernment, I hope this series of publications out of Global DARE Conferences will inspire, encourage and empower mission, theology and movements towards liberation and reconciliation!

Revd Dr Jooseop Keum
CWM General Secretary

This book was supported by the Council for World Mission (CWM) through its DARE Programme (Discernment and Radical Engagement)

Acknowledgements

This book enters the world thanks to the outpouring of support from the Council for World Mission through the Discernment and Radical Engagement (DARE) initiative. I extend my deep appreciation to General Secretary Revd Dr Jeeseop Keum and Deputy General Secretary Dr Sudipta Singh for their dedication to producing knowledge from the global South and for their confidence in this book project. I appreciate SCM Press for providing a platform for global scholars' quest for liberation and for publishing this book. I am grateful to Mr Sithembiso Zwane, who provided energy and insight at an earlier stage of this project. My sincere thanks also go to CWM's Mission Secretary the Revd Dr Graham McGeoch for his tremendous support, which made our collective intellectual labour come to fruition.

As a biblical scholar and transnational feminist theologian, I am indebted to the teachers and colleagues who have taught me cultural studies and theories of practices of ordinary people. I am eternally grateful for my late matriarchs, my grandmother and mother, who led me through Shamanist, Buddhist and Confucian rituals in my formative years. These rituals hybridized my Christian faith and practice, which is rooted in *minjung* and ecumenical traditions. I want to thank our contributors for their outstanding collaboration in co-creating a discourse of ritual based on praxis in various contexts. Their intellectual, spiritual and artistic brilliance and integrity shine throughout these texts and in their committed work worldwide. I wish to offer a libation to their ancestors and the communities who have journeyed with them in their struggles for liberation.

Jin Young Choi

I

Ritual Knowledge and Performance from the Margins

JIN YOUNG CHOI

Liberation and Ritual

Peruvian liberation theologian Gustavo Gutiérrez passed away on 22 October 2024, when I was completing the manuscript of this volume. It seems that today we live in an era in which liberation sounds obsolete; one can hardly grasp from and for what one needs to be liberated. Yet, this is not because there is no empire or dominating structure to resist. Instead of the direct conquest of territories, the ways powers operate have changed through decentralized and complex structures of economic control and global governance since the 1990s. Despite continued political projects of occupation and settler colonialism, rituals have played significant roles in global and national political economies.

The long history of the relationship between empire and ritual can be traced back to ancient empires' use of rituals (Price, 1985). Rome's rule expanded beyond the Mediterranean to Europe, Western Asia and North Africa. However, such victories were not exclusively achieved by military conquest or coercive central administration, but were also bolstered by rituals such as the imperial cult, public festivals and games designed to demonstrate the emperor's status and power and the empire's hierarchy, as well as reinforce the subjugation of conquered peoples.

This does not mean that all rituals are in the service of empire. In fact, we do not define ritual as either entirely oppressive or liberating. From rites of passage to patterned actions in a group, ritual is essential to human life, as it creates a shared everyday world of human interaction, shapes human experience and imbues meanings. Whether religious or secular or observed in everyday routine or national ceremony, rituals function to organize or disrupt social life in embodied ways through people's performances. However, since we engage rituals from the margins and liberation perspectives, we attend not only to religious and cultural but also to ideological functions of ritual. The preferential option for the poor – the core of Latin American liberation theology, as well as Gutiérrez's legacy – is not only an ethical but also an epistemological commitment, which applies to our inquiries of rituals based on social analysis of 'the poor, the exploited classes, the marginalized races, all the despised cultures' (Gutiérrez, 1973, p. 241). However, liberation theology is not a closed intellectual project but has evolved at various junctures of history, responding to emancipation and liberation movements, which are still ongoing.

Since September 2023 in Bangkok, when we started this collective project sponsored by the Council for World Mission, it has been clear to the participants that we would be undertaking a decolonial knowledge project on rituals and rites. Despite the diversity of our disciplinary training and discursive activities, we shared a commitment to critically analyse and reflect on rituals for liberation in a transdisciplinary manner. When attempting to construct a knowledge of ritual from the global South and the margins of the metropolis where we are located, like any contextual theologian, we grant epistemological privilege to our experiences. When critical scholars, creative practitioners and dedicated activists bring our epistemologies from our practices to contribute to disciplines, discourses and movements, we also struggle against linguistic imperialism, epistemic inequalities and internalized colonialism.

When we speak about our communal experiences of oppression and empowerment through rituals, we sometimes find contradictions due to our different identity formations and social locations, making our work inevitably intersectional and boundary-crossing. For instance, traditional rites are considered oppressive against women but have been reclaimed against the normalizing forces of colonialism backed by Western Christianity. Our approaches to rituals are diverse and multifaceted. While some authors use ritual theory or ethnographic research methods to analyse ritual practices and phenomena, others' approaches are autobiographical, describing their encounters with indigenous rituals. Some writings are evocative in a ritualistic sense or provide practical guidelines for transformative rituals. We interpret, critique, and perform rituals in our own cultures and communities, and such acts are discursive and performative, that is, theory-laden and theory-making. Theory and practice are inseparable; we do theory.

Then, do we need to know or engage in the ritual theory produced in the West, which often perceives and objectifies non-Western societies as archaic, uncivilized, or static? Not only does ritual produce ideological forms of knowledge, but the anthropologist Talal Asad notes that ritual theories, such as the view of ritual as symbolic activity, are historical constructions inextricably related to 'modern Western assumptions about the self and state' (1993, pp. 55–79; Bell, 1997, pp. 79–80). The term 'liturgy', once regarded as a higher form of religion in contrast to primitive or aboriginal forms of practice, is another example of the construct of ritual as a Western phenomenon (Bell, 1992, p. 6).

What follows is a brief overview of ritual theory. This overview is undertaken not to recentre Western epistemology but to acknowledge that no knowledge is produced in a vacuum but in the contact zones of cultures and histories, in which we attempt to postulate ritual knowledge in praxis. In doing so, we spell out the distinctiveness of our contexts and commitments in engaging rituals and ritual studies. We believe in transformative possibilities of our collective knowledge based on accountability to our communities as well as for ourselves as a ritual community.

Discourses of Ritual

Ritual studies has been established as a discipline in conjunction with anthropology, sociology and history since the 1980s with *Beginnings in Ritual Studies* (Grimes, 1982) and the *Journal of Ritual Studies* (since 1987; Bell, 1998, p. 207). However, scholars, especially in the sociology of religion, had already discussed the significance of ritual in the early twentieth century in terms of the religious, the symbolic and the social. First, ritual has been viewed as the human experience of the sacred, antithetical to the profane. The sacred-profane distinction constitutes the root of all religions (Eliade, 1987; Bell, 1997, p. 24). In this dichotomy of the sacred and the profane, rituals are usually centred around the sacred. Rituals function to secure the sacred from the profane by reinforcing the boundary between them. The symbolic demarcation between the sacred and the profane is extended to the social and bodily levels, dividing pure and impure and the inside and the outside (Douglas, 2002, pp. 142, 150–9). Second, according to Clifford Geertz, who defines culture as a system of symbols and meanings, religion is also understood as a 'cultural system' (1993, pp. 87–125). Symbolic expression in religion and ritual communicates the shared beliefs and values of that cultural system. Last, the symbolic system of meanings and values based on a hierarchical classification is central to structuring and maintaining the social order. The system of religion and ritual functions to 'adjust its internal interactions, maintain its group ethos and restore a state of harmony after any disturbance' (Bell, 1997, p. 29). Scholars explain that rituals sustain social cohesion and stability by imbuing collective consciousness (Durkheim, 1965, p. 420), organizing social boundaries and order (Douglas, 2002), or symbolically resolving conflicts and restoring harmony (Girard, 2013).

However, the model of ritual as maintaining group or social unity cannot explain the conflict embedded in any society, for which Victor Turner (1969) proposes two models of social organization: structure versus *communitas*. In rituals, like rites of passage, participants within a 'structured' society based on socioeconomic or political status enter into *communitas* – a 'relatively unstructured' society in which those lowly and marginalized lose their (ab)normal identity and appear to be liminal entities (1969, p. 96). They may find social bonds among equals and, even temporarily, experience the reversal of social order and empowerment. However, when returning to the dominant society, such members of *communitas* are subject to labels like 'polluting' and 'dangerous' (Turner, 1969, p. 109).

Religious-symbolic and social-functionalist views, which are not mutually exclusive, have limitations. Whereas the former holds that ritual is a universal phenomenon, generally assumed as the autonomous set of activities whose patterns are applicable across times and cultures, the latter emphasizes the role rituals play in conforming and integrating those placed on the other side – the profane, the polluting and the dangerous in the community. These views overlook the complex web of power relations and dynamics of domination and subordination. Not all communities based on norms and boundaries set through rituals welcome those who do not have the normalized body, ability, or means to participate in those rituals and ceremonies. Thus, rituals are not merely symbolic expressions or reflections of social values. Instead, they enact the values and beliefs of the community and generate systems of social relationships.

If, as Catherine Bell explicates, 'ritualization' is a 'particular way of organizing social relationships', the agency of those who participate in rituals through their performative acts should not be ignored (Bell, 1997, p. 39; cf. Gluckman, 1962, p. 24). This view highlights ritual as a social action, not limited to cultural performances or religious institutional activities. Despite the tendency of rituals to constantly seek unity, participants do not always comply with prescribed ritual actions but may turn ritual into the site of struggle. Thus, in some ritual performances, community members engage in a symbolic struggle with the more extensive social system. For instance, a Black football player's taking a knee during the national anthem at games became a symbolic gesture of protest against racial injustice.

Louis Althusser's concept of Ideological State Apparatuses (ISAs) provides additional insight into the ideological nature of ritual as social action. In contrast to the Repressive State Apparatus, which operates by violence, the ISAs function by embodying ideology in concrete practices. ISAs are institutions that 'ensure subjection to the ruling ideology' (Althusser, 1971). According to Althusser, religious practices and rituals are part of the mechanisms of ISAs through which ideology is constantly reproduced and reinforced. Participating in rituals, individuals internalize the values and norms of the ruling ideology and play the role of maintaining the extant power structures. Although Althusser's idea of rituals as ideological practices brings to light the materiality (not just symbolic) of religious practices and rituals, it raises the question of the agency of participants in rituals because it assumes that their beliefs and daily practices are determined by the dominant ideology.

The subject's agency is critical in transforming relations of domination and subordination within society. Paradoxically, because of the repetitive and regulatory nature of normative performances, there is the potential that performativity can subvert or transform normative structures. For instance, gender identity is constructed through repeated social acts and performances like rituals. Despite the 'performative construction of gender within the material practices of culture', this naturalized category can be disrupted by performing gender in ways that contradict or defy normative gender expectations and express fluid identities, as exemplified in drag performances (Butler, 1990, pp. 34–5). By exaggerating gender norms, queer performances expose the constructedness of gender and decentre normative frameworks.

While subjects are formed through rituals that preserve dominant ideology and normalize structures, through performativity individuals have the agency to navigate, negotiate and resist the norms that shape and redefine their identities. While Bell affirms the function of rituals to sustain social norms, values and collective identities, she also emphasizes individual agency in 'everyday production of goods and meanings, [in which persons] acquiesce yet protest, reproduce yet seek to transform their predicament' (1997, p. 83). Thus, ritual is not merely a set of prescribed actions or symbolic expressions but a space where potential subversion can occur, exposing the constructed nature of social norms, challenging normative power, and creating new possibilities for identity, community and society.

However, caution is needed regarding the significance of the 'performing subject' in neoliberal capitalist society. Byung-Chul Han argues that the neoliberal regime spurs the compulsion of production accompanying the 'compulsion to perform well', mainly through digital communication, which is 'communication without community' (2020, pp. 12–13). Instead of individualized performative acts that present and produce only the 'authentic' self and hence a culture of collective narcissism, we attempt to form a ritual community – a 'community of common listening and belonging' in a collective form of perceiving the world and performing for liberation (Han, 2019, pp. 16–26, 31). When capitalism manifests as a (pseudo)religion, or when a religion serves capitalism, we struggle to redefine, recreate and reengage rituals to restore a sense of community.

While ritual scholars examine rituals from various perspectives, which emphasize sacred domain, symbolic meaning, social function, cultural performance, or social action, our orientation towards rituals is communal, liberationist and decolonial. As a way of constructing knowledge of ritual from the margins, this volume organizes ideas that intersect with rituals, such as gender, colonialism, historical trauma, liberation struggles and ecology. Readers do not need to follow the order of the chapters; they may start with the most relevant and appealing topics, and examining connections and gaps within and across texts. Instead of simply providing a summary of each chapter, I will connect the ideas present and construct a flow of arguments throughout texts, highlighting each chapter's implications for liberation in its own social context, encouraging readers to recognize disparate theories and practices of ritual but simultaneously find overlapping themes and ideas.

Gender Oppression and Ritual

In a patriarchal society, rituals function to normalize gender oppression. When religious rituals secure the sacred from the profane, the dichotomy is extended to the social grouping that sets the boundary between the pure and impure. The impure are not only the outsiders of the community. When they are in the community, their existence makes it potentially dangerous, which requires their temporary seclusion and purifying rituals. Gifta Angline Kumar examines religious rituals in Kerala and Odisha, India, which control and use female sexuality to naturalize gender roles and norms (Chapter 2). For example, in the veneration of the celibate deity Lord Ayyappan in the Sabarimala Temple in Kerala, women between the ages of ten and fifty, which encompass menstruating years, are prohibited from entering the temple to safeguard chastity. Upon experiencing their first menstrual cycle, young women in Odisha are confined to their homes, prohibited from interacting with others and forbidden to engage in cooking activities. Often justified on religious grounds or using scriptural texts, custom and tradition ensure women's conformity to conventional gender roles, which can be the source of powerlessness and pain. Such rituals are seen as being practised for the common welfare of the people and become customs enforced by discipline. Kumar exposes the pervasive nature of such discriminatory rituals against women in various parts of India. She calls for a critical evaluation and reformation of religious practices and traditions to promote gender equality and challenge discriminatory norms.

Similarly, Ajungla Jamir deals with the impact of religious rituals and ceremonies on gender while finding multiple layers of oppression when women participate in rituals in both Northeast India and Mainland contexts (Chapter 3). Such complex situations, which she calls 'cultural crossroads', require an intersectional approach that includes qualitative methods. She focuses on the 'Northeast women' of India as a reference point to study how normalization processes of rituals within their own cultures and religions affect them. Taboos within Northeastern indigenous rituals and ceremonies, such as the Post-Transplantation Festival and the Feast of Reconciliation, have an especially profound impact on gender roles and participation. In addition to exclusion in their tribal rituals, Northeast women are called the derogatory term 'chinky', and they face discrimination in mainland India due to different food customs in the wider culture and dress codes in Christian worship. Jamir asserts that prejudices towards Northeast women are deeply intertwined with the broader spectrums of caste, race, social hierarchy and colonialism in Indian society. She proposes a transformative approach to rituals that focuses on women's agency, reimagining tradition, ethical considerations and intersectional advocacy.

The discussions of Kumar and Jamir concentrate on the role of rituals in organizing social order through symbols and taboos, as in the purificatory bath of a girl as a puberty rite, in which the symbolic act of cleansing reinforces the gender ideology of female (im)purity and modesty. Such rituals are intended to promote social cohesion and stability but at the expense of women, who are inferior in the gender hierarchy. It seems impossible to subvert patriarchy, especially when it is buttressed by mechanisms of ISAs, such as religious practices and rituals. Thus, these authors' strategy is to expose how cultural hierarchies based on gender and other factors are naturalized as they seek ways of critically reinterpreting and transforming traditional rituals, creating space for women's agency, advocacy and active participation.

Colonialism and Indigenous Spiritualities of Liberation

Rituals integrate traditional society and sustain its order, while excluding and oppressing certain groups of people. However, as colonialism convulsed the order of a traditional society, colonial experiences call for a serious reconsideration of one's own tradition. When European colonial forces, with Christianity, swept countries in Africa and the Middle East, Asia and the Pacific, and the Americas and the Caribbean, they suppressed native religions and practices, thereby annihilating their spirits and spiritualities. Whereas traditional cultures themselves contain oppressive elements in conjunction with such other social systems as patriarchy and caste in these regions, colonialism, as supported by Christian scriptures and doctrines, devalued and demonized traditional religions and practices. The norm of what it means to be human was manufactured with the image of a white man. In this regard, colonial rule is the imposition of colonial divisions of humanity and of the universal (read: European) cultural system based on reason, civilization and freedom. As Cedric J. Robinson's term 'racial capitalism' (1983) denotes, the process of extracting social and economic value from racialized people and people of colour was driven by the economic motivations facilitating colonial violence. However, colonizers could not exterminate the spirit of the colonized and racialized, who have resisted colonial powers in various ways – through direct oppositional movements and cultural resistance, or both. They, as the agents of resistance and change, transform and reinvent traditions and rituals. Three essays in this volume provide perspectives that embrace native cultures, regarding tradition as not entirely oppressive but as a means of countering colonial forces and affirming their identities.

Christel Zogning Meli examines the identity trajectories of the (neo)-traditionalist entrepreneurs she has interviewed during her qualitative field study since 2022 (Chapter 4). Those adherents to a (neo)traditionalist paradigm in Afro-militant associations in Brussels, Belgium, abandoned their Christian faith in favour of African spirituality because, as the supreme religion, Western Christianity exercised symbolic imperialism, by which it relegated the beliefs and ritual practices of colonized peoples to the rank of superstition and archaism. For certain Afro-militants, the

West's 'civilizing' activities in Africa and the Christianization of African societies are regarded as 'epistemicides'. Meli analyses how the scenarios of leaving Christianity for a 'return to the sources' produce cultural metamorphoses, collective changes in values, and so-called normative attitudes, giving rise to a growing dissident movement within the Black community. It is interesting to observe that while (neo)traditionalists rupture dominant Christian norms, they (counter)normalize 'African spiritualities' by reappropriating African cultural traditions and ancestral beliefs. Meli examines these entrepreneurs' normalization strategies in the real world and online to reaffirm and symbolize their belonging to those new traditionalist movements and to promote a freedom of belief and ritual practice that breaks with the Christian colonial heritage.

Johnathan Jodamus reclaims *Pinksterkerk* (literally Pentecostal church), a phenomenon of African Pentecostalism in postcolonial South Africa (Chapter 5). Against the background of legacies of colonialism, enslavement and apartheid, he explores the spirituality of *Pinkster* in the Cape Flats, which refers to Black and Coloured townships in Cape Town. Camissa Africans, the term some adopt as an alternative to Coloured people, are stereotyped with violence, gangsterism and social degradation. However, as indicated in the title 'The Absurdity of Joy', Jodamus argues that the townships and *Pinksterkerk* are filled with rich and life-affirming religious and cultural rituals. In this distinctive type of African Pentecostal religion in Cape Town, their embodied rituals, such as jubilant dancing, soulful singing and rhythmic drumming, create a space of liberation where practitioners foster their collective identity and assert their agency in order to resist the dehumanizing effects of poverty and deprivation. The rituals of the *Pinksterkerk* are deeply embedded in ancestral Camissa African spirituality. Moreover, the culturally-hybrid forms of ritual not only appear to contest colonial normalizing narratives of the negative social script of Coloured people but, on the discursive level, he further argues that indigenous Camissa African forms of spirituality must be recognized as a Black spirituality of liberation.

The question of tension between reimaging the African past and the imposed religion of Christianity in the present is not easily resolved. Whereas the cases mentioned above of African descendants in diasporic and post-apartheid societies demonstrate that traditional rituals are not necessarily oppressive but can be reclaimed and reappropriated to resist colonial legacies and their continuing impact, others preserve their tradition in hybrid rituals. As presented in Ángel F. Méndez Montoya's essay about Rarámuri worship, the phenomenon of inculturation is more patent in some indigenous cultures as the worship during the Holy

Week incorporates indigenous rituals such as dancing, drinking and feasting (Chapter 6). He calls such rituals an 'ecclesial third space'. In both Jodamus's and Montoya's writings, embodied aspects of ritual like dancing are critical. The latter emerged from the author's experience of visiting the Rarámuri community at the Jesuit missions of Samachique in the Tarahumara mountain range in northern Mexico in 2023. The Rarámuri culture and religiosity dating back to pre-colonial times are still preserved in their rituals, particularly their rituals of dancing and sharing food and drink. Montoya provides a thick description of how the indigenous culture and Catholicism in Mexico manifest as a hybrid form of Christian-Rarámuri inculturation and are physically experienced by this community. The Catholic-Rarámuri religious rituals and practices have survived even after more than five hundred years of colonial Christianity because of the communities' location, with relatively fewer colonial influences since the arrival of the Spanish missionaries.

Trauma, Spectrality and Ritual

Whether indigenous traditions are invigorated or enculturated through rituals of the colonized, their bodies and agency emerge as vital in ritual spaces where the past is summoned in the name of tradition to preserve a collective identity. Homi Bhabha describes a hybrid subject such as the Coloured South African inhabits 'the rim of 'in-between' reality' or 'Third Space' in which their cultural identity, a difference 'within', becomes a 'symbol for the disjunctive, displaced everyday life of the liberation struggle' (1994, pp. 18–19; Choi, 2015, p. 24). Hybridity as cultural identity differs somewhat from the liminality conceptualized in ritual studies, which is universal and eventually has a formative function within society. Hybrid subjects in colonial/postcolonial contexts signify an 'unhomely presence' in 'interstices between the historical past and its narrative present', in which the unspoken, unrepresented past haunts the present (Bhabha, p. 22). In this hybridized temporality, which manifests as haunting, the return of the obliterated colonial scene serves as a disruptive intervention in the present (Gordon, p. 142; Choi, 2015, p. 78). In some regions of the globe, brutal violence is obscured by (moving and) removing people's bodies and identities, which results in no space for mourning. Haunting serves as a form of cultural memory of the colonial past that disrupts the postcolonial present.

Miguel M. Algranti's essay deals with spectrality as an obscured past in Latin America, focusing on Argentina (Chapter 7). Since more than

30,000 young activists disappeared during the 'National Reorganisation Process' of the Argentinian military regimes in the 1970s, the figure of *los desaparecidos* (the disappeared) has haunted the country transversally. Algranti interrogates the case of 'Antivisita', an artivist performance authored by two of the victims of state terror, Mariana Eva Perez and Laura Kalauz, with a guided visit through the spectral dimensions of Escuela Mecánica de la Armada (ESMA), the former Clandestine Centre of Detention, Torture and Extermination. As Algranti participated as a performer and dramaturgic collaborator in the play, he provides a critical analysis of ritual and trauma through spiritism, a performative model, and the lens of the Theology of the People (Teología del Pueblo). He argues that 'Antivisita' employing a spiritualist séance is a political act through which the participants connect with the dead, rather than a religious act. Embracing the Theology of the People's emphasis on culture and popular piety, Algranti contends that popular rituals as a spontaneous site of social grief have their instrumental-affective, embodied dimension in engaging with the unresolved spectrality of the disappeared.

Popular rituals are sites of spectral engagement and resistance where communities reconstruct their identities in the aftermath of violence and navigate the ongoing presence of the past in their daily lives. For Teresa L. Smallwood, however, such popular religiosity is claimed to be sacred. Among the sacred religious traditions of African-derived peoples in America, she reclaims and restores 'conjure' as a sacred ritual practice (Chapter 8). Indebted to womanist and feminist theories and methodologies, she examines the socio-historical antecedents of 'conjure' as a heuristic tool. Jacques Derrida's *hauntology* is also helpful in demonstrating that the spectres of 'conjure' are discernible in the current religious topography of African American religious practitioners. Focused upon the work of Tracey E. Hucks, Dianne Stewart, Charles H. Long and Yvonne Chireau, Smallwood posits that womanist 'conjure' is a normative, holy and discernible 'religious good' that offers insight, intrigue and paths into the mysteries of a revelatory God. This is shown most notably in the manifestation of African-derived peoples' ancestral yearnings for freedom *from* domination and oppression and freedom *to* express religious experience without limitation, which evolved in the middle passage as a continuation of their African spiritual practices as well as through the centuries since the legal abolition of enslavement in the Americas. Moreover, 'conjure' represents one of many spiritual border-crossings linking ancient spirituality with the miraculous, the aesthetic and the ghostly, creating a synergy that instantiates 'black girl magic' and gives rise to the full embodiment of the freedom yearned for and now being experienced.

Ritual as a Site of Struggle and Transgression

Engaging with the spectres of the past through rituals or performative practices offers a transformative space for those deprived of official channels of remembering and mourning. Haunting, reflecting the collective memory of colonized subjects, points to their resilience and yearning for emancipation in ritual practices. It displaces boundaries between past and present, private and public, and sacred and secular. The concept of haunting or conjuring in ritual contributes to liberation theology, which is grounded in the lived experience of the oppressed. Transgression also occurs in the public sphere, often through deliberately prepared ritual processes. While we have observed in a local current of the theology of people in Argentina, liberation theology in South Africa has also evolved, as the Kairos Document (1985) conceptualized a trajectory from people's theology to prophetic theology to public theology. Part of what was envisaged by 'public theology' was the formal liturgical theology of churches.

Thirty years after political and juridical liberation, however, Gerald O. West sees little progress in the liturgy of churches towards reflecting the people's theology of those struggling for survival, liberation and abundant life (Chapter 9). He regards religion, and particularly church rituals, as dominant-dominating ideologies because they, like ISAs, aim to secure the subjugation of the most vulnerable community, in this case, people living with HIV in South Africa. The church's Bible studies, accompanied by liturgies, are a salient example of sustaining the dominant ideo-theological trajectories of most African churches by condemning, stigmatizing and marginalizing those people. West demonstrates how particular Bible-related liturgy fails to reflect the realities of the poor and marginalized. Examples addressed in his essay include 'the Lord's Prayer' (Matt. 6.9–13; Luke 11.1–4), 'the prayer of humble access' (Mark 7.24–31), a marriage liturgy (Ruth 1.16) and a eucharistic liturgy (1 Cor. 11.23–26). These liturgies come from a number of church traditions, both overtly liturgical traditions (e.g., Anglican and Baptist) and those that would not consider themselves liturgical (e.g. Pentecostal). Then, he calls for liberating liturgy, offering the Ujamaa Centre's Contextual Bible Study (CBS) as an ideo-theological resource and also a ritual process for a faith-based community's reworking and creation of liberating liturgies, what West calls 'infrapolitical rituals of resilience' (Scott, 1990, p. 184).

Whereas West testifies to how a Bible study as a ritualized process can contend with religion as a pervasive ideology but also create a liberating space, Lynnette Xiangling Li demonstrates secular civic spaces in Singapore turning into sites where rituals of creative resistance, as well as ideological contestations, occur (Chapter 10). In authoritarian and illiberal democratic nation-states like Singapore, the government's use of extreme legislation and disciplinary measures is designed and executed to suppress political dissidents and defiant critics. The threat of punishment forces civic obedience and compliance, which are required for nation-building. Li observes how protests as politics of rights manifest as rites when protesters employ rituals of resistance using mediums such as songs, a mirror and a smiley face drawn on paper. An aspect of ritual in these performances is to flip the script of conscripted obedience, loyalty and domestication of subjects while dislocating and transgressing structure (i.e., British colonialism) and anti-structure (i.e. postcolonial nation-building sought by the ruling party leadership). This reveals that the oppressive power also performs 'carefully calibrated coercion', which simultaneously incites creative rituals of resistance on the part of the silenced, surveilled and punished. Protesters utilize the 'oppositional gaze', calculated silence, or even docility, as in the Pink Dot movement, which Li calls 'queer rites'. Such gestures of compliance do not lack or abandon agency, but instead, ritualized passivity is transgressive and transformative in that such radical rituals of resistance inspire, provoke and conscientize the active participants and the audience who have been domesticated and silenced. Such socially observable rituals sometimes involve co-performers like law enforcement officers.

Both West's and Li's cases, whether in the ecclesial setting or the public sphere, emphasize ritualization as a 'culturally strategic way of acting' or the ritual process itself, which requires intentionally designed and developed liturgies or rituals amid the socio-historical conditioning of oppression and violence (Bell, 1992, pp. 7–8). Religion is shaped by politics, and the political and ideological also manifest as the religious. When rituals have social functions, ideological questions reach beyond their symbolic dimensions. Accordingly, the ritual process demands raising critical consciousness or conscientization of communities, whether faith-based or civic, often accompanied by resilience or docility – a form of agency of participants in rituals. The lesser in their class status, health, power and privilege negotiate authority, self and society in ritualized ways of acting, often transgressing binary logic and normativity. These and other essays affirm the significance of community, or *communitas*, but the community is not limited to a group of people. Our engagement with ritual should be extended to show how humans can be in communion with other-than-human beings.

Rituals of Healing and Planetary Thriving

Cláudio Carvalhaes questions rituals after the Anthropocene – our time as defined by climate chaos (Chapter 11). He starts with an analysis of colonialism and its project of conquest and pillage. Within colonialism, the notion of coloniality is essential to understanding the ways of destruction we live in now, since we operate under the modes of exchange developed within colonial capitalism. This capitalistic process has created a spirit that orients our ways of being in a world marked by consumerism, competition and profit. Carvalhaes argues that we are under the devastating spell of this spirit of climate colonialism, which creates many forms of death and loss. In such devastating ecological crises, he calls on all religions to take part in helping with a multiplicity of rituals for the transnational dispossession of this capitalist captivity. Then, he develops the notion of grief as a response to the colonial capitalist spirit and shows how we must pursue healing and liberation through many forms of rituals. Carvalhaes finally demonstrates the need to first sense the world and understand what is happening so that rituals of healing and transformation can enact a different spirit from that of capitalism.

The analytical, autobiographical and poetic writing of S. Lily Mendoza draws on insights from indigenous and native studies and from her own first-hand encounter with indigenous ritual (Chapter 12). She understands ritual not as a human-initiated endeavour intended primarily for human edification but as a response to the earth's own beauty and virtues. Such a distinct understanding of ritual leads her to see humans not as the sole subject who sees and knows the world but equally as the object for other sentient beings' seeing and knowing. Mendoza's participation in indigenous rituals – such as a sun ceremony on a Pueblo people's territory, instances of ritual tutelage with indigenizing communities both in the homeland and in the diaspora, and a ritual at the Detroit River – illumines the intimate connection between all beings, human and otherwise, and with the earth amidst the assault of our disenchanted modern culture. She argues that returning to a ritual way of living is a deep probing into the much bigger questions of the requisites for planetary thriving. Our species' role is to keep the wholeness of life engendered in ritual enactments going through the liberating power of encounters with the natural world as human beings' most important Other.

Carvalhaes's enactment of rituals of the Spirit of life in solidarity with non-humans and Mendoza's articulation of human relationship with the earth invites us to philosophical and theological thinking of a 'reciprocal economy, not one where God is the "ungiven Giver" and humanity has nothing to offer in return, but rather a reciprocal mutuality' (Grau, 2024, p. 55). Sacraments such as the Eucharist contain deep reciprocal potentials, reminding us of the greater sharing of the creation. Such a ritual of reciprocal economy is radically differentiated from the capitalist ritual of compulsion to produce the narcissistic self. Rituals are processes of embodiment and bodily performances, which comprise feelings – a 'collective feeling ... Faced with the experience of loss, the community imposes the mourning upon itself. Such collective feelings consolidate a community' (Han, 2019, p. 11). Grieving amidst impending global catastrophe and crying in deep gratitude and joy in the face of a magnificent Presence can happen simultaneously to ritual.

Closing Words and an Invitation

Since traditional rituals in many societies are entangled with patriarchal norms and other intersecting factors such as status, class and caste, exposing and critiquing how gender conformity and oppression operate in those rituals should be followed by claiming women's agency and advocacy, as well as reforming rituals (Kumar and Jamir). In postcolonial contexts, in which the legacy of colonialism and imperial Christianity still affects the psyches and cultures of the colonized, traditions like African spiritualities are revisited, reclaimed and reappropriated. While some employ counter-normalization strategies, other traditional and indigenous cultures seek to preserve the agency of the colonized in their embodied performances and cultural identities in the in-between spaces of traditional spirituality and colonial Christianity (Meli, Jodamus and Montoya).

However, tradition is not always traceable or reclaimable. While visiting suppressed histories and traumas of state terror and enslavement, readers are invited to attentively listen to the voices of those whose histories are eradicated through engaging with the dead in popular rituals or conjuring practices (Algranti and Smallwood). Rituals give rise to the unconscious and heal trauma. However, the continued wounding of vulnerable populations in many societies also demands counter-rituals as a site of struggle against oppressive normalizing power (West and Li). Neoliberal global capitalism is an irresistible force in the current historical moment, which brought about global climate disaster. This volume's last and urgent call is to acknowledge the agency of the earth and solidarity with other-than-human beings (Carvalhaes and Mendoza).

Our experiential and cultural knowledge affirms that ritual is situational and historically specific, which is contrary to the claim for the universal structure of culture and ritual that leads to discovering ritual patterns (Bell, 1997, pp. 8–10). Some basic ideas about ritual, such as its role in stabilizing and transgressing social order and norms, are present elsewhere in these texts. Still, our motivations, inquiries and contentions converge towards engagement with rituals of resistance and for liberation. When it is said that ritual promotes stable individual identity, social cohesion and group norms, racially and geopolitically marginalized subjects perceive not only the violence inherent in ritual mechanisms that manage the violence amid power struggles (cf. Kitts, 2018), but also reappropriate rituals recognizing their limits. This volume's distinctive contribution is to explore ritual's intersections with mechanisms and forces of power such as patriarchy, tradition, colonialism, authoritarianism and capitalism on the one hand and ritual's potential for reformation, resistance, resilience and restoration on the other. In doing theory and performing rituals, our work collectively deconstructs multiple binaries – sacred/profane, clean/unclean, normal/abnormal, West/East, civilizing/civilized, religious/political, private/public, symbolic/material, human/non-human, and so on. Rituals exclude and normalize, but they have the power to change. We invite you to discursive and performative ritual spaces where painful histories are revisited, traumas of oppression and exploitation are healed, and impossible futures of coexistence and flourishing are reimagined. Join us in singing and dancing, feasting and fighting, being haunted and grieving, resisting and rebirthing.

References

Althusser, Louis, 1971, 'Ideology and Ideological State Apparatuses' (Notes Towards an Investigation) [1970], in *Lenin and Philosophy, and Other Essays*, pp. 121–76, trans. Ben Brewster, London/New York: Monthly Review Press.

Asad, Talal, 1993, *Genealogies of Religion: Discipline and Reasons of Power in Christianity and Islam*, Baltimore: Johns Hopkins University Press.
Bell, Catherine, 1992, *Ritual Theory, Ritual Practice*, New York: Oxford University Press.
Bell, Catherine, 1997, *Ritual: Perspectives and Dimensions*, Oxford: Oxford University Press.
Bell, Catherine, 1998, 'Performance', in *Critical Terms for Religious Studies*, ed. Mark C. Taylor, pp. 205–24, Chicago: University of Chicago Press.
Bhabha, Homi K., 1994, *The Location of Culture*, London/New York: Routledge.
Butler, Judith, 1990, *Gender Trouble: Feminism and the Subversion of Identity*, London/New York: Routledge.
Choi, Jin Young, 2015, *Postcolonial Discipleship of Embodiment: An Asian and Asian American Feminist Reading of the Gospel of Mark*, Postcolonialism and Religions, New York: Palgrave Macmillan.
Douglas, Mary, 2002, *Purity and Danger: An Analysis of Concepts of Pollution and Taboo*, London: Routledge.
Durkheim, Émile, 1965, *The Elementary Forms of the Religious Life* [1915], trans. J. W. Swain, New York: Free Press.
Eliade, Mircea, 1987, *The Sacred and the Profane: The Nature of Religion*, New York: Harcourt Brace Jovanovich.
Geertz, Clifford, 1993, *The Interpretation of Cultures*, New York: Basic Books.
Girard, René, 2013, *Violence and the Sacred* [1979], London: Bloomsbury Academic.
Gluckman, Max, 1962, *Essays on the Ritual of Social Relations*, Manchester: Manchester University Press.
Gordon, Avery, 1997, *Ghostly Matters: Haunting and the Sociological Imagination*, Minneapolis: University of Minnesota Press.
Grau, Marion, 2024, 'Regifting the Divine Economy: Transitioning Petroleum-Based Energy Regimes', in *Assembling Futures: Economy, Ecology, Democracy, and Religion*, ed. Jennifer Quigley and Catherine Keller, pp. 46–63, New York: Fordham University Press.
Grimes, Ronald L., 1982, *Beginnings in Ritual Studies*, Lanham, MD: University Press of America.
Gutiérrez, Gustavo, 1973, *A Theology of Liberation: History, Politics, and Salvation*, Maryknoll, NY: Orbis Books.
Han, Byung-Chul, 2020, *The Disappearance of Rituals: A Topology of the Present* [2019], trans. Daniel Steuer, Cambridge: Polity.
Kitts, Margo, 2018, *Elements of Ritual and Violence*, Cambridge Elements: Religion and Violence, Cambridge: Cambridge University Press.
Price, S. R. F., 1985, *Rituals and Power: The Roman Imperial Cult in Asia Minor*, Cambridge: Cambridge University Press.
Robinson, Cedric J., 1983, *Black Marxism: The Making of the Black Radical Tradition*, Chapel Hill, NC: University of North Carolina Press.
Scott, James C., 1990, *Domination and the Arts of Resistance: Hidden Transcripts*, New Haven, CT: Yale University Press.
Turner, Victor, 1969, *The Ritual Process: Structure and Anti-Structure*, Ithaca, NY: Cornell University Press.

PART I

Gender Oppression and Ritual

2

The Impact of Religious Rituals and Ceremonies on Gender

GIFTA ANGLINE KUMAR

Introduction

The Sabarimala Temple, believed to be the abode of Lord Ayyappan and situated in the Periyar Tiger Reserve within Kerala's Western Ghats mountain ranges, is renowned for its unique religious customs. Devotees observe a 41-day penance, abstaining from worldly pleasures before embarking on a pilgrimage to the shrine. Lord Ayyappan is venerated as a celibate deity, leading to the traditional prohibition of women between the ages of 10 and 50 (encompassing menstruating years) from entering the temple to safeguard chastity. This restriction on women's entry, enforced through various measures, ignited a widespread national debate due to its evident discriminatory nature, entwined with notions of purity and pollution, menstruation, taboo and patriarchy.

The issue extends beyond Kerala, resonating with the broader problem of gender-based discrimination in religious practices across India. Examining the scenario in Odisha reveals a similar plight for women. Upon experiencing their first menstrual cycle, they are confined to their homes, prohibited from interacting with others and forbidden to engage in cooking activities. This chapter examines the challenges faced by women in Kerala and Odisha, underscoring the pervasive nature of discriminatory rituals against women in various parts of India and highlighting issues of chastity, seclusion and the regulation of female sexuality. This chapter calls for a critical evaluation and reformation of religious practices to promote gender equality and challenge discriminatory norms.

Religion is a powerful force all around the world. For women, religion can be an institution of limitation, oppression and even violence. It can also be a space of welcome, empowerment and resistance – sometimes at the same time. Of course, women's experiences of religion differ greatly, not only across religious traditions but also across race and ethnicity, nationality, sexuality, social class, ability and age. Women's position within societies is regulated by religious institutions at the family and community levels. Custom and tradition, often justified on religious grounds, ensure women's conformity to conventional gender roles, which can be the source of powerlessness and pain. Most rituals are practised for the common welfare of the people and become customs of discipline. When they are coated with God's word, they become stronger and are honoured as unquestionable. Therefore, rituals and ceremonies can have both inclusive and exclusive effects on society. While they can serve as unifying and meaningful practices that bring people together, they can also be used to discriminate and exclude certain individuals or groups. This chapter deals with the impact of religious rituals and ceremonies on gender with special reference to women in Odisha and India.

Context

The Sabarimala temple is an immensely popular pilgrimage site. Devotees observe a 41-day penance, abstaining from worldly pleasures before embarking on a pilgrimage to the shrine. Lord Ayyappan is venerated as a celibate deity, leading to the traditional prohibition of women between the ages of 10 and 50, encompassing menstruating years, from entering the temple to safeguard chastity (Iwanek, 2018). This restriction on women's entry, enforced through measures such as demanding age proof and deploying police personnel to prevent their access, ignited a widespread national debate due to its evident discriminatory nature. The issue extends beyond Kerala, resonating with the broader problem of gender-based discrimination in religious practices across India (Prasad, 2018).

Examining the scenario in Odisha reveals a similar plight for women. Upon experiencing their first menstrual cycle, they are confined to their homes, prohibited from interacting with others, forbidden to engage in cooking activities, and remain secluded for seven days. Subsequently, a ritual is performed to publicly announce the woman's first menstruation. This practice mirrors the challenges faced by women in Kerala and Odisha, underscoring the pervasive nature of discriminatory rituals against women in various parts of India.

In the context of Odisha, religious rituals are deeply intertwined with the region's diverse cultural and religious traditions. The dual nature of rituals necessitates a nuanced approach to appeal to those working towards gender liberation in the region. Hence, I have adopted a literature review and phenomenological method to explore the impact of religious rituals and ceremonies on gender in Odisha and find out how it intersects globally.[1]

Concepts of Purity and Pollution

The Case of Menstruation as Impure

Anthropologist Mary Douglas explains that the idea of purity and ritual uncleanness exists in all societies, and what is considered clean or pure in one context may be viewed as unclean or impure in another. For instance, in many cultures, menstrual blood is seen as polluting, and as a result, menstruating women are prohibited from participating in certain social and religious activities (Douglas, 2002, cited in Upadhya, 2017, pp. 101–2). Though menstruation is natural, it becomes the subject of various religious, cultural and gendered discriminative norms concerning purity, decency, responsibilities, taboos and stigma, manifested in the loss of gender rights and human lives (Upadhya, 2017, p. 102). Menstruation can make women feel restricted and isolated as though they are being punished or excluded (Upadhya, 2017, p. 108). Some societies view a woman's monthly period with disgust as impure, while ignoring or accepting a man's sperm discharge as something normal. Biologically, both menstruation and sperm discharge are natural bodily processes. Yet, men's sperm discharge has historically not been subjected to the same level of scrutiny or cultural taboos as menstruation.

Notions related to purity and pollution play a major role in Leviticus, probably more so than in any other book of the Hebrew Bible. A detailed law concerning the ritual of purity of both men and women is laid down in the priestly legislation. A notable distinction emerges regarding purity laws governing menstruation and sexual emissions. Leviticus 15.16–18 acknowledges male emissions, indicating a temporary state of ceremonial uncleanness, primarily focused on ritual purification rather than moral judgement. However, the following passage (15.19–24) delineates regulations concerning menstruation, labelling women as unclean during their menstrual period and imposing restrictions on their activities and interactions. During her period, a woman is considered impure and may not go near sacred spaces like the altar. Women during their period of fertility are permanently impure to some extent. This discrepancy underscores a patriarchal bias where female bodily functions are viewed as more impure or shameful compared to male functions. The law that determines the period of impurity of a woman at childbirth is another explicitly discriminatory expression of ritual uncleanliness. Seven days of impurity are prescribed for a mother who has borne a son, and her purification lasts for thirty days; but for a daughter it is fourteen days and her purification is sixty-six days (Lev. 12.1–5; Hnuni, 2009, p. 215).

Women are excluded from the role of priesthood, and it is open to debate whether women had an official role in worship. The Holiness Code is silent about this. While Exodus 38.8 mentions 'women who ministered at the door of the tent of meeting', but the text does not further explain the nature of their ministry. Women's exclusion from priesthood probably had the question of ritual purity as its background. Since physical wholeness and ritual purity are essential conditions for sacred ministry (Lev. 21—22, cf. Ezek. 44.15–31), women's uncleanness during regular menstruation and at childbirth must have been responsible for their exclusion from priestly office (Hnuni, 2009, p. 214). The notions of purity and pollution in Leviticus have contributed to discriminatory customs within certain religious traditions.

Menstruation subjects women to a sort of imprisonment and banishment. This maltreatment of women is rooted in a patriarchal culture of discrimination that denies women equal status to men (Upadhya, 2017, p. 108). This patriarchal culture consists of gendered language and imagery used in religious books or scriptures, limited roles in marriage and family ceremonies, limitations on public speaking, exclusion from leadership roles, restrictions on participation in religious rituals and dress codes. For instance, 1 Corinthians 14.34–36 instructs women to remain silent in churches and subordinate to men. When these religious teachings intersect with cultural views on menstruation, they compound the silencing effect on women in public spheres. Religious teachings often influence broader social and cultural norms. Discriminatory customs based on Leviticus and other biblical texts can extend beyond religious settings, shaping societal attitudes and contributing to the marginalization of women during menstruation.

Menstruation and Patriarchy

In societal views, menstruation is viewed as impure and detrimental to women's lives. Despite several variations, it becomes abundantly clear that there are many restrictions on menstruating women, based on the beliefs of the people that this particular bodily process makes women distinctly inferior to men (Pandey, 2015, pp. 205–6). These ideas are manifest in practices where menstruating women are secluded and restricted in their movements. The orientation of the body is based on the concept of purity and the protection of females. The woman has to keep within the laws regarding pollution and purity for life. When women go to lead a sexually active life, they feel their bodies are subordinate and continue to be a source of pollution. The female body absorbs the sins of the husband and any danger to him. The proponents of the argument believe that women produce 'perishable bodies' and men produce 'enduring symbols'; therefore, men are superior to women and must control women (Pandey, 2015, pp. 205–6). Female sexuality is controlled to maintain the super status of men.

This biased view comes from a society that favours men and does not honestly acknowledge this reality. Women might tolerate this humiliation because they have been conditioned to accept it in a male-dominated society (Samson, 2014, pp. 186–7). It is, therefore, clear that it is a male chauvinistic society oppressing women by upholding the ritual of the monthly period as impure and ignoring rituals regarding men. Women are therefore subject to atrocious acts of untouchability, partiality and alienation.

The biological and social-cultural comprehension of issues and problems embedded with gender and sexuality differs according to societies and cultures. Social-cultural norms and practices explaining gender and sexuality are deeply embedded in every level of patriarchal society and frequently influence human rights, the decisions of legislative and judicial bodies, law enforcement and health care services. The problem of menstruation discrimination remains grim: not all societies treat menstruation as a natural biological phenomenon because of its perceived ritual uncleanness. Instead, it becomes the subject of various religious, cultural and gendered discriminative norms concerning purity, decency, responsibilities and stigma that are manifest in the loss of gender rights and human lives (Upadhya, 2017, p. 102).

Purity, Pollution and Female Sexuality in the Context of Sabarimala and Odisha

In India, even mere mention of the topic of menstruation has been taboo in the past, and even to this date, cultural and social influences appear to be a hurdle to the advancement of knowledge on the subject. Culturally, in many parts of India, menstruation is still considered to be dirty and impure. Further, in the Hindu faith, women are prohibited from participating in normal life while menstruating. She must be 'purified' before she is allowed to return to her family and do the day-to-day chores of her life. Many girls and women are subject to restrictions in their daily lives simply because they are menstruating. Not entering the 'puja' (ritual worship) room is the major restriction among urban girls, whereas not entering the kitchen is the main restriction among rural girls during menstruation (Garg and Anand, 2015).

As such, the ideas of purity/impurity were present all over Hindu society for centuries, in domestic as well as public life, in any exchange of food and water, in the practice of occupations, in kinship and marriage, in religious action and beliefs, in temples and monasteries, and in myriad different contexts and situations. These ideas played a crucial role in separating one caste from another and arranging them in a hierarchy, that is to say, in ordering the basic structure of the society. A Hindu man or woman's life was permeated by ideas of purity/impurity from the moment of birth to the moment of death, and every day from the moment they got up from bed till they went to bed. Hindu civilization is sometimes called a civilization of purity and pollution, and the Hindu psyche is believed to be pathologically obsessed with them. One has only to conjure up an image of the orthodox Hindu taking different kinds of purificatory baths and their frequency. The highest degree of purity was attributed to gods and goddesses; their abodes, the temples, were therefore protected from every conceivable source of impurity. In the same manner, temple priests were considered the purest men and had to observe the rules of purity/impurity meticulously (Shah, 2007, pp. 355–6).

Pollution can be temporary or permanent, voluntary or involuntary, affecting anyone in society. Specifically, women experience temporary pollution during their first menstruation and childbirth. This makes them untouchable and untouching during this time, almost like the lowest untouchables. The idea is to protect them from harmful influences and prevent contamination of others. People believe evil spirits are attracted to this impurity. Women in this state should avoid actions that increase impurity, especially avoiding certain foods. The end of pollution is marked by purification ceremonies to restore normal ritual status (Ferro-Luzzi, 1974).

The way society views women's sexuality has been complicated, especially when it comes to religion and culture in India. In the past, some societies admired women for their ability to have children and valued signs of fertility. Roles related to reproduction and sexuality were interconnected. In some places, there were even rituals where men mimicked menstruation. In the context of purity and pollution in India, however, women are perceived to have a polluting influence on men during sexual intercourse. Entering the inner sanctum of a temple is considered to defile the sacred space and anger the guardian deity. Additionally, touching men on their heads or shoulders is viewed as causing pollution, affecting both ordinary men and those believed to possess extraordinary powers, leading to the loss of these abilities (Ortner, 1973, p. 50).

The Sabarimala temple does not allow women in, and this rule perpetuates the idea that women should be responsible for controlling their sexuality. The Sabarimala temple justifies its ban on women by claiming religious autonomy. Despite being considered a *Brahmacārin* or divine celibate, someone who practises *Brahmacharya* should not feel threatened by the presence of women (Krishnan, 2006). *Brahmacharya* is the celibate student stage of life. The term *Brahmacārin* can mean 'one who is celibate'; the idea behind this, common to all Indian religions, is that to remain celibate is to be unpolluted by sex and to control sexual energy which, usually understood as the retention of semen, can be redirected for a religious purpose (Flood, 2017, p. 63). However, in modern democracy, discrimination based on gender or caste is not acceptable. Concepts like 'sacredness' or 'security' should not be used to support unfair practices. In today's India, sacredness and female sexuality are still linked in people's minds, contributing to unequal treatment and reinforcing gender biases. It is important to work towards ending these discriminatory practices for a fairer and more inclusive society.

Likewise, the Paroja community of Odisha follows puberty rites for girls, involving a seven-day seclusion post-menarche. The term 'Paroja' in Odia, also pronounced as Paraja, Parja, or Poroja, refers to common people distinct from former ruling chiefs. Legend has it that Rajas (kings) and Prajas (common people) once lived as brothers but diverged in lifestyle. The Paroja community speaks Parji, a form of Gondi influenced by local languages like Odia or Telugu, now commonly using 'Desia' (Marinescu, 2023, p. 67). The girl undergoes a purificatory bath, symbolizing cleansing, and receives new clothes and cosmetics. The rites reinforce traditional gender roles, emphasizing female purity and modesty. Pregnancy brings taboos and restrictions for the well-being of the woman and safe delivery. Childbirth involves rituals, cutting the umbilical cord and a period of seclusion until the cord dries. Afterwards, purification rituals are conducted, and the family welcomes the newborn with celebrations and offerings to family deities. Hence, the seven-day seclusion during menstruation and post-childbirth seclusion may lead to social isolation for women. Limited interaction with males during these periods could impact women's social relationships and opportunities for engagement within the community. The taboos and restrictions imposed during pregnancy may influence women's daily activities and diet. Engaging in daily chores until advanced stages of pregnancy might affect maternal health, potentially leading to physical strain. The seclusion and specific practices during menstruation and childbirth may contribute to feelings of stigmatization or reinforce societal views on women's roles. Limited access to modern medical practices could impact maternal and child health outcomes.

The following are the areas where gender discrimination is found in many states of India, due not only to the concept of purity and pollution but also to the teachings that are found in religious books and scriptures of the Indian religions.

Discriminatory Practices

Social Restrictions

In Odisha, I had a conversation with a few girls belonging to Hindu and Adivasi religious traditions who expressed the belief that it is appropriate to restrict women from participating in religious activities during menstruation. Consequently, these girls refrained from entering places of worship, adhering to the notion that the female body is considered impure during this period. They held the conviction that entering sacred spaces could compromise sanctity, potentially bringing bad luck. Despite being rooted in age-old traditions, they felt that such practices should be upheld.

To better understand the day-to-day experience of women facing discrimination based on purity and pollution, I employed a phenomenological approach to observe the girls' kitchen activities. They disclosed that they are still not allowed to cook or fetch potable water during menstruation. The duration of this restriction varies from three to five days. While the girls acknowledged and validated the limitation on entering religious places, they collectively opposed restrictions within their homes. They expressed discomfort with the idea that family members would become aware of their menstrual status, causing them shame. Some girls also shared experiences of elders in their families prohibiting them from leaving the house during menstruation due to the fear of attracting negative spirits or bad omens. Regarding their daily routines during this period, the girls asserted that their rest and activities remain the same as on other days. These practices continue in many places in Odisha, not only among Hindus but in other religious traditions as well.

Limited Roles in Marriage and Family Ceremonies

In Christian weddings and family rituals, women are often portrayed as submissive wives and mothers, following traditional gender roles. This can strengthen the idea of male dominance and restrict women's freedom and independence within marriage and family life. People see it as something sacred, perfect and unconditional, and some even believe it is a union arranged by a higher power, often saying, 'Marriages are made in heaven' (Rao, 2018, p. xi). In a patriarchal context like India, a woman is said to be fruitful and blessed only if she bears a child in her marital phase of life, or else she is considered to be a curse to the family and to society. Due to her barrenness, she is prevented from participating in any socio-religious or cultural events. She is made to internalize the patriarchal norms very strongly, leading her to actively isolate herself from society (Keerthana, 2014, p. 1).

According to my phenomenological research in interaction with my school and college friends, it is not the same for men in a patriarchal context like India. Men are not judged or excluded from society based on their ability to have children. The societal pressure and consequences related to fertility and childbearing are primarily experienced by women in such contexts. This reflects gender inequality and discrimination against women. The issue of purity and pollution is often exacerbated in these contexts. Women who do not conform to the expected roles, such as being childless, are considered a curse to the family and society. This categorization further marginalizes these women, reinforcing the idea that their worth is solely determined by their adherence to traditional gender roles.

In many societies, traditional notions of purity have been linked to women's roles in maintaining the sanctity of the private sphere, particularly through their roles as wives and mothers. When women challenge or seek to participate in public spaces traditionally reserved for men, they may be perceived as violating these purity norms. This perception can lead to the marginalization and stigmatization of women who aspire to break free from traditional gender roles. The enforcement of purity norms often results in the control of women's bodies and behaviours, reinforcing the idea that certain spaces are inherently impure or inappropriate for women to inhabit. This contributes to the perpetuation of gender-based discrimination and silencing, as women are discouraged from participating fully in public life. The intersection of religious beliefs, traditional gender roles, and the concept of purity and pollution creates a complex web that continues to marginalize and limit the agency of women in various societal spheres globally.

Restriction on Participation and Leadership Roles

The combination of menstrual taboos and religious restrictions reinforces gender stereotypes and fosters feelings of shame and inferiority among women. This not only affects their participation in religious gatherings but also extends to secular settings where women may feel hesitant to assert themselves or speak out. It also points out that these beliefs have been used to justify the unequal treatment of women in both religious institutions and society, often through the manipulation of religious texts.

According to Ninian Smart, religion is a constantly adapting tradition (Smart, 1973, p. 15). Throughout its history, it has manufactured hierarchical structures and inequality in line with the vested interests of affluent communities. Women and Aboriginals have been most victimized in such a process (Giri, 2018). Exclusively male-centred leadership in the church has been developed gradually in the course of history. In 1 Corinthians 14.34–36, Paul states, 'Women should be silent in the churches. For they are not permitted to speak but should be subordinate, as the law also says. If there is something they want to learn, let them ask their husbands at home. For it is shameful for a woman to speak in church.' There are other passages in the New Testament that discriminate against women by setting boundaries of laws and codes for them, such as in Colossians 3.18–19, where wives are admonished to be submissive to their husbands: 'Wives, be subject to your husbands.' In the early period an egalitarian church slowly became a hierarchal one, and ministry was exclusively in the hands of male-ordained clergy (Longkumer, 2018, p. 122). Some men use women's biological roles in childbearing and procreation as excuses to exclude them from equal participation in the church's ministry (cf. 1 Tim. 2.13–15). The exclusion of women is justified based on interpretations of these biblical texts or traditional understandings of gender roles.

In addition to religious conditioning, cultural stereotypes persist that portray women as less capable leaders than men. Female leaders will likely be refused by persons with traditional gender role attitudes, preferring women to be housewives and mothers. The unreasonable excuse many men often make is that 'it is unthinkable for carrying women to conduct holy communion, to give baptism and travel from one place to another, so it is not good to accept women as pastors and in other leadership roles'. By suggesting that women's physical capabilities or natural functions render them unfit for roles such as administering sacraments or leading congregations, this mindset perpetuates harmful stereotypes and reinforces gender-based discrimination. In my personal experience serving as a teacher in a Bible college, there were instances when I was asked to read scripture for programmes. However, I was instructed by the bishop not to ascend to the pulpit or stage for this task. Instead, I was directed to remain at ground level while reading. This instruction left me puzzled, as I could not discern the reason behind it. It seemed as though there was a perception that women, including myself, were considered spiritually unfit or impure to ascend the stage for such readings. This exclusion reinforces gender hierarchies and limits women's involvement in the spiritual and liturgical life of the community.

In general, women experience top-down, hierarchical and patriarchal leadership which is not only negative but also disempowering and dominating. In such a style of leadership, authority is exercised as power over, reinforcing power structures that continue to oppress, exclude, marginalize and silence women (Longkumer, 2018, p. 121). To this day women's participation in leadership in different spheres of life is unsatisfactory. Even though women have been active participants and members in different walks of life and despite the fact that capable women have come out in different societies and churches, it remains taboo to appoint women in a position of a leader. Women have been ordained as pastors in some Indian churches, such as the Church of North India, the Church of South India, the Methodist Church and in a few Churches in Northeast India. But these instances are like a drop of rain in the vast ocean. Ordination is one thing; women are prevented from having any role in the decision-making bodies. At the highest level of decision making, the General Assembly or Annual Meeting or Synod, sometimes not even a single woman representative will be there among hundreds of members (Hnuni, 2009, p. 38). Since people with a traditional mindset would endorse traditional role allocation between women and men, one could assume that these persons feel uncomfortable about women in high-status positions, which affects subordinates' perceptions of female leaders. These traditional gender stereotypes have been very resistant to change even today in the attitudes of the people. Thus, women in leadership issues bring conflicts and tensions; their presence at that level divides opinions among the people regarding women's leadership

(Longkumer, 2018, pp. 116–17). However, diverse religious practices worldwide reflect varied attitudes towards women's leadership, while legal and societal norms range from progressive to restrictive.

Control of Female Sexuality through Dress Codes

Women's central role as wives, mothers and transmitters of cultural and religious beliefs makes it important for their behaviours to be regulated, in particular their sexuality, since the paternity of their children is of prime concern to patriarchal societies. Most human religions, from tribal to world religions, have treated the woman's body, in its gender-specific sexual functions, as impure or polluted and thus to be distanced from sacred spaces and rites dominated by males. The need to control women's impure sexuality is linked to male physical and mental violence against them, ranging from sexual violence inflicted on child and adult females at home and outside the home, to the policing of women's dress codes and modesty (Sweetman, 1998, p. 4).

Religions establish dress codes to clearly show what they consider moral and modest. People in power within the church use these dress codes to impose their beliefs on others. These codes serve to identify the group members and also to maintain male-dominated control. When religions use dress to uphold tradition, they tend to oppose fashion, which is constantly changing. Religious attire evolves slowly because they see fashion as a distraction from focusing on personal salvation and emphasize conformity instead (Arthur, 1999). In the context of religion, clothing can be divided into two categories: sacred and secular (or profane). Sometimes, what is considered sacred clothing is actually a garment that has cultural importance related to gendered power. In patriarchal religions, where men are often seen as responsible for enforcing religious rules, certain garments become associated with sacredness because of the rules and dress codes they follow (Arthur, 1999). Hence, some Christian communities impose strict dress codes or expectations of modesty on women during religious ceremonies. These expectations can place the burden of responsibility on women for controlling the thoughts and actions of others, perpetuating harmful ideas about female sexuality and reinforcing gender-based discrimination. So, these practices have negative effects on women in society and restrict their involvement in religious matters.

Strict dress codes often reinforce traditional gender roles, portraying women as solely responsible for upholding modesty and purity. This perpetuates the idea that women's primary role is to maintain societal norms of chastity and virtue, while men are often exempt from similar expectations. The way these dress codes are enforced often makes it seem like women are the only ones responsible for making sure men behave themselves. This idea reinforces the belief that women are inferior and that they have to be careful not to tempt men. It is like saying women are to blame if men cannot control themselves, which is not fair at all. This not only undermines women's agency but also contributes to a culture of victim-blaming, where women are held accountable for the actions of others. Women may feel compelled to adhere to strict dress guidelines out of fear of social stigma or religious condemnation. This limits their ability to express themselves through clothing and undermines their right to make personal decisions about their appearance and attire. Imposed dress codes often reflect and reinforce patriarchal norms within religious institutions.

Religion and Transformation

As Sujith Kumar Chattopadhyay points out, 'Women were basically viewed with an objectified, fragmented and dehumanizing approach' (Chattopadhyay, 2018, p. ix). Inequality and degradation of women are often sanctified in religious traditions. Women in almost all the religions of the world have similar low-ebb experiences and dehumanizing tendencies. Religion professed turned out to be irrelevant and oppressive for various sections of society, especially for women, and that is how reform became a pressing necessity even for the very existence of any religious tradition in the world (Krishnan, 2018). Oppressive interpretations of religious texts promoted by male-dominated religious institutions can be challenged by alternative interpretations of religious writings.

Thus, Bridget Walker suggests feminist theologies as: 1) a quest for alternative traditions which will include women as well as men; 2) feminist theology as a transformation of male symbols and search for inclusive symbols used for God and humans that can be compared and linked to other liberation theologies reclaiming religion for the poor (Walker, 1998, p. 20; Hnuni, 2009, p. 214). In her 1990 lecture on Feminist Theology in Bangalore, Rosemary Radford Ruether also brings out three processes in her methodology of feminist theology: 1) a critique of androcentrism and misogyny; 2) a quest for alternative traditions; and 3) a search for the transformation of models (cited in Hnuni, 2009, p. 1). Similarly, R. L. Hnuni argues that feminist theology seeks to analyse the effect of the exclusion of women and negative anthropology about women in the shaping of the understanding of God, nature, sin, grace, Christology, redemption and ecclesiology (Hnuni, 2009, p. 9). The core ideas of religion, often expressed in the words of a deity or prophet, can inspire positive social, economic and political change. Religious faith motivates the thoughts and actions of women and men throughout the world; most religious movements have their roots in reformatory visions, which focus on the inner ethical motivations of the person, rather than their external bodily state, and respect for all persons, regardless of gender or ethnicity (Sweetman, 1998, p. 4).

Reforming Faith: Rethinking Purity and Pollution

Feminist theologians assert that merely rediscovering faith is inadequate because religions evolve based on the specific conditions of their time, shaped by politics, economics and social attitudes. They contend that codes and practices from the past must be reformed to align with the present social context. Movements advocating for women's ordination apply this concept. In feminist theology, the emphasis is on uncovering women's identity from their own experiences, diverging from conforming to a patriarchal culture. This approach seeks both personal and social transformation. To reform the purity and pollution concept present in various religious traditions, feminist theology encourages a re-evaluation of these notions (Walker, 1998, p. 20). Therefore, I argue that reforming the traditional beliefs surrounding purity and pollution within faith systems is imperative for promoting women's empowerment and their inclusion in leadership roles both within religious institutions and society at large. Instead of viewing certain practices as impure or contaminating, there is a call to recognize the inherent equality of all individuals, challenging discriminatory beliefs and fostering inclusivity within religious contexts. This transformation aims to create a more egalitarian and just spiritual space, acknowledging the worth and contributions of everyone, regardless of gender, in a global context.

Rejecting the Spiritual Notions Tied to Purity and Pollution

Rejecting spiritual notions tied to purity and pollution is crucial for advancing gender equality and challenging patriarchal norms entrenched in religious practices. In many cultures, including parts of India, menstruation is associated with impurity, leading to restrictions on women's activities such as offering prayers, touching holy books, and even preparing food. These beliefs are rooted in cultural myths and taboos surrounding menstruation, perpetuating notions of women as unclean and contaminated. According to Kumar and Srivastava (2011), women who participated in rituals reported that during menstruation the body emits some specific smell or ray, which turns preserved food bad, so they are not allowed to touch sour foods like pickles.

Cultural norms and religious taboos on menstruation are often compounded by traditional associations with evil spirits, shame and embarrassment surrounding sexual reproduction. In some cultures, women bury their clothes used during menstruation to prevent them from being used by evil spirits. In some parts of India, strict dietary restrictions are also followed during menstruation: sour foods such as curd, tamarind and pickles are usually avoided by menstruating girls. It is believed that such foods will disturb or stop the menstrual flow (Garg and Anand, 2015). The rejection of organized religion by many women is often linked to the perception of it being deeply entwined with a pervasive patriarchy rooted in violence. In this context, the patriarchy within organized religion is seen as a contaminating force, symbolizing impurity (Walker, 1998, p. 20).

In some parts of India, bodily excretions are believed to be polluting, as are the bodies when producing them. All women, regardless of their social caste, incur pollution through the bodily processes of menstruation and childbirth. Water is considered to be the most common medium of purification. The protection of water sources from such pollution, which is the physical manifestation of Hindu deities, is, therefore, a key concern (Garg and Anand, 2015). This highlights the possible reason why menstruating women are not allowed to take a bath, especially for the first few days of their menstrual period. It is believed that if a girl or woman touches a cow while she is on her period, the cow will become infertile – leading girls to associate their own bodies with curse and impurity.

Hence, rejecting the spiritual concepts associated with purity and pollution can significantly contribute to enhancing the full personhood of women. By discarding these antiquated notions, we can dismantle the barriers that have long confined women to subordinate positions within religious hierarchies. These concepts often perpetuate harmful gender stereotypes and restrict women's agency by prescribing rigid roles based on notions of purity and impurity. Consequently, women are often excluded from leadership roles and denied opportunities for active participation in decision-making processes within religious institutions.

Moreover, rejecting these spiritual notions of purity and pollution aligns with the principles of equality and justice, fostering an environment where women are recognized as equal participants in matters of faith and spirituality. Embracing a more inclusive and egalitarian interpretation of religious teachings can pave the way for women to assume leadership positions and contribute their perspectives to the development and evolution of religious doctrines and practices. Furthermore, by challenging these traditional beliefs, we can foster a more inclusive and welcoming environment within religious communities, one that celebrates the diversity of human experiences and acknowledges the inherent worth and dignity of all individuals regardless of gender. This, in turn, can contribute to the broader movement for gender equality and social justice by promoting greater acceptance and respect for women's rights and autonomy.

To overcome this perceived contamination and achieve gender equality, a transformative journey is essential. This involves re-evaluating and reshaping religious practices and structures that reinforce patriarchal norms, recognizing them as sources of impurity in need of purification. It also requires adopting inclusive practices, acknowledging past injustices, and creating spaces within religious traditions where women can freely express their spiritual experiences without the constraints of patriarchal norms. Through these changes, individuals and religious communities strive to challenge and dismantle patriarchal elements viewed as pollutants, while preserving positive aspects that resonate with personal spiritual paths. Education and awareness programmes can play a crucial role in promoting gender equality within religious settings. Ultimately, the goal is to cultivate a more equitable and spiritually enriched global faith expression, embracing intersectionality as a crucial framework to address interconnected systems of oppression and privilege that affect people across diverse identities and experiences worldwide.

Conclusion

While religious rituals and ceremonies have the potential to be empowering and unifying, they can also reinforce harmful gender stereotypes and discrimination. This chapter calls for a critical evaluation and reformation of religious practices to promote gender equality and challenge discriminatory norms. Religious institutions should re-examine their language, imagery, and rituals to ensure they are inclusive and empowering for all genders. Encouraging women's active participation in leadership roles and decision-making bodies will not only foster a more diverse and equitable religious community but also enrich the faith with different perspectives and talents. This imperative for change resonates globally, intersecting with various cultural contexts and social dynamics, thereby underscoring the universal relevance of fostering gender-inclusive religious spaces and practices.

In addressing these challenges globally, it is essential to acknowledge that many Christian traditions already embrace gender equality and strive to challenge discriminatory practices. The task is to extend these inclusive practices to all religious communities and denominations, fostering an environment where gender equity is embraced as a fundamental tenet of religious teachings. To achieve this, religious leaders and communities must engage in open dialogue and engage in theological discussions that challenge patriarchal interpretations and oppressive norms recognizing the intersectionality of gender issues within diverse global contexts.

Note

1 Phenomenology in qualitative research is a study of a phenomenon, event, situation or development, like religious expression in words, acts and expressed intentions as they actually appear and emerge in religious traditions, through a thorough and detailed analysis like a personal interview. Cf. Lott (2001), pp. 36–7.

References

Arthur, Linda B., 1999, *Religion, Dress and the Body*, Rhode Island: Berg Publishers.
Chattopadhyay, Sujith Kumar, 2018, *Gender Socialization and the Making of Gender in the Indian Context*, New Delhi: Sage Publications.
Douglas, Mary, 2002, *Purity and Danger, An Analysis of Concepts of Pollution and Taboo*, London: Routledge.
Ferro-Luzzi, Gabriella Eichinger, 1974, 'Women's Pollution Periods in Tamilnad (India)', *Anthropos* 69 (1/2), p. 114.
Flood, Gavin, 2017, *An Introduction to Hinduism*, Cambridge: Cambridge University Press.
Garg, Suneela, and Tani Anand, 2015, 'Menstruation Related Myths in India: Strategies for Combating It', *Journal of Family Medical Primary Care* 4 (2), pp. 184–6, https://doi.org/10.4103/2249-4863.154627 (accessed 3.3.2025).
Hnuni, R. L., 2009, *Vision for Women in India: Perspective from the Bible, Church and Society*, Bangalore: Asian Trading Corporation.
Iwanek, Krzsztof, 2018, 'India's Sabarimala Temple and the Issue of Women's Entry', *The Diplomat*, 3 October, https://thediplomat.com/2018/10/indias-sabarimala-temple-and-the-issue-of-womens-entry (accessed 21.1.2025).
Keerthana, Shuba, 2014, 'A Sermon for Advent a Feminist Perspective, Hannah's Cry: A Quest for God's Reign', in *Women from the Pulpit*, ed. Atola Longkumer and P. Mohan Larbeer, Bangalore: BTESSC.

Krishnan, Giri, 2018, 'Women's Role and Participation in Contemporary Hindu Religious Movement in the Context of "Gender Socialization"', in *Religion and Women: Pilgrims in Search of Justice and Equity*, ed. Lalchawiliana and K. Lalchhuanawma, Aizawal: Lengchhawan Press, pp. 54–77.

Krishnan, Kavita, 2006, 'Sacred Spaces, Secular Norms, and Women's Rights', *Economic and Political Weekly* 41 (27/28), pp. 2969–71.

Kumar, A., and K. Srivastava, 2011, 'Cultural and Social Practices Regarding Menstruation among Adolescent Girls', *Society of Work Public Health* 26 (6), pp. 594–604.

Longkumer, Limatula, 2018, 'Women in Ecclesial Leadership: A Justice Issue', in *Religion and Women: Pilgrims in Search of Justice and Equity*, ed. Lalchawiliana and K. Lalchhuanawma, pp. 109–26, Aizawal: Lengchhawan Press.

Lott, Eric, 2001, 'Approaching a Religious Tradition', in *Religious Tradition of India*, ed. P. S. Daniel et al., pp. 1–45, Delhi: ISPCK.

Marinescu, Angelica Helena, 2023, 'Society, Culture and Natural Surroundings: Indigenous Knowledge and Practices of the *Dongria*, *Dhuruva* and *Poroja* Tribes of Rayagada and Koraput Districts, Odisha, India', *Revista Română de Sociologie* 1–2, pp. 61–82.

Ortner, Sherry B., 1973, 'Sherpa Purity', *American Anthropologist* 75 (1), pp. 49–63, https://www.jstor.org/stable/672339 (accessed 21.1.2025).

Pandey, Seema, 2015, *Women in Contemporary Indian Society*, New Delhi: Rawat Publications.

Prasad, Akshita, 2018, 'The Sabarimala Issue is About Gender and Patriarchy, and Our Denial Won't Change That', *News, Sexism and Patriarchy, Society*, https://www.youthkiawaaz.com/2018/08/the-sabarimala-issue-is-about-gender-and-patriarchy-and-our-denial-wont-change-that/ (accessed 21.1.2025).

Rao, Naveen, 2018, 'Marriage: Traditions, Changes and Future', in *Marriage, Traditions, Changes, Challenges Ahead*, ed. Bendanglemla Longkumer, pp. xi-xvi, Sandeshharika LTC: ISPCK.

Samson, Kausalya, 2014, 'Transgression –The True Spirituality', in *Women from the Pulpit*, ed. Atola Longkumer and P. Mohan Larbeer, pp. 185–90, Bangalore: BTESSC.

Shah, A. M., 2007, 'Purity, Impurity, Untouchability: Then and Now', *Sociological Bulletin* 56 (3), pp. 355–68.

Smart, Ninian, 1973, *The Science of Religion and the Sociology of Knowledge*, Princeton: Princeton University Press.

Sweetman, Caroline, 1998, 'Editorial', in *Gender, Religion and Spirituality*, ed. Caroline Sweetman, pp. 2–6, Oxford: Oxfam.

Upadhya, Prakash, 2017, 'Mestruation Pollution Taboos and Gender Based Violence in Western Nepal', *The NEHU Journal* 15(2), July–December, pp. 101–11.

Walker, Bridget, 1998, 'Christianity, Development, and Women's Liberation', in *Gender, Religion and Spirituality*, ed. Caroline Sweetman, pp. 15–22, Oxford: Oxfam.

3

Cultural Crossroads: Women's Ritual Participation in Northeast India and the Mainland

AJUNGLA JAMIR

Introduction

The world is a mosaic of diverse ethnicities, religions, languages, cultures and regions. Within this rich tapestry, rituals and ceremonies hold significant importance in upholding various cultures, reinforcing cultural norms, values and identities. These practices, deeply rooted in society, promote social unity and safeguard heritage. By transmitting rituals and ceremonies to successive generations, cultural continuity is ensured. However, for women globally, some of these practices inadvertently reinforce harmful normalization procedures that adversely affect them, be it their well-being, cultural identity, or social status, to name only a few.

This chapter sheds light on women's experiences globally concerning rituals and ceremonies within their native communities. In doing so, it focuses on the women of Northeast India as its reference point to study how these normalization processes of rituals and ceremonies within their own cultures and religions affect women in public spaces and religious institutions. Specifically, two rituals are considered: the Post-Transplantation Festival, which serves as an expression of gratitude towards the divine and a plea for blessings on agricultural endeavours; and the Feast of Reconciliation, which promotes peaceful co-existence between hostile communities. Besides these, the experiences of Northeast women regarding food customs and dress codes in Christian worship in the mainland Indian context are also examined. The central question revolves around reimagining these normalization processes to foster inclusivity and empowerment for women, countering tendencies of marginalization and exclusion.

Methodological Standpoints

This chapter resorts to a comprehensive analysis of cultural, religious and socio-political contexts in the South Asian milieu of India. A feminist liberation perspective provides a lens through which power structures and gender dynamics of the practices under investigation are critically analysed. Simultaneously, the historical analysis traces the evolution of rituals and ceremonies, elucidating how these practices have been shaped by historical events, colonial influences and socio-political transformations. Through a meticulous examination of these theoretical trajectories, this chapter discerns continuities and changes in rituals over time, thereby unravelling the intricate interplay of various factors that have contributed to the contemporary experiences of Northeast women in India.

Intersectionality is a key methodological standpoint used in this chapter. It holds that individuals hold multiple identities that intersect and influence their experiences. It considers factors such as gender, class, sex, ethnicity, race, religion and geographical location, to name a few. This approach allows for a nuanced understanding of how the unique intersectional identities of Northeast women contribute to their experiences in rituals and ceremonies both in their native land and in the context of mainland India.

Through qualitative methods such as interviews, participant observation and analysis of cultural texts, this chapter gained insights into the lived experiences of women, uncovering nuances and variations in their participation in rituals and ceremonies. Lastly, personal narratives are integrated into this chapter to illustrate the real-world impact of cultural and religious practices on Northeast women. These narratives provide a relatable context for readers, fostering empathy and a deeper understanding of the challenges faced by women in general and Northeast women of the South Asian context of India in particular.

Understanding 'Northeast' in View of Mainland India

In India, the term 'Northeast' was established when the Indian Parliament passed the North Eastern Areas (Reorganization) Act of 1971. Later, the term was formalized with the creation of the North Eastern Council in the same year (Baruah, 2003, pp. 922–3). Since then, the term 'Northeast' has been a collective geographical and administrative category referring to the eight federal states of India, namely, Arunachal Pradesh,

Assam, Manipur, Meghalaya, Mizoram, Nagaland, Sikkim and Tripura. The region covers about 263,179 sq. km, which is about 7.89% of the total geographical area of India. The population of Northeast India is heterogeneous, consisting of approximately 65 million people, representing many ethnic groups with many different religions, languages, cultures, etc. (*Northeast Now*, 2023). According to government records, Northeast states are considered among the most backward states in India, receiving 'preferential treatment in government grants and loans' (Tuniyi and Wouters, 2016, p. 6).

Due to its distinct geo-political location, most mainland Indian people view Northeast states with suspicion and reservation. The term 'mainland Indian people' (or mainstream/mainline Indian) is commonly used throughout India to differentiate Northeast people from those in other parts of India. The necessity for a separate designation when referring to 'India' underscores 'the ontological gap between the people of the Northeast region and the rest of India' (Angelova, 2015, p. 153).

Northeast Tribal Rituals and Ceremonies

Northeast India harbours over 200 distinct tribal community groups, with many adhering to Christianity, Hinduism and/or Primal religion. Each community diligently preserves and upholds its unique traditions through a myriad of traditional rituals and ceremonies. This rich diversity challenges the pinpointing of a singular practice, as each community upholds its distinct rituals and ceremonies (D'Souza, 2012, pp. 22–3). Despite these differences, a common thread lies in the pervasive influence of taboos that guide these rituals and ceremonies.

Deeply interwoven within the fabric of indigenous rituals and ceremonies, taboos serve as fundamental guidelines governing behaviour, interactions and the execution of sacred rituals (Soto, 2011, pp. 71–5). Within indigenous cultures, taboos encompass a wide range of prohibitions, restrictions and obligations that dictate acceptable behaviour within the community. These taboos extend to various facets of life, including food, language, relationships and restrict actions such as seeing, doing, hearing and wearing clothes (Loly, 2022, p. 165). Integral to rituals, taboos play a crucial role in ensuring their proper performance and preserving the sanctity of the occasion. They often delineate who can participate in specific ceremonies, dictate the sequence of rituals, and specify the requisite attire or offerings. One significant aspect of taboos within Northeastern rituals and ceremonies is their profound impact on gender roles and participation. In many Northeast cultures, taboos impose stringent restrictions on the roles and behaviours of both men and women during these sacred events. Regrettably, it is often women who bear the brunt of these taboos, with restrictions disproportionately affecting them. This disparity is palpable in widely practised customs within Northeast tribal communities, such as the Post-Transplantation Festival and the Feast of Reconciliation.

Post-Transplantation Festival

Various cultures around the world observe post-transplantation festivals or agricultural festivals.[1] The Hopi tribe in North America celebrates a similar festival known as the *Soyal* ceremony, which marks the winter solstice and involves prayers for a successful planting season (Dorsey and Voth, 1901). In addition, other East Asian countries such as the Chinese and the Vietnamese observe a traditional harvest festival known as the Mid-Autumn Festival or the Moon Festival, which involves offerings of food, mooncakes, and prayers to deities for a successful harvest. The underlying themes of gratitude, blessings for agriculture, and rituals to appease divine entities are common in all these cultures.

Likewise, many Northeast tribal communities in India also observed the Post-Transplantation Festival. In the Northeast Indian context, this festival serves as an expression of gratitude towards the divine and a plea for blessings on agricultural endeavours. The festivities typically span three to four days, with one specific day reserved for a ritual performed exclusively by men. While the festival's name varies in each dialect, its essence remains consistent throughout the communities. This festival features a pivotal ritual, which takes centre stage on its eve. Among the Poumai Naga community, this ritual is termed *Loutouju*, which literally means 'food eating'. Participation in this ritual is exclusive to menfolk, yet it remains voluntary, not mandatory for every man. Consequently, elderly men and people with disabilities abstain from participation, while women and children are unable to partake directly. In fact, during this practice, any form of female involvement or assistance in male activities is strictly proscribed.

However, women can seek divine mercy, blessings and protection while not participating in the ritual. Those men who partake in this ritual manage their own dietary needs, while others rely on women as usual. Each man individually carries out the tasks of fetching water, cooking with fresh firewood on a new hearth, and kindling a fire using bamboo and wood. Women are prohibited from consuming any remnants of the meal. The central purpose of this ritual is to implore the divine for martial prowess, strength and good fortune in the individual's life. Following the conclusion of the festival, the men who participate in this ritual meticulously clean their pots, adorning them with a specific leaf cover before hanging them beneath the roof for the forthcoming year. On the first day following the festival's conclusion, the men of the community take on the responsibility of cleansing all pathways leading to the village. Once this task is accomplished, village priests perform a symbolic gesture to the divine by releasing a cock as an offering. The ritual's irony and prejudice stem from its focus on securing divine favour solely for the man conducting it, disregarding the family as a whole and women in particular (Loly, 2022).

Feast of Reconciliation

Rituals promoting reconciliation, unity and peaceful coexistence are not unique to any single culture or country but are found in various forms across different societies throughout history. The *Mato Oput* ritual observed among the Acholi people of Northern Uganda as a means to bring about reconciliation provides one such example. This ritual involves a multi-stage ritual for restoring relationships between communities affected by wrongful killings. It begins with the perpetrator community seeking mediation from a third party, who communicates details of the killing to the victim community. Truth-telling, genuine accountability and compensation follow, testing the sincerity of the perpetrators. The central ritual, *Mato Oput*, involves drinking a bitter root concoction symbolizing the bitterness of death. This is followed by restoring relationships through symbolic gestures and the sharing of food. Finally, societal transformation occurs as witnessing communities join in festivities, marking a fresh start and collective healing (Mwaka, 2023, pp. 11–12).

Similar to the *Mato Oput* practised by the Acholi people of Uganda, the Feast of Reconciliation is a significant event observed among many tribal communities in Northeast India. Among these communities, the *Aksü* feast, whose literal translation means 'pig dead' or 'pig killed', holds particular importance for the Ao Naga tribe of Nagaland, India. *Aksü* is generally observed as a 'feast organized by killing pigs as a sign of political supremacy as well as protection' (Imchen, 1993, p. 194). Additionally, *Aksü* is also an act of showing love, through which reconciliation and peace are built between conflicting villages/groups. It reaffirms the bond of friendship, loyalty and love between different factions within and between the community (Takatemjen, 1998, p. 117). The *Aksü* feast typically follows a structured procedure when held between two conflicting villages or groups seeking a peaceful resolution:

1. Representatives from each conflicting party meet to discuss and address the issues at hand. After a thorough inquiry, the guilty party is identified, and arrangements are made for reconciliation.
2. The offending party, known as the guest group, is welcomed into the accused village by council members. Each member of the guest group is assigned a host family to stay with during their visit.
3. Various gatherings and house visits are organized, allowing members of both parties to interact, share meals and participate in traditional rituals such as the *kimak* procession, which is a ceremonial procession or visitation to various households within the village. Council members lead these activities to ensure the smooth progress of the reconciliation process.
4. On the third day, a pig is ceremonially slaughtered by the host village council members. The process follows specific customary techniques, and the divided portions of the pig are presented to the guest group. If satisfied, the guest group offers a symbolic payment known as '*aksü kupen*' to the host council members as a sign of acceptance and satisfaction with the ceremonial pig killing.
5. The final day of the *Aksü* feast ceremony, known as *ankep* or *yimkep* day, features various traditional speeches and ceremonies, typically led by important community figures such as the *Ung* (priest) and the *Samen* (village chief) from both groups. They discuss the history of their villages, their friendship and prospects of camaraderie. It is a time for reflection, reconciliation and celebration of shared identity and heritage.

Various other tribes in Northeast India have their own versions of the Feast of Reconciliation under different names. For example, the Chakhesang Naga tribe refers to it as *Küchene*, meaning the Feast of Peace-making, while the Sumi Naga tribe calls it *Alu Pekili*, signifying reconciliation. Despite the diversity of names, the essence of the ceremony remains constant. Unlike fixed annual festivals, this ceremony, in general, occurs once, forever binding the communities (Takatemjen, 1999, pp. 106–7). Rituals such as the sharing of communal meals and drinks, the exchange of gifts, visits between villages, and symbolic acts of forgiveness are integral parts of the ceremony. The practices surrounding these rituals vary significantly, reflecting the unique cultural contexts, histories and traditions of different communities.

One common thread among many indigenous rituals is the exclusion of women from active participation in these historic proceedings, as seen in ceremonies such as the Ao Naga's *Aksü* and the Poumai Naga's *Loutouju*. This exclusion can be traced back to deeply entrenched cultural norms and traditional practices associating them with impurity and transgressions. Historically, many societies have been patriarchal, meaning that power and decision-making authority have been predominantly held by men. This patriarchal structure often extends to indigenous rites and rituals, where men are seen as the primary agents of these rituals and ceremonies.

In Northeast tribal communities, cultural norms and customs dictate that women's roles are primarily domestic, while men are responsible for public affairs and decision-making. As a result, women are excluded from decision-making bodies. Instead, they are relegated to the kitchen space for cooking and singing songs of praise during the feast, thereby being only indirectly involved in the ceremony. This exclusion is problematic for several reasons. Firstly, it goes against the principles of equality and equity, which advocate for the equal participation and representation of all members of society, regardless of gender. Excluding women from rituals and ceremonies deprives them of a voice in decisions that directly impact their lives and communities. It also perpetuates gender inequalities and reinforces the idea that women's perspectives and contributions are less valuable than those of men. Overall, the exclusion of women from such rituals not only perpetuates gender-based discrimination but also limits the effectiveness and inclusivity of reconciliation processes within communities. This has led to men predominantly leading and benefiting from rituals, while women are pushed to the margins. This exclusion maintains gender hierarchy and sidelined women as passive observers rather than active participants in these rituals and ceremonies.

Experience of Northeast Women in Mainland Indian Rituals and Ceremonies

In the last three decades or so, a large population of Northeast people migrated to mainland Indian cities, such as Delhi, Mumbai, Bangalore, Kolkata etc., for better education, job/employment avenues and similar opportunities. The population of Northeast people in mainland India constitutes a little over one million (Lusome and Bhagat, 2020, p. 1134). The Northeast women in mainland India signify one of the weakest sections of the national population. The cases of discrimination and various kinds of exploitation and oppression against them in mainland India are alarming. There are cases and stories being told by the Northeast tribal women about the ways the mainland Indian people hypothesize and fetishize their body, food, language, dress, region, religion and culture. In many instances, the identity of the Northeast people by many mainland Indian people is often marred by misunderstanding. This misapprehension arises due to their distinct geographical location, unique physical attributes, including skin tone and Mongoloid features. This frequently leads to misidentifications as Chinese, Japanese, Korean, Nepalese, or even derogatory terms like *Chinky*. Racism against Northeast people is unfortunately not uncommon in mainland India. They are often treated as outsiders, facing a sense of alienation within their own nation. Intrinsically, the Northeast women in mainland India often suffer more marginalization based on gender, race, class and ethnic disparities than their male counterparts. Whether in public spaces or workplaces, they are constantly at risk, facing objectification due to their appearance. Given this hostile environment, participating in and feeling accepted within the rituals and ceremonies of mainland India becomes an especially daunting task for Northeast women. To illustrate this point, I would like to highlight two specific areas, food and Christian worship.

Food-Based Discrimination

Food plays a pivotal role in understanding the integration of rituals and ceremonies into Indian culture. Specific foods are integral to Indian rituals, whether as offerings to deities, communal sharing, or part of communal gatherings. In this sense, food takes on a deeper significance, carrying multiple meanings that are deliberately chosen and managed to uphold and affirm ritual traditions. The discrimination against Northeast people in participating in mainland Indian rituals and ceremonies stems from the clash of the 'food code' between the Northeastern communities and the vegetarian norms upheld by the mainland Indian communities. The term 'food code' refers to the dietary practices and restrictions observed by different cultural or regional groups in India, particularly in the context of rituals and ceremonies. Mainland Indian rituals and ceremonies such as the *Upanayanam* (Thread Ceremony) and *Homa* (Fire Sacrifice Rituals), particularly emphasize vegetarianism as a central tenet. The *Upanayanam* ceremony is a significant rite of passage in Hinduism, particularly for boys from Brahmin or Kshatriya and Vaishya communities. Historically, girls are often excluded from this ceremony. While the ceremony primarily focuses on the initiation of boys into the study of the *Vedas* and other sacred scriptures, there are certain food codes associated with it (Sundareswaran, 2015). For instance, the meals served during the ceremony and associated rituals are typically vegetarian. It includes *sattvic* food such as grains, fruits, vegetables, dairy products, nuts and seeds. This adherence to vegetarianism aligns with broader Hindu beliefs in *ahimsa* (non-violence) and purity. It symbolizes the purity of the body and mind, preparing the initiate for spiritual learning and growth. Another important ceremony is the *Homa* which is a sacred Hindu practice involving offerings of food such as grains, fruits, ghee (clarified butter), herbs and other plant-based substances into the consecrated fire. In general, it is the priest who performs this ritual on special occasions. The ingredients used in these rituals are strictly vegetarian, and the act of offering them to the fire is believed to purify the environment and create a harmonious connection between the material and spiritual realms (Lubin, 2015).

Both rituals are deeply ingrained in the symbolic purity, spirituality and commitment to non-violence associated with vegetarianism. Consuming non-vegetarian foods during these sacred occasions is seen as impure and disruptive to the spiritual atmosphere of the ceremony. When an individual from the Northeast attempts to engage in mainland Indian rituals while adhering to vegetarian norms, they often face exclusion and discrimination from mainland Indians, including those actively involved in the ceremonies. This exclusionary attitude arises from the perception that Northeastern participants are ineligible to partake due to their dietary differences. Consequently, Northeastern individuals, especially women, are marginalized and excluded, both because of their gender and the inability to accommodate their dietary preferences within the context of mainland Indian rituals and ceremonies. This discriminatory behaviour reflects a broader issue of intolerance towards diversity within the cultural framework.

The issue of food-based discrimination further extends to racism, particularly concerning the distinctive aromas and flavours of Northeastern cuisine. Northeastern dishes typically incorporate fermented spices, beans, bamboo shoots, vegetables, pulses, dry fish, smoked meat and fermented foods. These culinary preferences differ from mainstream Indian cuisine, often leading to misconceptions, ridicule and offensive comments from those unfamiliar with their foods. Discriminatory instances encompass derogatory remarks and stereotypes such as calling them dog-eaters, bat-eaters, barbaric etc. (Singh, 2023).

In India, the culture of deeming certain foods as undesirable or primitive originates from class distinctions, where those of higher caste perceive their diet as superior to that of lower-class individuals (Mishra, 2022). According to Kikon (2021, p. 280):

> The prejudiced treatment emanating from ignorance of the eclectic food cultures in Northeast India and the lack of knowledge about the region often means racism is downplayed. It seems to suggest that Indian racist culture is a result of citizens who are unaware about diversity, while reiterating caste sensibilities about pure and impure food cultures as the norm. Here, casteism and racism feed off each other. The disgust towards food that communities from Northeast India consume signifies how caste authority and privilege reproduce politics of purity and civic order.

In this context, these attitudes and perceptions contribute to the targeting of Northeast people, particularly women, for violence and discrimination due to their cultural practices, including food habits. In essence, prejudices towards Northeast food cultures are deeply intertwined with broader spectrums of caste, race and social hierarchy in Indian society. These spectrums are employed by mainland Indian people to validate hierarchal ideology, promoting a sense of superiority over Northeast people, particularly Northeast women.

Experience in Mainland Indian Churches

Moving forward to the experience of Northeast women in mainland Indian churches, it becomes evident that cultural differences extend beyond festivals and dietary practices to encompass attire and customs within religious settings. Church traditions are often entwined with rituals and ceremonies. The customs within the Indian Christian traditions have evolved through a combination of colonial legacies and indigenous socio-cultural influences. For instance, the practice of singing classical Christian hymns in Indian churches can be traced back to Western origins. When European and American missionaries introduced Christianity to India, they brought along their religious practices, including the singing of hymns. Indian converts embraced these musical traditions as part of their newfound faith, and over time, the practice of singing classical Christian hymns became entrenched in Indian church traditions. Conversely, distinct dress codes for men and women are reflections of local cultural norms. The dress code regulations during worship in Indian churches reflect wider societal expectations concerning gender roles and dress norms. Across many Indian communities, there are traditional expectations that dictate appropriate attire for men and women, especially within religious contexts. These social conventions shape the dress codes upheld in churches, distinguishing between male and female attire during worship.

It is notable that the traditions of certain mainland churches such as the Church of North India (CNI) and the Gossner Evangelical Lutheran (GEL) Church place considerable importance on dress codes, extending to clergy, service leaders and women. This affirms the claim that dress codes are consequential in Christian rituals and ceremonies, as they are deeply ingrained in worship practices. The dress code followed by Northeast women often diverges from the expectations upheld by many mainland Indian churches. They often opt for attire such as their traditional dress called *mekhela*[2] or Western-influenced dresses during worship services. This choice reflects both cultural preferences and personal comfort. On the other hand, mainland Indian women, particularly in the above-mentioned church traditions, typically wear the *saree*[3] along with a cassock when participating in religious activities. The disparity in clothing choice inadvertently results in discrimination against Northeast women in mainland India, manifesting in various forms such as racial slurs, mockery, ridicule and reinforcement of stereotypes like being uncultured or immodest. In addition to these prejudices, Northeast women are frequently barred from taking leadership roles and participating in worship services due to their attire not meeting the prescribed dress code, a problem rarely encountered by Northeast men.

In numerous instances, certain churches in mainland India have imposed their dress codes and customs onto Northeast women, insisting on practices such as removing footwear and veiling the head. I, too, have personally experienced such restrictions in one of these churches. During a particular visit to a church with my students, I was given the opportunity to deliver a sermon. With a strong sense of cultural pride, I chose to wear my traditional *mekhela*, only to be met with ridicule and disapproval. I was then compelled to cover my head while speaking from the pulpit, highlighting the extent to which such practices can be enforced, even in matters as personal as religious expression. These experiences underscore the tensions that can emerge when differing cultural practices intersect within a religious setting. They illuminate the complex interplay between local customs and religious rituals. Moreover, these encounters serve as poignant reminders of the intricate challenges faced by Northeast women when their deeply personal expressions of faith clash with firmly entrenched traditions within religious institutions. Such instances not only reflect the struggle for cultural autonomy and religious identity but also prompt critical reflections on the inclusivity and adaptability of religious spaces. Furthermore, when these customs are imposed on individuals from different cultural backgrounds who do not traditionally adhere to them, it perpetuates a hierarchy where those who adhere to the dominant cultural norms hold authority over those who do not, further marginalizing minority groups.

Reforming Rituals for Liberation

While rituals and ceremonies foster social unity and preserve cultural heritage, the processes of normalization often distort their intended goal of promoting humanity and liberation, leading to discrimination against certain sections of the population in society. The exclusion of women from active participation in the above-mentioned rituals and ceremonies reinforces patriarchal power dynamics within the community. Men predominantly lead and benefit from rituals, while women find themselves marginalized and relegated to the margins. This normalization of gender hierarchy further solidifies patriarchal structures, restricting women's agency and limiting their participation in decision-making processes. Addressing these normalization processes requires a formative approach towards rituals for true liberation. This entails adopting a nuanced strategy that upholds cultural traditions while also tackling inequalities perpetuated by certain practices. Drawing from the insights provided in the preceding discussion, here are some suggested steps that can be undertaken.

Centring Women's Agency

'Women's agency' refers to the ability of women to act independently, make choices and exert influence over their lives and the communities they are part of. In the context of this chapter, women's agency includes actively participating in rituals and ceremonies, shaping and influencing these practices according to their beliefs, values and needs. Rather than relegating specific roles solely to men, such as those traditionally performed during ceremonies like the Post-Transplantation Festival and the Feast of Reconciliation, it is imperative to promote gender-inclusive participation and restructuring rituals to integrate women into all facets of planning, preparation and execution. By doing so, communities enrich their cultural tapestry and amplify diverse perspectives. This entails not only inviting women to assume leadership positions but also creating an environment where their contributions are valued, their ideas solicited, and their voices heard in the decision-making processes surrounding rituals. Conversely, the exclusion of women from ritual spaces perpetuates homogenized representations of traditions, limiting the breadth of insights and inhibiting the evolution of these practices. Therefore, prioritizing women's participation and representation in ritual contexts is not merely a matter of fairness; it is a strategic imperative for fostering inclusivity and advancing gender equality within communities. Empowering women to claim agency in rituals paves the way for a more equitable and harmonious society where their voices are heard, their contributions are valued, and community well-being is nurtured.

Reimagining Tradition

Rituals often serve as mirrors reflecting and reinforcing entrenched gender norms and roles. To genuinely liberate communities, there is a pressing need for a transformative shift in how rituals are perceived and practised. This transformation requires communities to embark on a journey of critical reinterpretation of traditional rituals, challenging established gender paradigms, and creating space for women's active participation and leadership. A crucial aspect of this reinterpretation involves reconceptualizing the roles traditionally assigned to women within rituals. Rather than being confined to passive roles or relegated to the sidelines, women should be empowered to take on active roles and leadership positions. For example, in ceremonies like the Feast of Reconciliation, aimed at nurturing unity and peace, it is essential to reimagine these traditions to ensure that all members, irrespective of gender, have opportunities to contribute to fostering relationships and resolving conflicts.

Conversely, central to this reformative process is fostering open dialogue within the community. This dialogue should delve into the roots of traditional rituals, unpacking the gender norms they perpetuate and advocating for transformative change. Importantly, this dialogue must actively solicit and incorporate women's perspectives, experiences and ideas on how rituals can be reconfigured to be more inclusive and empowering for them. By embracing this inclusive approach to ritual reinterpretation, communities stand to achieve outcomes that are not only more meaningful but also sustainable for everyone involved. It is through this collective reimagining of traditions that communities can break free from the constraints of outdated gender norms and pave the way for a more equitable and just future.

Engaging with Taboos

Undertaking a critical examination of taboos entrenched within Northeast rituals and ceremonies is an indispensable stride towards cultivating inclusivity and redressing systemic inequalities entrenched within sacred spaces. This endeavour requires a meticulous and critical examination of the taboos prevalent in these rituals, particularly those that contribute to the marginalization or confinement of certain groups, notably women, within Northeast communities. By interrogating the underlying rationale underpinning these taboos, including their historical, cultural and religious factors, Northeast communities can assess their relevance, applicability and validity in contemporary contexts. Additionally, they can unravel ingrained assumptions and biases, paving the way for a more nuanced understanding of cultural practices and their broader implications.

Moreover, critical examination of taboos necessitates an inclusive approach that involves consultation and dialogue with a spectrum of community stakeholders, including women, religious leaders, elders and other vested parties. This inclusive methodology ensures that a diverse array of perspectives is considered, amplifying voices that have historically been marginalized and enriching the discourse with a multiplicity of insights. Embracing such inclusivity not only fosters a sense of ownership and empowerment among community members but also facilitates meaningful engagement and collaboration towards effecting transformative change. By coalescing collective wisdom and harnessing the collective agency of its members, Northeastern communities can chart a course towards rituals and ceremonies that are not only reflective of their cultural heritage but also embody principles of equity, justice and inclusivity.

Navigating Ethical Considerations

Ethical considerations serve as a guiding light in the transformative process, particularly in confronting the pervasive discrimination faced by Northeast communities within the broader fabric of Indian society. Upholding the inherent rights, dignity and autonomy of individuals hailing from these communities becomes paramount, demanding a concerted effort to confront and dismantle discriminatory attitudes and behaviours rooted in ignorance and prejudice. Navigating this ethical terrain involves a steadfast commitment to cultural sensitivity, fostering understanding, respect and acceptance of the diverse culinary traditions and religious practices that enrich the tapestry of Indian culture. It is about recognizing that food is not merely sustenance but a vessel of culture, identity and heritage, with each region contributing its unique flavours and customs to the mosaic of Indian cuisine. Moreover, combating racism and casteism must be intrinsically woven into the fabric of the reform agenda. Acknowledging the interconnectedness of these forms of discrimination is vital for addressing the root causes of inequality and injustice embedded within Indian society's framework.

By adhering unwaveringly to ethical principles and cultivating a culture of integrity and compassion, communities navigate this complex terrain with purpose and conviction. In doing so, they chart a course towards dismantling systemic barriers to equality, nurturing trust, and fostering cohesion among all members of society, irrespective of their background or identity. Finally, by cultivating spaces that are welcoming and accommodating to diverse cultural expressions of faith, churches can foster a sense of belonging and empowerment among Northeast women, enabling them to fully participate in religious activities and leadership roles without fear of discrimination or prejudice.

Intersectional Advocacy

In addressing the challenges faced by Northeast women in mainland Indian rituals and ceremonies, intersectional advocacy emerges as a pivotal instrument for advancing social justice initiatives. The migration of Northeast communities to mainland Indian cities has shed light on the multifaceted discrimination experienced by these women, who navigate various social contexts as migrants and citizens. They often confront misunderstandings and misrepresentations of their identity and cultural practices, perpetuating marginalization and exclusion within mainland Indian society. Intersectional advocacy recognizes the complex interplay of gender, race, ethnicity, class and religion in shaping these experiences and aims to address them holistically. By forging alliances with other social justice movements, including those focused on gender, racial, indigenous and marginalized community rights, advocates amplify the voices of Northeast women and strive to dismantle discriminatory practices in rituals and ceremonies. Recognizing that oppression is intersectional and interconnected, collaborative efforts with diverse marginalized communities, including Northeastern and South Indian women, as well as other Asian and minority groups across the globe are imperative. Through such collaborative endeavours, advocacy efforts are enriched, and a concerted push is made towards developing effective strategies for dismantling discriminatory practices and fostering equity in ritual spaces.

Conclusion

In summary, this chapter sheds light on the intricate relationship between rituals and ceremonies, revealing their profound impact on gender dynamics, cultural norms and the shaping of identities. By closely examining Northeast Indian rituals and their repercussions for women, alongside the struggles faced by Northeastern women within the mainland Indian context, a pressing need for transformative action is apparent. While rituals and ceremonies serve as conduits for cultural heritage and fostering social cohesion, they often reinforce harmful norms that marginalize and sideline women. To tackle these issues, the chapter advocates for a transformative approach to rituals that focuses on women's agency, reimagining tradition, ethical considerations and intersectional advocacy. By prioritizing women's participation and leadership in rituals, the cultural fabric of the Northeastern community is enriched and gender equality is promoted. Moreover, reinterpreting traditional practices by confronting taboos and combating discrimination necessitates a commitment to ethical principles and intersectional collaboration with other social justice movements.

In essence, the chapter calls for a paradigm shift in how rituals are conceptualized and practised, emphasizing inclusivity, empowerment and liberation for all members of society. While this journey presents challenges and resistance, embracing the opportunity for change is essential. By reforming rituals for genuine liberation, communities meaningfully create sacred spaces that truly reflect the values of inclusivity and equality. Ultimately, this collective endeavour contributes to the establishment of a more harmonious and just society where individuals from all backgrounds and identities can thrive and fully participate in cultural and religious practices.

Notes

1 For example, in Japan, there is an ancient Shinto harvest ritual known as 'Niiname-sai' or the 'First Fruits Festival', where the Emperor or the priest offers newly harvested rice to the gods to give thanks for a bountiful harvest and to pray for the nation's prosperity.

2 The *mekhela* is the traditional dress of the Northeast tribal women in Nagaland and elsewhere too. It is a rectangular piece of cloth that is pleated and wrapped around the waist, resembling a sarong. Notably, in numerous churches throughout Northeast India, the *mekhela* takes precedence as the chosen attire for worship in the pulpit.

3 A *saree* (also spelled *sari*) is a traditional garment worn by women in various South Asian countries, including India, Bangladesh, Nepal and Sri Lanka. It consists of a long piece of fabric, typically ranging from four to nine metres in length, that is draped elegantly around the body. The *saree* is typically paired with a blouse (*choli*) and an underskirt (petticoat). *Sarees* are often worn during various occasions, from everyday wear to special events, festivals, weddings and formal gatherings.

References

Angelova, Iliyana, 2015, 'Building a "Home" Away from Home: The Experiences of Young Naga Migrants in Delhi', *Journal of the Anthropological Society of Oxford* 7 (2), pp. 153–67.

Baruah, S., 2003, 'Nationalizing Space: Cosmetic Federalism and the Politics of Development in Northeast India', *Development and Change* 34 (5), pp. 915–39.

Dorsey, G. A., and H. R. Voth, 1901, *The Oraibi Soyal Ceremony: The Stanley McCormick Hopi Expedition, Anthropological Series* 3 (1), The Field Columbian Museum, pp. 2–59, http://www.jstor.org/stable/29782025 (accessed 21.1.2025).

D'Souza, A. B., 2012, 'Tribal Theology in the North East: Some Suggestions from Sociology', in Y. Vashum, P. Haokip and M. Pereira, eds, *Search for A New Society: Tribal Theology for North East India*, pp. 21–8, Guwahati: North Eastern Social Research Centre.

Imchen, P., 1993, *Ancient Ao Naga Religion and Culture*, New Delhi: Har-Anand Publications.

Kikon, D., 2021, 'Dirty Food: Racism and Casteism in India', *Ethnic and Racial Studies*, 45 (2), pp. 278–97.

Loly, P. S., 2022, *The Gospel of Matthew as Instructions for a Peripheral Community: A Tribal Reading*, Delhi: ISPCK.

Lubin, T., 2015, 'The Vedic *Homa* and the Standardization of Hindu *Puja*', in *Homa Variations: The Study of Ritual Change across the Longue Durée*, ed. Richard Payne and Michael Witzel, pp. 143–66, Oxford Ritual Studies Series, Oxford: Oxford University Press.

Lusome, R., and R. B. Bhagat, 2020, 'Migration in Northeast India: Inflows, Outflows and Reverse Flows During Pandemic', *The Indian Journal of Labour Economics* 63, pp. 1125–41.

Mishra K., 2022, 'Why Food Has Emerged as a Divisive Factor for People from Northeast', *Outlook India*, 10 August, https://www.outlookindia.com/national/why-food-has-emerged-a-divisive-factor-for-northeast-indians-in-india-news-193094 (accessed 15.1.2025).

Mwaka, A. D., 2023, 'Reconciliation Among the Central Luo of Northern Uganda: The Ingredients and Process of Mato Oput', *Cogent Social Sciences* 9(1), pp. 1–27.

Northeast Now, 2023, '20 Reasons Why a Visit to Northeast India is a Must', https://nenow.in/why-a-visit-to-northeast-india-is-a-must (accessed 15.1.2025).

Singh, B., 2023, 'North East Students' Organisation and Congress Demand Protection for Northeast Indians', *The Economic Times*, retrieved July 25, 2023, https://economictimes.indiatimes.com/news/politics-and-nation/north-east-students-organisation-and-congress-demands-protection-for-northeast-indians/articleshow/74780958.cms.

Soto, S. L., 2011, *Tribal Theology of Integral Humanhood: A Resource from Shamanism of the Nagas*, Delhi: ISPCK.

Sundareswaran, N. K., 2015, 'The Upanayana Ritual in the Satapathabrahmana', in *Texts and Rituals: Issues in Indology*, pp. 41–67, Kochi: Sukrtindra Oriental Research Institute.

Takatemjen, 1998, *Studies on Theology and Naga Culture*, Delhi: Indian Society for Promoting Christian Knowledge for Clark Theological College.

Takatemjen, 1999, 'Theology of Reconciliation: A Naga Perspective', in A. W. Longchar and L. E. Davis, eds, *Doing Theology with Tribal Resources: Context and Perspective*, pp. 103–16, Jorhat: Tribal Study Centre, Eastern Theological College.

Tuniyi, Z., and J. J. P. Wouters, 2016, 'India's Northeast as an Internal Borderland: Domestic Borders, Regimes of Taxation, and Legal Landscape', *The NEHU Journal*, XIV(1), pp. 1–17.

PART 2

Colonialism and Indigenous Spiritualities of Liberation

4

African Spiritualities and the Normalization of Ancestral Rituals in Brussels' Afro-Diasporic Contexts

CHRISTEL ZOGNING MELI

Introduction

In 2017, a sociological study titled *Citizens with African Roots: A Portrait of the Belgo-Congolese, Belgo-Rwandans and Belgo-Burundians* showed that Afro-descendants denounced the silences and taboos linked to Belgium's colonial past.[1] The people interviewed noted 'the importance of not reducing Africa to the colonial episode (end of the nineteenth century) or to the arrival of Europeans (end of the fifteenth century), ignoring the existence of kingdoms and civilizations' (Demart et al., 2017, p. 166). On a religious level, the argument of memorial revindications and 'historical justice' could also be evoked. Indeed, with the Christianization of African societies, the peoples in them suffered epistemicides, i.e. the annihilation, devaluation and silencing of their knowledge systems (Miano, 2020, p. 151). Historian Sophie Dulucq points out the almost total denial of local ways of life, the destruction of places of worship and animist symbols, and the prohibition of customs supposed to offend Christian morality (Dulucq, 2004, p. 68). According to Dulucq, a renewed reading of history could argue that the thinking of the time prevented missionaries from perceiving the symbolic violence at work in colonial relations, as they had no doubts about the 'civilizing mission' and the absolute superiority of Christian civilization endowed with norms, practices and customs par excellence (Dulucq, 2004, p. 70). Nevertheless, for many Afro-descendants, memories of colonization and the ambiguous role played by certain missionary institutions in its expansion have left their mark on the collective memory, and still leave deep wounds.

In any case, this is the historical frame of reference that prevails in the testimonies of the Afro-descendants interviewed in our field investigations.² In the postcolonial context, the 'phenomena' of leaving Christianity are generated by the experience of symbolic, cultural and spiritual conflicts caused by Western Christianity's relations of power and domination over non-Christian African traditions. As Kirafiky Mbog, one of our interviewees, writes in her first book:

> Each people expressed its vision of the world, of the *Divine*, of Life. Each developed its own way of communing with the *Spiritual*. Religious imperialism is manifest when one people or religious community elevates its vision or way of doing things above and to the detriment of those of others. (Mbog, 2022, p. 53)

Religion, and Christianity in particular, are seen as foreign paradigms with which these Afro-descendants no longer wish to identify (Mbog, 2022, p. 21) and are experienced by them as a form of alienation from which they must free themselves. To resist this alienation, they must 'regain awareness of their past, their culture, their traditions, their spirituality and their vision of the world' (Auque-Pallez, 2022, p. 69). Gradually, an emancipatory awakening of consciousness seems to be taking place within the Brussels' Afro-diasporic community.³ It manifests itself in a dynamic of visibility of new spiritual-cultural paradigms elaborated or reinterpreted by Afro-descendants who provocatively identify themselves as 'ex-Christians'. By distancing themselves from biblical truth regimes and 'postcolonial religious Afroculture' (Coyault, 2021), these 'former Christians' would begin the reconstruction of their own narratives through a rebirth, a return to their sources or 'African spiritualities'.⁴ The latter are made up of revisited ancestral practices or reinvented rituals – enabling them to construct a new imaginary, this time in accordance with their African identity and their own pragmatic and spiritual-cultural expectations.

The intention of this article is not to spell out the salient features and characteristics of the ancestral rituals and practices in question, as their number multiplies in proportion to the plurality of 'African spiritualities'. They reflect diverse constellations of meanings and uses, where inventiveness and borrowings are interwoven in a spiritual-cultural intermingling. Rather, using Afro-militant associations as a starting point, we describe and analyse the agency of new (neo)traditionalist entrepreneurs and the strategies they deploy in the real world and online to normalize new ritual and ceremonial practices derived from

African spiritualities in the Brussels religious landscape.[5] In this struggle for recognition, what is at stake is the creation of a space for freedom, information, the transmission of traditional knowledge and heritage, and initiation, enabling Afro-descendants of the Black community in an identity crisis to rebuild an improved spirituality.

The argument is structured in three stages. The first is an attempt to understand the term 'African spiritualities', from which the ancestral practices and rituals derive and are normalized. Second, I will outline the identity trajectories of the (neo)traditionalist entrepreneurs we interviewed, analyzing how the scenarios of leaving Christianity for a return to the sources produce cultural metamorphoses, changes in values and collective attitudes, and give rise to a growing dissident movement within the Black community. Finally, faced with the solid anchoring of Christian belief in the Belgian religious sector, I will examine the normalization strategies implemented by these entrepreneurs, on the one hand to reaffirm and symbolize their belonging to a (neo)traditional movement or an African cult group, and on the other to promote freedom of belief and ritual practice that break with the Christian colonial heritage.

Between Continuity and Discontinuity: An Attempt to Define 'African Spiritualities'

The expression 'African spiritualities', as designated by the (neo)traditionalist entrepreneurs we met, is a polysemous and rather vague category that covers complex and plural realities. Indeed, each people has its own specific traditions, rituals, beliefs, ceremonies and cosmogonies. So, there is not one but many 'African spiritualities'. These can be seen in continuity and discontinuity with traditional African belief, which 'in its initiatory form is a practical and ritual knowledge in which the initiate himself verifies his beliefs by observing what takes place in his body' (Mukaminega, 2023, p. 4). And such traditional belief has 'no priestly clergy, no single place of worship, no taught doctrine and no authoritative written text' (Kibora and Langewische, 2019, p. 21).

From the viewpoint of continuity with traditional African belief, 'African spiritualities' is for the people interviewed to summon up and legitimize the variety of traditional African religions and the rituals as follows:

- Bwiti is a religious tradition originating from the Mitsogo people of southern Gabon. It is an initiation society organized into small local communities led by a 'father initiator' (Bonhomme, 2007, p. 2; 2018, p. 155).
- The Vodou (or Vodoun) religion is based on the worship of spirits and ancestors and on polytheism associated with the forces of nature (Rieucau, 2019, p. 609). In the Fon language, Vodoun designates ancestral and tutelary divinities, invisible powers linked to nature and human activities (Souty, 2004).
- The Orisha cult is the traditional religion of the Yoruba-Anago. Orishas are Afro-American deities originally from Africa and, more specifically, from Yoruba religious traditions. They are worshipped in Benin and Nigeria (Rieucau, 2019, p. 607).
- The animist religion of the Dogons in Mali worships the creator God Amma and immortal ancestors (Sanogo and Coulibaly, 2003, p. 142).

Traditional practices that constitute key elements of African religious thought, such as ancestor and spirit cults, feasts for the dead, libations, initiation ceremonies and journeys, healing dances, purification, protection rituals, etc., are thus the subject of a powerful revival of interest in the discourses of (neo)traditionalist entrepreneurs, even if there are major differences in approaches, styles and discursive content due to the diversity of influences on intra-African traditional belief.

Discontinuity, on the other hand, would refer to a revisiting of rituals, beliefs, cosmogonies or ancestral African traditions, to the invention or 'bricolage' of traditional elements (Mary, 2000, p. 39).[6] Kemite (or Kamite) neo-traditionalism is a striking illustration of this. Kemitism is a set of beliefs and practices that draws on the wisdom and religion of ancient Egypt. There are several currents that originated in the United States in the twentieth century, in the movements of Pan-Africanism and Afrocentrism, with many points in common in terms of their sources, theologies and rituals. The word is based on the root *'kemet'*, which in ancient Egyptian means 'black land' or, according to Cheikh Anta Diop, 'land of the Blacks' (Diop, 1979, p. 46). Kemitism in Europe's French-speaking world emphasizes the links (languages, beliefs, rituals) between Egyptian and African cultures. In the legacy of Diop and his vision of an African renaissance, proponents of Kemitism, considering that their ancestors came from the Nile Valley, assimilate a return to African traditions with a return to ancient Egypt. To define oneself as a Kemite means 'to claim an identity autonomous from Western ideological categories' (Auque-Pallez, 2022, p. 69) or, as Jean-Philippe

Omotunde (one of the thinkers of Kemitism) puts it, 'to withdraw from all extra-Kamite cultural, spiritual and intellectual tutelage' (Omotunde, 2010, p. 1). In order to 'define oneself by oneself, for oneself' (Auque-Pallez, 2022, p. 70), this spiritualist movement promotes a form of reappropriation and revendication of one's origins, a return to Egypt in all domains. As Diop points out, such a return 'is the necessary condition for reconciling African civilizations with history, for building a body of modern human sciences, for renovating African culture' (Diop, 1981, p. 12). It should be noted that the meaning of Kemitism also takes on 'different forms, depending on the ways in which it is mobilized by militants: an Africanity of active resistance on the ground; a filiation with ancient Egypt; an autonomy of knowledge completely divorced from any Western ideology, or a concrete practice of Kemite spiritual rituals' (Auque-Pallez, 2022, p. 76).

Influenced by Kemitism, master Djehouty Mwamba, one of our contacts in the field, advocates a 'traditional, multimillennial and Kamite' teaching that enables its initiates 'to pass from the stage of ontological virtuality to that of ontological plenitude' and 'to travel on their boat with Hou (creative speech, command, etc.), Sia (knowledge, creative intelligence, etc.) and Heka ('magical' force of vital energy, etc.)' (Facebook post, 1 November 2020).[7] The originality and complexity of his 'bricolage' dynamic consists in recovering symbolic material marked by its previous use (Mary, 2000, p. 40) and handling representations referring to originals that are difficult to access because they are so distant in space or time (Manzon, 2022, p. 1). In this case, 'Hou', 'Sia' and 'Heka' represent deities from Egyptian mythology. In the end, master Djehouty Mwamba's reflection focuses on the inventiveness of a new paradigm that combines the deconstruction of Christian beliefs that draw on the Bible,[8] with a form of (neo)traditionalist esotericism that emphasizes the inner, in-depth experience of a spiritual teaching (prayers to the ancestors, meditation, invocation, trances, fasting, libations, offerings, initiation ceremonies, etc.).

Religious Dissidence and Mergence of 'Religious Virtuosos' and 'Nodal Actors'

Kirafiky Mbog, Momi M'Buzé and Djehouty Mwamba (aka Apôtre Nabi Mwamba) are emerging referential figures in our field of investigation who are part of a logic of exit from Christianity towards 'African spiritualities'.[9] As 'Religious virtuosos' in the Weberian sense (Weber, 1996,

p. 358)¹⁰ and 'nodal actors' (Argyriadis, 2012, p. 58), they construct their own trajectory and indicate possible bifurcations in the Black community. 'Despite a shared commitment to mobilizing followers behind "African tradition" to challenge "foreign" religions', neo-traditional worldviews are sometimes 'diverse in terms of background, teachings, practices, development and followers' (de Witte, 2012, p. 174).

At the intersection of several worlds or systems of meaning, they 'embody postures of dissent' (Coyault, 2021) enabling them 'to access a position of prestige and/or of power at all scales' (Argyriadis, 2012, pp. 58–9). They hold a 'powerful influence over those who do not have a musical ear for religion' (Weber, 1996, p. 362), so much so that they could be recognized by some as emblematic figures of identification, endowed with an alternative religious or cultural authority, capable of becoming in the long term 'new prophets' or 'supreme guides' (Argyriadis, 2012, p. 59) of the new forms of spirituality they are helping to (re)construct. The strengthening of alternative religious or cultural authority is facilitated by a self-designation mechanism that enables nodal actors to assert themselves and express skills and aspirations, the combination of which enables them to support their own religious identity or cultural project (Argyriadis, 2012, p. 59). Momi M'Buzé, a pan-African and Afro-centric activist, prolific novelist and member of the Afrofuturist movement, calls himself an 'African prophet'.[11] According to him, his project is to design Africa's future by constructing liberated imaginaries with which his audience[12] can identify, in order to '(re)construct an image of themselves and of the World, a New Kamite Paradigm that corresponds to them socially, politically, economically, in terms of identity, philosophy and spirituality'.[13] For his part, Djehouty Mwamba, founder of the 'Mystery School, cradle of wisdom',[14] constructs his character and position through a double logic of self-designation. A 'master of wisdom of Kemite spirituality' when dispensing his multi-millennial and essentially African traditional teachings (Facebook post, 19 October 2020), he also calls himself apostle Nabi Mwamba – Nabi meaning prophet in Hebrew – when in contact with his Pentecostal congregation.[15] Having attended his teachings, his pupils refer to him as 'master Neb', Neb being the ancient Egyptian equivalent of Nabi (interview, 20 February 2023).

I note here the hybrid and original nature of this virtuoso's spiritual project, which is rooted in two a priori opposed and irreconcilable visions, in the manner of 'in-between characters, like those prophet-bricoleurs of Africa, often former catechists or seminarians' (Mary, 2000, p. 41). At the crossroads of Christianity and Kemitism, the originality and complexity of Djehouty Mwamba's approach consists in 'building' a new form of spirituality on the basis of an innovative reappropriation of biblical texts, considered by him as 'a plagiarized copy of the original'. And it constitutes the anchor point for going back to the source, to ancient Egypt, 'the veritable cradle of the Kamite being' according to him. He even admits his affection for Christianity and biblical texts: 'Christianity doesn't shock me; I like it a lot. My approach is to show with evidence that Christianity comes from ancient Egypt. I teach how to return to Black African spirituality from the biblical text' (interview, 20 February 2023). This ongoing process of religious deconstruction is part of a trajectory in which borrowings from existing traditions generate an unprecedented recomposition. By way of illustration, the Kamite teachings he gives to his students borrow several liturgical and ritual elements from charismatic-type communities: introductory prayer, teaching, prayer of appropriation, glossolalia,[16] trances, offering and closing prayer.

Djehouty Mwamba, Momi M'Buzé and Kirafiky Mbog work[17] on the content of their messages to gain legitimacy as agents of alternative spiritual-religious or cultural authority. As this is gradually recognized, they can gain the respect and support of Afro-descendants and show the way to the philosophies and practices of African spirituality.

Ancestral Rituals and Normalization Processes: Challenges and Identity Issues for Afro-Descendants

There are no societies without rituals. Indeed, rituals define, accompany and consolidate every type of community, whether they represent geographical, religious, cultural, or symbolic territories. Their importance in the construction of identity should, therefore, be noted. As Claude-Marie Dupin points out, they are the glue that binds human groups together, providing a framework for the stable marking of life's important transitions, demonstrating the roots of the group considered and each individual's belonging to those roots (Dupin 2009, p. 54). Rituals are diverse, ranging from religious and cultural to rituals of passage, initiation, healing, protection and purification. Numerous works address the question of ritual in the fields of social psychology, psychoanalysis, ethnology, ethology and sociology. According to Jean Maisonneuve, in ethnology and sociology, ritual refers to 'a set (or type) of prescribed or forbidden practices, linked to magical and/or religious beliefs, ceremonies and festivals, according to the dichotomies of sacred and profane, pure and impure' (Maisonneuve, 1999, p. 6). For him, ritual linked to faith, the sacred and the body is a codified system of practices 'with lived meaning and symbolic value for its actors and witnesses' (p. 12). For Momi M'Buzé, sacred things ultimately represent the 'historical narrative', primordial identity, spiritualities and beliefs of the Kemites (Facebook post, 27 December 2023).[18] Ritual is thus intimately linked 'to the actors' own experience, and thus to the set of situations, feelings and representations they both 'express and regulate' (Maisonneuve, 1999, p. 13). Before being practical, it is and makes sense. It is therefore through ritual that (neo)traditionalist agents express their sense of belonging and their filiation to African culture and ancestral traditions.

The quest for their original identity often involves a ritual name change. As one of the credos of twentieth-century African-American political and spiritual movements puts it, 'the name means everything' (Guedj, 2010). Changing one's name is therefore a symbolic act that seals the new birth and the transition to African spirituality, and invites the construction of a new identity, this time assumed. The Western first name, representing the 'subjugated identity', is abandoned and replaced by another from one or other African language – not necessarily the language of their country of origin – and whose meaning carries significance in the visible and invisible world (Guedj, 2010). Momi M'Buzé, for example, comments: 'I've taken back my first name Momi, before I was called Hervé. Hervé means absolutely nothing. Momi in the "Ngombé" language means "man, virility"' (interview, 30 February 2022).

Moreover, ritual as 'prescribed order' (Picard, 2002, p. 251) or 'order of the cosmos' (Cuisenier, 2006, p. 17)[19] can present a 'theocentric' and 'sociocentric' vision (Sanogo and Coulibaly, 2003, p. 143)[20] that materializes, as Kirafiky points out, the relationship or communion with the divine, the ancestors, the *Ba tuu pêg*, the divine in ourselves and in others (Mbog, 2022, p. 87).

> In the African imagination, the cosmos represents the habitat of visible and invisible forces, the seat of primordial energy. Cosmic order is perceived here as the way of being and manifesting of primordial energy, of the supreme being, or the order of orders. From knowledge of this order and communion with the universe, the African hopes to draw the vital energy, balance and harmony he lacks. The quest for order and the desire for balance and harmony are embodied in religious practices and rituals. (Latoki, 2010, p. 2)

It is from this perspective that (neo)traditionalists reclaim and reappropriate their ancestral beliefs and African cultural traditions: ancestor and spirit worship, feasts of the dead, libations, initiation ceremonies and journeys, purification rituals, meditation, prayers, healing dances, the adoration and veneration of things and objects from the material world, and so on.

Faced with the spectre of denial of recognition and continued stereotyping of (neo)traditional rituals, the latter will then 'explicitly seek public recognition for traditional religion ... to counter global and local Christian-derived stereotypes that frame it as "fetish," "juju," or "black magic"' (de Witte, 2012, p. 174). The concept of normalization takes on its full meaning here. It is evoked by Michel Foucault in the context of social control or disciplinary power. In a speech he gave at the Collège de France in 1978, he declared:

> Disciplinary standardization consists in first laying down a model, an optimal model that is built according to a certain result, and the operation of disciplinary normalization consists in trying to make people, gestures and acts conform to this model, the normal being precisely what is capable of conforming to this norm, and the abnormal, what is not.[21]

When 'ex-Christians' abandon the optimal model or religious norm, they engage in the 'abnormal' and are subjected in return to epistemic injustice and socio-religious exclusion by the followers of the institutions that constructed it. Activists of intensive Christian belief, like Tito Mutyebele, pastor of a postcolonial evangelical megachurch 'New Jerusalem', can publicly call African spiritualities and their rituals 'folklore that interests witchcraft followers and people who want to pray to spirits'.[22]

On social networks, the hashtags 'normalize the fact of' are multiplying to criticize established norms and enable collective thinking to evolve. When various minority groups, victims of disqualification, retake the concept of normalization to gain in recognition and visibility, normalization is a means by which new or previously disqualified philosophies, conceptions, practices and behaviors become 'normal', legitimate or conforming to the norm in a given social group. Normalization process theory 'provides a set of sociological tools to understand and explain the social processes through which new or modified practices of thinking, enacting and organizing work are operationalized in healthcare and other institutional settings'. Although this theory is primarily used in medical sociology and science and technology studies, it is also applicable to other fields. It can be useful in analysing various situations. Here are some important points to consider.

> Practices become routinely embedded – or normalized – in social contexts as the result of people working, individually and collectively, to enact them ... The work of enacting a practice is promoted or inhibited through the operation of generative mechanisms (coherence, cognitive participation, collective action, reflexive monitoring) through which human agency is expressed ... The production and reproduction of a practice requires continuous investment by agents in ensembles of action that are carried forward in time and space. (May et al., 2009, p. 2)

To think of the normalization or integration of ancestral practices and rituals in the context of socio-religious change means to give to the agents working for its implementation and effectiveness a strong militant dimension, in which phenomena of religious dissidence are mobilized, concrete struggles against reductive assignations are waged and innovative procedures are developed to valorize and integrate African spiritual-cultural heritage in the long term. When Kirafiky speaks of the spiritual reconstruction of Afro-descendants, she understands freedom as a progressive struggle: 'It is not something you ask for, but something you take, something you give yourself little by little, accepting the responsibility that comes with it; because to free oneself is to (re)become responsible for one's actions and choices' (TikTok post, 16.12.2023).

Normalization thus requires a personal and collective agency that articulates the phenomenon of resistance to an established norm with the mobilization of ideas and actions to act on the world, society and the beings that make it up, to influence them, transform them and ultimately allow the integration of new systems of meaning.

Black Agency, Transnationality and Normalization Strategies

Transnational Communication and Visibility Strategies

The awareness-raising strategies of (neo)traditionalist entrepreneurs are transnational in scope. In the age of new communication technologies and social networks, the construction of their systems of thought and the spiritual and cultural meanings and practices derived from them are also transmitted and exchanged beyond the borders of Belgium. The use of social networks multiplies their virtual interactions not only with Afro-descendants but also with Afropeans and Africans.[23] The preferred spaces and platforms used to make visible and transmit their spiritual-religious and cultural projects are associative groups and events, conferences, courses, online discussions and interviews (podcasts), and social networks such as Facebook, YouTube, Instagram, TikTok, X (Twitter), Patreon, etc. Our virtuosos mobilize a virtual community of nearly 30,000 people,[24] not counting the plethora of virtual accounts of other traditionalist activists who benefit from publicity or communication support on their platforms.

Cooperation Among Afro-Descendants (Neo)Traditionalists

Like all social and political activists, Afro-descendant (neo)traditionalists seek to establish their opinions and spiritual and cultural philosophies through offensive and defensive actions. The liberationist quest is not just a personal one, nor does it play a part in the self-construction or self-invention of these 'ex-Christians'. It is also societal and communitarian. It is about changing the game. To implement not only logics of religious rupture or deconstruction of dominant Christian norms but also logics of restoration of revived ancestral codes and rituals (worship of deserving ancestors, libations, prayers), these (neo)traditionalist entrepreneurs, empowered by the religious/spiritual authority that characterizes them, establish cooperative relationships. Associations, online groupings and networks of the Black community sharing the African traditionalist vision and its general objectives, which tended towards isolation or identitarian withdrawal, initiate original synergistic connections to achieve their goal. In solidarity with each other, they formed a bloc to better assert themselves against the militants of Christian belief by deconstructing the imperialist schemes of Western Christianity and the practices of religious assimilation processes. We are also witnessing a form of mutual support at events and on social networks. Sharing, commenting, or 'liking' each other's posts and events is a way of adhering to all forms of Kemite discourse or ancestral beliefs, despite possible divergences, and showing that the unity of African identity is possible in difference. On the Facebook page of the 'École des mystères berceau de sagesse', Djehouty Mwamba and his team validate and post publications from other accounts with (neo)traditionalist content, such as those of Thérésa Bouams[25] and Tshiwala Ngalula Kalengayi.[26] The cooperation between Djehouty Mwamba and Tshiwala Ngalula Kalengayi reflects a shared understanding of the imperative to exit Western Christianity and the need to implement ritual and ceremonial practices to mark the transition to ancestral spiritualities.

> Couldn't the seemingly perpetual misfortune of Africa be explained by the fact that we spit on the memory of our ancestors by glorifying their executioners and accepting their dogmas instead of our ancestral spirituality? P.S.: Every January 08, our initiatic and esoteric circle organizes a rite, a ceremony to BREAK these chains and to UNLOCK those who make the SINCERE and RESPONSIBLE vow to leave these churches and to free themselves from their mortifying dogmas. (Facebook 2023)[27]

The same school also manages a public transnational group called 'Sagesse plurimillénaire'.[28] This group, which had 676 followers as of 20 December 2023, is presented by its administrators as an initiatory circle of passionate enthusiasts of the classical African humanities[29] for the Kamite renaissance. Anticonformists and freethinkers, their vocation is to popularize their ideological and philosophical current, described as 'plurimillennial'. The practices presented to the group include healing rituals, salt protection rituals, and instructions for their use. The philosophical and intellectual solidarity of the spiritual-religious entrepreneurs has the effect of making their thoughts and practices more visible and raising awareness among Afro-descendants. And although the movement is still in its embryonic stages, it already seems to be ringing alarm bells in evangelical and conservative (neo)Pentecostal circles. Indeed, many believers, especially young Afropeans attending Belgian post-colonial Afro-descendant churches, are reportedly abandoning their Christian faith in favour of African spirituality. Although the leaders of these churches do not speak out officially and tend to downplay the phenomenon, our initial research within these communities suggests that it is very real. Personal initiatives are emerging. Online podcasts are popping up to explore the phenomenon, which is adding complexity to the landscape of Afro-religious culture.[30]

Self-Training, Education and Transmission of the Spiritual-Cultural Heritage to Afro-Descendants

For (neo)traditionalist entrepreneurs, the normalization of philosophies and practices that are little known, misunderstood, and even denied by some Afro-descendants involves education, which they believe has the merit of curbing the obscurantisms at play. Self-taught, they are constantly 'searching' for historical, scientific and archaeological information to support or justify their religious dissidence. The individual agency gives rise to a self-forming activity in each of these actors, which in the socio-cognitive perspective focuses on the relationship to training and the concept of self-directed learning (Jézégou, 2014, p. 271). According to Jézégou, using Malcolm Knowles' definition, self-direction is a process in which an individual 'takes the initiative, with or without the help of others, to determine his or her training needs, to identify the human and material resources required for training, and to select and implement learning strategies' (Jézégou, 2014, p. 272). It is through self-directed learning that (neo)traditionalist entrepreneurs ensure the acquisition of knowledge and the coherence of their reflections, and that they can make available to their communities, students, initiates and followers, course contents, articles (paid and unpaid) and books that, on the one hand, help to open up spaces for training and self-definition and, on the other hand, provide keys to facilitate the logics of transition and conversion. The biblical passage 'My people are destroyed for lack of knowledge' (Hos. 4.6a), often used by Djehouty Mwamba during his classes (participant observation, 5 March 2023), allows him to insist on the need to be 'motivated to study, to work seriously' (Facebook, 1 November 2020) in order to equip oneself responsibly and to undertake the gradual (re)construction of a free identity, as every (neo)traditionalist entrepreneur reveals to us in the interview of the imperialist culture of Christianity.

> I had to search, question myself, work on myself, on my mind, with my heart to emancipate myself from Christian religious dogmatism and find my spiritual-religious balance. I'm still working on cultivating myself and developing my spirituality, because it's a never-ending process. As I like to say: life is a continual learning process. (Mbog, 8.7.2021)[31]

Kirafiky's first self-published work, *Retour à l'Essence-Ciel*, serves as a means of transmitting spiritual and cultural heritage to Afro-descendants through her social networks, in which she actively engages. The author invites her readers to approach religious and spiritual life differently and to 'restore a spiritual vision and practice that promotes harmony, integrity and unity' (Mbog, 2022).[32] In terms of ritual, she reveals the importance of prayer, fasting and meditation. According to her, these are ancestral practices that transcend all religions and are accessible to everyone (Mbog, 2022, p. 203). Prayer enables Afro-descendants to remember who they are, and especially the cosmic order of which they are a part (Mbog, 2022, p. 189). On her Facebook (posts[33]) and Instagram (live direct[34]) accounts, Momi celebrates, through teachings addressed to her community, Kwanzaa, an African-American cultural holiday created by the political activist Maulana Karenga in response to the celebration of Christian Christmas. For the latter,

> Kwanzaa thus came into being, grounded itself and grew as *an act of freedom, an instrument of freedom, a celebration of freedom and a practice of freedom*. It was an act of self-determination and self-authorization; a means of cultivating and expanding consciousness and commitment; a righteous reveling in our recaptured sense of the sacredness, soulfulness and beauty of our Black selves; and the practice of principles that engenders and sustains liberated and liberating ways to understand and assert ourselves in the world.[35]

As such, (neo)traditionalist entrepreneurs search for religious and spiritual life, which is an alternative to imperialist Christianity for transmitting the spiritual-cultural heritage to Afro-descendants.

Digital Conversation and Personalized Support for Neophytes

Very active on social networks, Kirafiky notes on her Patreon page: 'As a content creator, I make available many of my reflections, knowledge, thoughts, advice, readings and inspirations, as well as my time and person, so that those who feel they need it can benefit from my journey and research.' His deconstructive publications on religious dogmatism, which currently have nearly 180,000 likes on TikTok alone, testify to the popularity of his emancipatory messages. In the comments section, Kirafiky engages in dialogue 'without any desire to proselytize', she says, with people who are seeking to build a healthy, progressive and self-centred spirituality. She answers questions, offers help or accompaniment (both real and virtual), and responds to the attacks often launched by members of certain evangelical currents. In November

2022, on Instagram, she made a publication formalizing her position as an 'identification figure':

> I got this dm[36] a few days ago. It's not the first time I've received this kind of dm, but it's the first time I've decided to take my courage in both hands and accept the fact that even though I'm not a guru or spiritual master, I do have some answers to offer to this kind of problem, having encountered it.[37]

Finally, the social processes and strategies observed in our study show that the process of normalizing ancestral practices and rituals specific to 'African spiritualities' is under way, even if the term is not used by (neo) traditionalist Afro-militants to describe their individual and collective agency. The mechanisms at work in collective agency thus make it possible, through the mediation of the definition of a common goal (Jézégou, 2014, p. 278), through the ongoing self-training and cooperation between (neo)traditionalists, and through the effectiveness of the transmissibility of a spiritual-cultural heritage thanks to their great power, to disseminate knowledge to future generations and to gradually transform the socio-religious environment rather than assimilate into it.

Conclusion

'Pass on the truth to the next generation ... Teach them early what we learned late' (Deo Gracias on the group 'Sagesse Plurimillénaire', 14.4.2020). While the notion of truth may be debatable even within Afro-militant (neo)traditionalist networks, the injunction to consolidate collective memory and transmission is important for the durability of African spiritualities and the rituals that derive from them. Memory enables the accumulation of knowledge by structuring facts, events and practices to forge identity and transmit knowledge over time (Ehrenfreund, 2019, p. 776). It is externalized 'in places, books, objects, rituals and practices' (Ehrenfreund, 2019, p. 777). There is thus a close link between collective memory, ritual practices, socio-religious identities and logics of transmission in the service of a community's interests. The conscious efforts of (neo)traditionalist actors and groups responsible for the intergenerational transmission of constructed or manipulated African knowledge facilitate their normalization process. As it gradually takes root and opens up new avenues towards more inclusive transnational societies, a double difficulty that is already present could intensify and divide the Black community. First, an internal difficulty, with the spectre of the extremism of the proselytizing and Afrocentric discourses of certain (neo)traditionalist propagandists in their quest for political, religious and cultural liberation. As for the external difficulty, it concerns the attitude of the dominant religious actors who, losing the privilege of being the norm, could be tempted to adopt more hostile behaviour in order to maintain their position. To address these tensions, further research is necessary to explore other conceptual tools to support this process of normalization. Useful concepts like interculturality will offer insights into the process of dialogue between Christian Afro-militants and (neo)traditionalists, as the intercultural approach involves a process of reciprocal transformation through horizontal and critical conversation, which challenges asymmetrical relationships, hierarchies, and relations of domination.[38]

I'm not at war with any religion, any pastor, any theologian. But what I'm asking for is a minimum of respect for what 'African spiritualities' represent, what an African traditionalist represent. (Momi, *Zone Shining* podcast, 18.5.2023)[39]

Notes

1 This study is published in French: Demart et al., 2017, *Des citoyens aux racines africaines: Un portrait des Belgo-Congolais, Belgo-Rwandais et Belgo-Burundais*. An Afro-descendant is a person of African descent, affiliated with the African diaspora.

2 The data and analyses presented in this chapter are based on field observations carried out within two Afro-militant associations in Brussels (Change and Pensons Bercail) since March 2022.

3 The term 'Afro-diasporic' refers to all people of African descent affiliated with the diaspora.

4 From an emic perspective, the expression 'African spiritualities' is used by Afro-descendants who attempt to name and express the systems of thought, spiritual experiences, and practices they appropriate. For more details, see the first part of this work: 'Between continuity and discontinuity: an attempt to define African spiritualities'.

5 I follow Jézégou's definition of agency: 'In its broadest sense, agency refers to the capacity of human beings to act intentionally on themselves, on others and on their environment.' (Jézégou, 2022, p. 41).

6 We leave the concepts of '*bricolage*' and '*bricoleur*' in French. One would mean 'do-it-yourself' and the other 'a do-it-yourselfer'. According to André Mary, who borrows the notion of *bricolage* from Claude Lévi-Strauss, 'the symbolic material recovered by the "bricoleur" is marked by its previous use; it is pre-

constrained, i.e. it retains in part the memory of its value (in the Saussurian sense of the term) and imposes on the configuration into which it integrates systemic effects that can lead to an unprecedented recomposition' (Mary, 2000, 40).

7 École des mystères berceau de sagesse [Facebook profile], https://www.facebook.com/profile.php?id=100064896303764 (accessed 15.1.25).

8 Particularly literalist biblical interpretations from Pentecostal fundamentalist circles.

9 In the context of this contribution, only three people affiliated with Afro-militant associative networks will be mentioned. Kirafiky is a 26-year-old Afro-militant thinker, author, singer and virtuoso of religious deconstruction. Momi M'Buzé is a 44-year-old prolific African fantasy author, accountant, pan-African activist and Afro-centrist. Djehouty Mwamba is a wisdom master of Kemite spirituality and a Pentecostal pastor.

10 'At the very beginning of any history of religion we find an important fact of experience: the unequal religious qualification of *men* ... The most valuable goods of religious salvation – the ecstatic and visionary capacities of shamans, sorcerers, ascetics and pneumatics of all kinds – were not within everyone's reach; their possession was a charisma that could be awakened in some people but not in all' (Weber, 1996, p. 358).

11 An interview with M'Buzé was conducted on 2 March 2023. He is the author of several books. See https://www.momimbuze.com/livres/ (accessed 15.1.25). Afrofuturism is a literary, aesthetic, and cultural movement that emerged in the diaspora during the second half of the twentieth century. It combines science fiction, techno-culture, magic realism, and non-European cosmologies, with the aim of interrogating the past of so-called peoples of colour and their condition in the present (Mbembe, 2014, p. 125).

12 He works mainly with young people, as he teaches African history to Afro-descendant children and young people in the association Change.

13 See his biography on https://www.momimbuze.com/bio/ (accessed 15.1.25).

14 See his Facebook page: École des mystères berceau de sagesse [Facebook profile], https://www.facebook.com/profile.php?id=100064896303764 (accessed 15.1.25).

15 He is responsible for a church called Heure du salut in Charleroi (Belgium), but he is also present in Lubumbashi (Democratic Republic of the Congo), Lusaka (Zambia) and Johannesburg (South Africa) (interview, 20 February 2023).

16 From the ancient Greek γλῶσσα (language) and λαλέω (to chatter), glossolalia is the speaking of languages incomprehensible to human reason. It is characteristic of the Pentecostal habitus.

17 Each of them points to the importance of thorough research in the historical, religious, archaeological and theological fields in order to refine the quality of their reflections.

18 His Facebook page was at https://www.facebook.com/mbuze.naym.momi, but is no longer available.

19 The term 'ritual' comes from the Latin *ritus*, meaning a cult, a religious ceremony, but also more broadly a usage, a custom (Maisonneuve, 1999, p. 3), a 'prescribed order' (Picard, 2002, p. 251). The Latin *ritus* has an Indo-European root *ar*, present in the Vedic Indian *rta* and in ancient Iranian *arta*, evoking 'the order of the cosmos' (Cuisenier, 2006, p. 17).

20 We borrow these two expressions from Zanga Youssouf Sanogo and Nabé-Vincent Coulibaly, in 'Croyances animistes et développement en Afrique subsaharienne', *Horizons Philosophiques* 13(2), pp. 139–52, https://doi.org/10.7202/801242ar (accessed 15.1.25).

21 Michel Foucault, 1978.

22 Pastor Tito Mutyebele's comments on the *Zone Shining* online podcast (YouTube interview, 11 May 2023) hosted by Mike Shining, an evangelical doctor and rapper, and indeed religious activist whose aim was to understand this 'return to the sources' that complexifies the landscape of religious Afro-culture. See Mike Shining, 2023, 'Why Afro-descendants are abandoning the Christian faith', YouTube, 11 May, https://www.youtube.com/watch?v=MokHFJ4XqtI (accessed 15.1.2025).

23 This is an emerging concept that applies to people of sub-Saharan descent who were born or raised in Europe. They are characterized by a dual African and European cultural heritage. See Miano, 2020, pp. 10 and 51. 'African' refers to anyone living in Africa.

24 Kirafiky has a community of about 20,000 subscribers on YouTube, Instagram, X (Twitter), Spotify and TikTok. Master Djehouty Mwamba has about 6,000 subscribers in his virtual community (Facebook), but only about ten people attend his face-to-face classes (observed on 5.3.2023 on the building of the Pentecostal church, 'Centre de réveil spirituel, Walesa Ministries in Anderlecht). About 4,000 people follow Momi on Facebook, Instagram, and X (Twitter).

25 See bouams_officiel [TikTok profile], https://www.tiktok.com/@bouams_officiel (accessed 15.1.2025).

26 See Tshiwala Ngalula Kalengayi [Facebook profile], https://www.facebook.com/kalengayi (accessed 15.1.2025).

27 Words are capitalized in the citation. See École des mystères berceau de sagesse [Facebook profile], https://www.facebook.com/profile.php?id=100064896303764 (accessed 15.1.2025).

28 See Sagesse Plurimillénaire [Facebook group], https://www.facebook.com/groups/214506453263430 (accessed 15.1.2025).

29 The expression 'African classical humanities' is used by Cheikh Anta Diop to designate the philosophical and religious contributions of ancient Egypt.

30 For example, Mike Shining, an evangelical doctor, rapper, and outspoken religious activist, hosted Kirafiky, Momi M'Buzé, and Tito Mutyebele, pastor of the evangelical megachurch 'New Jerusalem', on his online podcast *Zone Shining* on 3 March 2022, and 11 and 18 May 2023, https://www.youtube.com/playlist?list=PL3JOgVVpEVObItSJVOucPkbG-Tpy1Xdof (accessed 14.5.2025).

31 Self-presentation of Kirafiky on the Patreon platform (https://www.patreon.com/kirafiky/about) before its recent closure.

32 From the book's presentation note (back cover).

33 See Momi M'buze [Facebook profile], https://www.facebook.com/mbuze.naym.momi (accessed 15.1.2025).

34 See Momi M'buze (momi_mbuze) [Instagram profile], https://www.instagram.com/momi_mbuze/ (accessed 15.1.2025).

35 The Pan-African rite is held annually from 16 December to 1 January and is based on seven principles and practices: *Umoja* (unity), *Kujichagulia* (self-determination), *Ujima* (collective work and responsibility), *Ujamaa* (economic

cooperation), Nia (purpose), *Kuumba* (creativity) and *Imani* (faith). See Kwanzaa Freedom Justice and Peace – Dr Maulana Karenga – Annual Founders Kwanzaa Message 12-21-23.pdf (officialkwanzaawebsite.org).

36 The acronym dm stands for 'direct message'.

37 See Kirafiky Mbg. (kirafiky), [Instagram post] (9 November 2022), https://www.instagram.com/p/CkvxdXvoyo4/?img_index=1 (accessed 15.1.2025).

38 'Interculturality' is an interesting transversal theme in several disciplinary fields. For example, the concept of 'alteritarian interculturality', which takes into account the other as a plural; see Lemoine, 2018.

39 See Momi M'Buzé, Shining Zone, 2023, 'Pourquoi les Afro-descendants abandonnent la foi chrétienne', YouTube, 18 May, https://www.youtube.com/watch?v=zBjvHz5Jiyc (accessed 15.1.2025).

References

Argyriadis, Kali, 2012, 'Formes d'organisation des acteurs et modes de circulation des pratiques et des biens symboliques', in Argyriadis Kali, Capone Stefania, de la Torre Renée and Mary André, eds, *Religions transnationales des Suds: Afrique, Europe, Amériques*, Louvain: Academia / IRD / CIESAS, pp. 47–62.

Auque-Pallez, Ysé, 2022, 'Libérer l'Afrique ou se libérer soi-même? Mobilisations politiques et identitaires des militants panafricanistes afrocentriques en Île-de-France', *Études de la Chaire Diasporas Africaines* 2, pp. 1–99.

Bonhomme, Julien, 2018, 'Incident autour d'un poteau. Rituel, script et performance dans le Bwiti du Gabon', L'Homme, 227–28 (3–4), pp. 153–78, https://www.cairn.info/revue-l-homme-2018-3-page-153.htm (accessed 15.1.2025).

Bonhomme, Julien, 2007, 'Transmission et tradition initiatiques en Afrique centrale', *Annales de la Fondation Fyssen* 21, pp. 48–60, halshs-00801895.

Coyault, Bernard, 2021, 'Militances, dissidence et dilettantisme religieux au sein de la population afropéenne de Bruxelles' (séminaire sur la 'Religion, circulations et migrations dans les Afriques', IMAf – EHESS), 17.5.2021 (contribution à paraître).

Cuisenier, Jean, 2006, '1. Du rite et de la cérémonie', in Cuisenier, Jean, *Penser le rituel*, pp. 17–36, Paris: Presses Universitaires de France, https://www.cairn.info/penser-le-rituel-9782130555674-page-17.htm (accessed 15.1.2025).

Demart, Sarah, et al., 2017, *Des citoyens aux racines africaines: Un portrait des Belgo-Congolais, Belgo-Rwandais et Belgo-Burundais*, Bruxelles: Fondation Roi Baudouin.

de Witte, Marleen, 2012, 'Neo-Traditional Religions', in *The Wiley-Blackwell Companion to African Religions*, ed. Elias Kifon Bongmba, pp. 171–83, https://doi.org/10.1002/9781118255513.ch10 (accessed 15.1.2025).

Diop, Cheikh Anta, 1959/79, *Nations nègres et culture*, Paris: Présence Africaine.

Diop, Cheikh Anta, 1981. *Civilisation ou barbarie: Anthropologie sans complaisance*, Paris, Présence Africaine.

Dulucq, Sophie, 2004, 'Action missionnaire et violence en Afrique subsaharienne du début du xix siècle aux indépendances', in *Religions, pouvoir et violence*, ed. Patrick Cabanel and Micheal Bertrand, pp. 61–73, Toulouse: Presses Universitaires du Midi.

Dupin, Claude-Marie, 2009, 'Les rituels: enrichissement de la vie', *Actualités en analyse transactionnelle* 130(2), pp. 53–6, https://doi.org/10.3917/aatc.130.0053 (accessed 15.1.2025).

Ehrenfreund, Jacques, 2019, 'Mémoire et transmission', in Régine Azria, Danièle Hervieu-Léger and Dominique Logna-Prat, *Dictionnaire des faits religieux*, pp. 776–81, Paris: Presses Universitaires de France / Humensis.

Foucault, Michel, 1978, 'Sécurité, territoire, population – Leçon du 25 janvier 1978', http://www.guillaumenicaise.com/wp-content/uploads/2014/08/foucault-le%C3%A7on-du-25-janvier-1978.pdf (accessed 14.5.2025).

Guedj, Pauline, 2010, '*What's my original name?*: Changement de nom, transnationalisation et revendications identitaires dans le nationalisme noir états-unien', *Nuevo Mundo Mundos Nuevos*, https://doi.org/10.4000/nuevomundo.59182 (accessed 15.1.2025).

Jézégou, Annie, 2014, 'L'agentivité humaine: Un moteur essentiel pour l'élaboration d'un environnement personnel d'apprentissage', *Sciences et Technologies de l'Information et de la Communication pour l'Éducation et la Formation* 21, Évaluation dans les Jeux Sérieux / Les EPA: entre description et conceptualisation, pp. 269–86, https://doi.org/10.3406/stice.2014.1099 (accessed 15.1.2025).

Jézégou, Annie, 2022, 'Agentivité', in Anne Jorro (ed.), *Dictionnaire des concepts de la professionnalisation*, pp. 41–4, Louvain-la-Neuve: De Boeck Supérieur, https://doi.org/10.3917/dbu.jorro.2022.01.0041 (accessed 15.1.2025).

Kibora, Ludovic and Langewische, Katrin, 2019, 'Qu'est-ce que la "tradition"? Qu'appelle-t-on religion traditionnelle?', in Degorde, Alice, Ludovic Kibora and KAtrin Langewische, *Rencontres religieuses et dynamiques sociales au Burkina Faso*, Dakar: Amalion, p. 17–38.

Latoki, Paul-Émile, 2010, 'La religion comme quête de l'ordre dans la société africaine traditionnelle', *Les cahiers de psychologie politique* 16, https://cpp.numerev.com/numeros/189-revue-16-recherche-empirique-janvier-2010 (accessed 14.5.2025).

Lemoine, Véronique, 2018, 'L'interculturel en réflexion pour la classe et ailleurs', *Recherches en didactiques* 1(25), pp. 77–92, https://doi.org/10.3917/rdid.025.0077 (accessed 15.1.2025).

Maisonneuve, Jean, 1999, 'Qu'est-ce qu'un rituel? Sens et problématique', in Maisonneuve, Jean (ed.), *Les conduites rituelles*, pp. 6–23, Paris: Presses Universitaires de France, https://www.cairn.info/les-conduites-rituelles--9782130419709-page-6.htm (accessed 15.1.2025).

Manzon, Agnieszka Kedzierska, 2022, 'Retour aux sources? Nouvelles formes de ritualisation et d'expertise rituelle en Afrique et ailleurs', *Annuaire de l'École pratique des hautes études (EPHE), Section des sciences religieuses* 129, pp. 1–6, https://doi.org/10.4000/asr.3973 (accessed 15.1.2025).

Mary, André, 2000, *Le Bricolage africain des héros chrétiens*, Paris: Cerf.

May, Carl R. et al, 2009, 'Development of a Theory of Implementation and Integration: Normalization Process Theory', *Implementation Sci* 4(29), https://doi.org/10.1186/1748-5908-4-29 (accessed 15.1.2025).

Mbembe, Achille, 2014, 'Afrofuturisme et devenir-nègre du monde', *Politique africaine* 4(136), pp. 121–33, https://doi.org/10.3917/polaf.136.0121 (accessed 15.1.2025).

Mbog, Kirafiky, 2022, *Retour à l'Essence-Ciel: Retrouver le chemin vers une spiritualité saine, une note après l'autre*, Bruxelles: Kirafiky Mbog.

Miano, Léonora, 2020, *Afropea: Utopie post-occidentale et post-raciste*, Paris: Grasset.

Mukaminega, Jeanine, 2023, 'L'afropéenne au carrefour des traditions, désobstruction du croire institutionnel: Transmission et dépassement' (colloque sur 'Nommer sa condition. Afropéanité et conditions féminines', FUTP-CARES, 20/10/2022), Bruxelles (contribution à paraître).

Omotunde, Jean Philippe, 2010, *Qu'est-ce qu'être Kamit(e)*, Paris: Menaibuc.

Picard, Dominique, 2002, 'Rites, rituels', in Barus-Michel, Jacqueline (ed.), *Vocabulaire de psychosociologie*, pp. 251–7, Toulouse: Érès, https://doi.org/10.3917/eres.barus.2002.01.0251 (accessed 15.1.2025).

Rieucau, Jean, 2019, 'Ouidah (Bénin): Mettre en tourisme la ville du binôme culture vaudou/mémoire de l'esclavage', *Les Cahiers d'Outre-Mer* 280(2), pp. 599–626, https://doi.org/10.4000/com.10733 (accessed 15.1.2025).

Sanogo, Zanga Youssouf, and Nabé-Vincent Coulibaly, 2003, 'Croyances animistes et développement en Afrique subsaharienne', *Horizons philosophiques* 13(2), pp. 139–52, https://doi.org/10.7202/801242ar (accessed 15.1.2025).

Souty, Jérôme, 2004, 'Le vaudou', *Sciences Humaines* 147(3), p. 31, https://www.cairn.info/magazine-sciences-humaines-2004-3-page-31.htm (accessed 15.1.2025).

Weber, Max, 1996, *Sociologie des religions*, Paris: Gallimard.

5

'The Absurdity of Joy': Reclaiming *Pinkster* (Pentecostal) Rituals as Decolonial Indigenous Expressions of Existence, Resistance and Solidarity

JOHNATHAN JODAMUS

Setting the Scene

I was reared in a conservative Christian home in an Assemblies of God (AOG) Pentecostal church, comprised mainly of poor and working-class Coloured people living in Mitchell's Plain on the Cape Flats in South Africa.[1] While grouped under the general AOG churches, the church I attended with my parents and my two older sisters was unique to the Cape Flats and known as *Pinksterkerk* (literal translation: Pentecostal church). I was drawn to this study not only because of my first-hand experience of *Pinksterkerk* in the AOG church of my youth but also because in the vast literature on African Pentecostalism and Black theology, with one or two recent exceptions, this particular phenomenon of *Pinksterkerk* is largely absent from the literature (Thompson, 2015; Engelbrecht, 2023; Jodamus, 2023). This chapter, therefore, has three goals:

1 To expand the scholarship of African Pentecostal studies by placing the study of *Pinkster* on its agenda
2 To present an alternative discourse to the prevailing narratives of despair and despondency prevalent in much of the literature concerning the social dynamics of the Cape Flats
3 To nuance and expand understandings of the notion of 'Black' within Black theology, through locating *Pinksterkerk* within the Camissa African spiritual tradition

Mellet explains (2022, p. 179):

> the word 'Camissa' comes from the Kora (Cape Khoe) *llkhamis sa*, meaning 'sweet water for us all'. It refers to the river that flows from Table Mountain down to the sea, a freshwater system with over 40 tributaries and springs that today runs beneath the city of Cape Town.

He further argues for a 'rejection of the term Coloured and refers rather to "Camissa Africans"', which he asserts 'is a non-colourist, non-racist and non-tribalist term'. The concept of Camissa is rooted in a tool known as the 'seven tributaries matrix', and 'within these seven identified tributaries we unpack the more than 195 streams of origin of Camissa Africans, and the ties that bind us to our fellow diverse African communities' (Mellet, 2022, p. 243).

The *Pinkster* churches scattered throughout the plains and concrete jungles that comprise the Cape Flats practise a distinctive type of African Pentecostal religion that is deeply embedded in the ancient, culturally hybrid context of Cape Town. This spirituality is practised against the background of legacies of colonialism, enslavement and apartheid (Mellet, 2020; Bam, 2021). Hence, using a decolonial Black theology approach, I will argue that the rituals of the *Pinksterkerk* are expressions of ancestral Camissa African spirituality, and that the *Pinksterkerk*, is therefore uniquely rooted in the Black theology tradition, which embodies a range of cultural expressions and spiritual practices.

Cultural and Religious Context

The Assemblies of God (AOG) must be understood within the cultural and religious context of the Cape Flats. While the AOG has its roots in the US, historian Patric Tariq Mellet notes (2022, p. 63):

> Unlike most of the evangelical and Pentecostal churches in South Africa, which were white churches with missions to black people, the AOG started among black people and spread to white people. It's black leaders thus had a lot more influence, even though the AOG quickly became controlled by whites with a conservative leaning.[2]

Despite the white oversight of the church, the AOG developed in uniquely indigenous *Pinkster* ways on the Cape Flats. The songs, the dances, and even the readings and spoken practices are localized both linguistically and culturally.

The dances are known as *koordans* or *jubel en juig*.[3] The latter is loosely translated as jubilant dancing. *Koordans* may be described as an energetic and ecstatic dance comprised of rhythmic, trance-inducing movements. It is a dance, mostly done in a group, which incorporates quick shuffling feet, stomping legs and moving arms pirouetted in a circle.[4] It is ritual dancing that utilizes the entire body with gyrations and sometimes even rhythmic running.

The repetitive choruses and songs are known as *koortjies* and are sung in Afrikaans with its distinctive Kaaps vernacular. Kaaps is the language predominantly spoken on the Cape Flats by Coloured people, and while Kaaps shares similarities with Afrikaans, it has its own integrity as a language with slave ancestry linked to Khoi, San, Dutch, Malay and Arabic linguistic heritage (Williams, 2021; Williams and Stroud, 2014). *Koortjies* have been translated as emphatic and boisterous praise songs (Engelbrecht, 2023). They are mostly a few (four to six) lines of choruses sung repeatedly using the expressive Kaaps vernacular and sung to the sound of rhythmical African *ghoema* drum-centred beats, accompanied by piano accordions, tambourines and banjos as further musical accompaniment.

The *ghoema* is an ancient traditional drumming instrument often heard during the annual Cape minstrel celebrations on *tweede nuwe jaar* (second new year). 'Traditionally held on the second or third day of January, Tweede Nuwe Jaar is a colourful and musically exciting event that sees minstrel bands from across the Cape arrive in bright and multicoloured costumes' (Dooms and Chutel, 2023) to mark the emancipation of slaves in Cape Town in 1834 when freed slaves danced and mocked their former slave owners.

It is clear then that *Pinkster* is an inherently local form of spirituality, that is, specifically Coloured. While the term 'Coloured' is contested, Mohamed Adhikari notes that (1994, p. 101):

> Contrary to international usage, in South Africa the term 'Coloured' does not refer to black people in general. It instead alludes to a phenotypically diverse group of people descended largely from Cape slaves, indigenous Khoisan peoples, and other blacks who had been assimilated to Cape colonial society by the late nineteenth century. Being also partly descended from European settlers, Coloureds are popularly regarded as being of 'mixed race' and hold an intermediate status in the South African racial hierarchy, distinct from the dominant white minority and the numerically preponderant African population.

In this chapter, I opt to frame *Pinkster* as Camissa African spirituality, diverging from the characterization of it solely as Coloured spirituality. This choice is motivated by Mellet's assertion that embracing the multifaceted Camissa African identity facilitates the restoration of obscured historical narratives. It is an act of restorative memory that counteracts prevailing perceptions that Coloured identities lack cultural depth or are exclusively linked to aspects of white heritage.

Such a focus on Camissa identity also contests contemporary popular essentialist ethno-nationalist framings of race, which tend to offer unnuanced accounts of the term 'Black' that restrict the notion of Black to those who are phenotypically African. As Zimitri Erasmus argued (2001, pp. 18–19):

> although the Black Consciousness Movement of the 1970s promoted blackness as an inclusive, positive political identity marking the racially oppressed and making visible the unearned privileges of whiteness, the politics of the time prevented this discourse from acknowledging the specificity of coloured experiences or the heterogeneity and locatedness of blackness. The Black Consciousness Movement tended towards a universal and single notion of being black which privileged black African experiences (narrowly defined) and papered over racial hierarchies and differential racialization among racially oppressed South Africans.

So to assert that *Pinkster* is a Camissa African spirituality is to reclaim it as part of Black theology and spirituality. Considering the distinctive characteristics of the localized Pentecostal religious practices observed on the Cape Flats, what analytical frameworks may best explain its role and positioning within the broader discourses of Black theology and African Pentecostalism? In their introduction to a special journal issue on Black Theologies, Sarojini Nadar and Demaine Solomons (2022) propose that Black theologies in their current iterations can be considered within three frameworks: 'existence, resistance and solidarity'. In this chapter, I wish to draw on and expand their frameworks to conceptualize the rituals and rhythms of *Pinksterkerk* as constitutive of Black theology and indigenous Camissa spirituality.

Existence

As Nadar and Solomons note (2022, p. 507),

> The task of Black theology is not just to *critique* the racist and socially unjust underpinnings of systems and structures or so-called universal Western theologies – it is to *create* theologies that arise proudly from Black existential and cultural experiences and to provide more nuanced conceptions of blackness.

If the task of Black theology is to also create theologies from Black cultural and existential experiences, then the creative ritual expressions of *koortjies* (choruses), *koordans* (dance) and *getuienis* (testimony) serve as markers of existential affirmation. In contexts that often seek to deny the humanity of Black people, it can be argued that these practices affirm the worth and dignity of each worshipper.

In a recent musicology PhD study, Inge Engelbrecht (2023) argues for the ownership of the *koortjie* and *koordans* as a Coloured cultural and spiritual practice linked directly to the Khoisan spiritual and music traditions. In other words, these rituals and rhythms constitute a form of cultural existence – a type of embodiment where the 'body is both context and content' (Pinn, 2010, p. 121). As Ashon Crawley (2008, pp. 308–9) similarly notes in his observations on performance theory and Black Pentecostalism in the North American context, such embodiment serves to consolidate identity. Relating this to the Cape Flats context, it could be argued that bodies, which apartheid sought to erase through its nomenclature of Coloured, are 'revisibilized' through the religious embodiment of *Pinkster*. In its most crude form, Coloured was reduced to bi-racial identity, which excluded Blackness and foregrounded whiteness (Dooms and Chutel, 2023, p. xvi). The *Pinksterkerk*'s existence then challenges the legacies of racist apartheid normalization patterns, which sought to script Black bodies in deterministic and suppressive ways (Pinn, 2010, p. 101).

Apartheid did not just script bodies; it also erased traditions and histories, and this remains particularly true for people designated as Coloured, whose rich cultural heritages were downplayed. The Cape Flats, historically marked by apartheid-era forced removals that formed a breeding ground for socio-economic malaise, experienced a profound disruption of traditional cultural practices and a 'whitewashing' that has left many disillusioned and with a feeling of cultural amnesia (Bam, 2021, pp. 203–30). *Pinksterkerk koortjies* (Pentecostal church choruses) or spiritual songs, emerged as a resilient form of expression within these communities. The gatherings not only foreground song but also blend Christian religious themes with other indigenous cultural elements like *rieldans* (reel dance) (Van Wyk, 2013; Arnolds and De Jager, 2013; Engelbrecht, 2023), which is derived from an ancient celebratory dance performed by the San, Nama and Khoi.[5] It is considered one of the oldest dancing styles of indigenous South Africa. Similarly, elements of the *Kaapse klopse* (Cape Town minstrels) also appear in these *Pinkster* rituals. *Klopse* refers to a 'celebration of escape in the late 1800s when formal slavery ended and freed men and women could celebrate occasions like the New Year in their own ways and on their own terms' (Dooms and Chutel, 2023, p. 62). *Pinkster* religious expressions thus created a unique fusion that resonates with the lived experiences and traditions of the people and provides a platform for the Cape Camissa communities to reconnect with their indigenous and ancient roots.

Within these existential claims lies a strong pull towards restorative memorialization (Jethro, 2021). Through music, dance and communal worship as participatory (Williams, 2016, p. 46), individuals can express their spirituality in a way that reflects both their Christian beliefs and their diverse cultural heritage. This synthesis helps bridge the gap between the introduced Christian faith and the indigenous spirituality that pre-dates it. For example, Mellet (2020, p. 152) asserts: 'In Cape Town one of the elements that survives of the African faith of the Masbiekers is the creolization of the word ngoma (drum) to ghoema and its associated drumming beat in Cape Jazz and Klopse music.' He also notes: 'Much of southern Africa below the equator is home to the Ngoma faith. This traditional faith, roughly translated as 'the way of the drum' (ngoma, also creolized to 'ghoema') is facilitated by the sangomas, who are diviners, and the faith has more than 3,000 years of history (Mellet, 2020, p. 22). According to Mellet, restorative memory is a precursor to restorative justice. Part of this restorative justice for me is to claim the recognition of indigenous spirituality and cultural meaning-making for local Camissa African communities on the Cape Flats. In this way, these practices become not only expressions of faith but also acts of self-affirmation, identity construction and cultural preservation.

Pinksterkerk koortjies and *koordans* on the Cape Flats thus serve as a powerful conduit for reclaiming indigenous cultural and religious identity amidst a violent past and an ongoing troubled present. Rooted in the rich and diverse history of the Cape Camissa communities, these religious gatherings by local *Pinksterkerk* communities create an opportunity for ritual and embodied expressions that are a vital aspect of preserving and revitalizing indigenous spirituality and cultural heritage. While reclaiming one's heritage is an important step in affirming existence, the embodied praxis also serves another purpose – disruption and resistance (Crawley, 2008).

Resistance

While often characterized as apolitical, Pentecostal expressions such as *Pinksterkerk* can also embody a profound form of resistance against colonial structures and social injustices. As shown above, at its core, the *Pinksterkerk* represents a fusion of indigenous Camissa African spirituality with Christianity, creating a unique syncretic faith that resonates deeply with its followers. This syncretism allows the *Pinksterkerk* to assert its independence from the colonial legacy of Christianity imposed by European colonizers and even the type of Pentecostalism forged by its American founders. By incorporating elements of African culture and traditions into its worship, it asserts the value and dignity of African identity as resistance to colonial erasure and as a sidestep from assimilation into American forms of Pentecostalism.

Furthermore, the performative nature of *koordans* disrupts traditional notions of religious authority and challenges the Eurocentric gaze that often devalues non-Western spiritual practices. In so doing, it empowers the *Pinksterkerk* communities to assert their autonomy and challenge the narrative that places Western Christian practices as superior. The ritual performance of *koordans* within the *Pinksterkerk* instead represents a dynamic form of resistance against colonial religion and traditional Christian theology.

Apart from the theological resistance, the vibrant music and dance central to *Pinkster* worship serve as forms of resistance against material forces of colonialism and social marginalization, as well. Through ecstatic praise and communal celebration, *Pinkster* congregants find solace, strength and solidarity in the face of adversity. The rhythmic drumming, energetic dancing and soulful singing create a space of liberation where individuals can express their collective identity and assert their agency against the dehumanizing effects of poverty and deprivation.

An example that stands out quite pointedly for me is one where, during a period marked by the institutionalized racial segregation of apartheid in South Africa, my parents embarked on one of their church 'mission' trips. On the way, they stopped at a filling station for refreshment. My mother, possessing a phenotypic appearance that aligned with the privileged racial category, i.e. she looked white (by virtue of the fact that her father was classified white, even though she was classified 'mixed'), was accorded the privilege of entering the garage shop via the main entrance. My father, characterized by a darker complexion, was told to use the rear entrance, designated for deliveries and 'servants'. The episode of humiliation and indignity notwithstanding, my parents insisted that they found solace in the fellowship and praise and worship for the rest of the trip. While some might contend that their framing of joy amidst the humiliation is typical of Pentecostal personal spirituality at the expense of political action for structural change, my parents insisted that the joy constituted resistance. Such was their joy that my father was known to be a *koordans voorloper* (dance leader) of the jubilant human train dance that was common in many of the services. Indeed, this may be perceived to be an 'absurd joy', and yet there is an agency in this embodied expression that cannot be ignored.

In her study of *koortjies* and *koordans*, Inge Engelbrecht comments '*hoe belangrik die kerk vir hulle was, vir die marginalized Coloured community*' (how important the church was for the marginalized Coloured community). One of the participants in her study notes:

> 'Because *hulle kan da [in die wêreld] uitgaan ... en dan kan iemand 'n altercation het met die*, you know, *apartheid police, or whatever, and but like die faith was that thing that no matter if they can die, soelank hulle naam da [in die paradys] is*.' This can be translated as: '[t]hey can go out into the world and even have an altercation with the apartheid police, and may even die, but as long as their names are written in paradise.' (Engelbrecht, 2023)

Engelbrecht asserts that Marie Jorritsma gave her an alternative perspective on this research participant's viewpoint. 'The preservation of this aural/oral evidence within this religious repertoire ... constitutes a strong statement of survival amid painful experiences of oppression and marginalization' (Jorritsma, 2016, p. 229).

My initial scepticism of my parents' proclivity towards joy in the face of indignity, akin to 'pie in the sky theology', has also gradually yielded to a more nuanced appreciation. Indeed, the collective joy, manifested through singing and dancing, emerges as an implicit assertion of human dignity, thus constituting a form of resistance against the pervasive racial dehumanization of the era. This spiritual resilience fosters a sense of community cohesion and collective action, which can lay the groundwork for social change and transformation.

Despite its ostensibly non-political stance, the *Pinksterkerk*'s vibrant music and dance inherently challenge the hegemony of mainstream church formations and confront the broader socio-political context of material oppression. Furthermore, the *Pinksterkerk*'s emphasis on spiritual empowerment and divine intervention provides a sense of hope and resilience. In a society where economic disenfranchisement and systemic racism are pervasive, the *Pinksterkerk* offers a sanctuary of faith and healing where individuals find comfort and inspiration to persevere in the face of deep hardship. These spaces are often forged in solidarity with one another, the final theme to which we shall turn.

Solidarity

Whereas Nadar and Solomons (2022) refer to solidarity as alliances between different forms of liberation theology, I am framing solidarity here as the bonds that are created between those who share their faith in the midst of challenging socio-economic conditions. *Pinksterkerk koortjies*, *koordans* and *getuienis* play a pivotal role in solidarity by forging bonds of communal support and collective identity amongst Cape Flats Coloured communities. The shared experience of these gatherings fosters a sense of belonging and solidarity among participants. The music and rituals create a communal space where individuals can not only express their cultural identity but also support one another in navigating the challenges faced by the community.

Through communal singing and dancing, *Pinksterkerk* congregants affirm their existence as valued members of a spiritual community. The shared experience of lifting their voices in harmony and moving together in rhythmic unison reinforces a sense of belonging and identity. In the act of singing and dancing together, worshippers transcend individual concerns and unite as a single body of believers. The rhythmic pulsation of the music and the synchronized movements of the dancers create a sense of shared purpose and mutual encouragement (not least of all because the nature of *koordans* requires one to move 'in-step' with the other).

On the Cape Flats, this solidarity often takes place in the midst of pain. This goes beyond the familiar Marxian notion that religion is the 'opium of the masses' type of reasoning. Indeed, there is validity in the momentary escapism argumentation that music and singing may bring (Dooms and Chutel, 2023, pp. 58–9), but there is also a deep joy that is ushered in through singing and dancing in these *Pinksterkerk* communities (Alexander 2009, p. 20; Kgatle, 2019). It is useful then to understand the rhythms and rituals of this church formation as a form of religious and cultural solidarity with adherents who experience the daily struggles of life on the Cape Flats. The inexplicable joy experienced in the rituals of dance and the joy of the music and singing offers a 'counternarrative' (Jorritsma, 2016, p. 242) to the depressing realities encountered by people who experience painful and violent situations daily both as material legacies of apartheid and systemic violence. For example, using performance theory together with feminist and queer theory, Crawley (2008, p. 308) notes how the Black Pentecostal church in North America offers 'sites of superfluous emotionalism' and the opportunity to rupture oppressive norms.

This spiritual rejuvenation and empowerment tactic was invigorating for adherents in the church where I grew up. Given the many social ills on the Cape Flats, with gangsterism and drug addiction as common problems plaguing the community (Van der Westhuizen and Sibulelo, 2021), it was almost absurd to see a bunch of people in such joyous celebration, 'the absurdity of joy' (Jodamus, 2022, p. 604). What did they have to be joyful about? Through rhythmic singing and spirited dancing, *Pinksterkerk* congregants reclaimed spaces of worship as productive ritual sites against the dehumanizing forces of racial segregation. The very act of gathering together to sing and dance in praise of God represented an embodied and bold defiance of the racial hierarchy imposed by the apartheid regime.

Furthermore, the content of *koortjies* often contained biblical themes of liberation, hope and justice, echoing the struggles of the Black community for freedom and equality. By vocalizing their aspirations for a better future through song, *Pinksterkerk* congregants found solace and strength in their shared resistance against oppression. In a different, though related manner, Scandrett-Leatherman (2011, p. 951–9), writing about the violence of lynching, has demonstrated how Black people resisted subjugation and dehumanization and transgressed these systems of oppression through the ritual of dance. He asserts that 'Afro-Pentecostal dance was (and is) an expression of life that resists the dehumanizing effects of violence' (Scandrett-Leatherman, 2011, p. 96). Some hopeful and justice-oriented *ou evangelie* (old Gospel) *Pinksterkerk koortjies* (Pentecostal church choruses) that I grew up hearing and singing include songs like:

- *Daar is môre in my hart* (there is promise in my heart).
- *Jesus is myne, hy is myne deur die beproeving* (Jesus is mine through the trials)

- *Soos 'n Brandende hout, hy haal my uit die vuur uit soos 'n brandende hout* (like a flaming piece of wood, he rescues me from the fire, like a flaming piece of wood).
- *Hierdie evangelie sal ek vas aan hou* (I'll hold steadfast onto this Gospel).
- *Verlossing het gekom op Golgotha* (Deliverance came on Golgotha).

These choruses were especially roused and stirred during the occasions of *evangelisasie dienste* (evangelistic outreach services) and often accompanied the ritual of *doop diens* (baptism) for new converts, but it could easily be stirred up among participants, and very often elderly women in the church were the leaders of this ritual performance, performed as and when 'the spirit moved'.

Another ritual of solidarity that accompanied *koortjies* and *koordans* and also occurred on the occasion of *doop diens* (baptism) was the ritual of *getuienis* (testimony). This rhetorical performativity often expressed solidarity of lived experience and provided an opportunity for encouragement and social affirmation. At these baptism occasions, it was customary for someone 'fired up by the holy spirit' to eagerly make their way to the front of the church to address the congregation with a personal testimony that would often rouse the applause of the community and serve as edification.

The practice of giving testimony, however, not only serves as a powerful rhetorical performance ritual that celebrates individual experiences of deliverance and redemption: it also fosters bonds of solidarity within the faith community. Through the sharing of personal narratives, believers stand up to recount stories of overcoming adversity, finding strength in their faith, and experiencing divine intervention in their lives. When individuals share stories of deliverance from drug addiction, financial crisis, or other challenges, they bear witness to the miraculous workings of divine grace.

Moreover, the act of giving testimony is inherently performative, as believers stand before the congregation to share their stories in a manner that is often emotive, impassioned and persuasive. This rhetorical performance aspect serves to engage the audience on both emotional and intellectual levels, eliciting empathy, admiration and solidarity. Through their testimonies, individuals not only recount their experiences but also actively shape the narrative of their collective redemption, framing their struggles and triumphs in ways that resonate with each other.

Furthermore, testimonies serve as vehicles for social critique and prophetic witness within *Pinkster* churches. As individuals recount their experiences of deliverance from addiction, poverty, or gangsterism, they implicitly challenge social structures and systems that perpetuate these injustices. For example, when I was growing up, it was common for reformed gangsters to be asked to give their testimony. One story that comes to my mind is when a local gangster, part of the 'Hard Living Kids' (HLK), which is a notorious gang on the Cape Flats, took to the front of the church to give his testimony. This same young man was often found at the nearby shop and had been accused of committing theft, which included stealing from members of our church. This new convert was now overcome with remorse and decided to take his opportunity to *getuig* (testify) as an opportunity to also apologize publicly to those whom he had wronged previously. This demonstration of God's transformative power, contrition and a commitment to reconciliation fostered a discernible moving atmosphere of forgiveness and communal solidarity within the faith community, thereby facilitating the cultivation of deeper interpersonal connections among the church adherents. In summary, *koortjies, koordans* and *getuienis* serve multiple purposes, functioning as acts of worship, sources of encouragement and catalysts for communal solidarity.

Conclusion

While much research in South Africa has been devoted to studying race in terms of its critical manifestations within oppressive and supremacist discourses, insufficient work has been done on Coloured identity and even less on *Pinksterkerk* communities on the Cape Flats. As Dooms and Chutel (2023, p. xii–xiii) argue, 'Not nearly enough has been written about Coloured identity in South Africa historically, and certainly not about the contemporary experiences of Coloured people in the context of a post-apartheid society seeking to redress the injustices of our brutal past.'

Similarly, I, too, have been developing and arguing for more nuanced conceptualizations of race beyond the Black/white binary within Black theological reflections (Jodamus, 2022, 2023). This research aims to bring more of these local voices to the fore. I hope that this fresh exploration of a manifestation of African Pentecostalism will be significant, not least of all, because Coloured religious experiences and practices have either been excluded or not nuanced in the scholarship produced within Black theology and African Pentecostalism.

In the context of the *Pinksterkerk*, a church with roots in indigenous African traditions, the ritual performance of *koortjies, koordans and getuienis* emerge as crucial elements in cultivating expressions of existence, resistance and solidarity within the context of Black theology. Through these practices, worshippers affirm their humanity and cultural identity, assert their agency in the face of oppression, and forge bonds of solidarity and joy within their communities. As embodiments of faith in action, the rituals of *koortjies, koordans* and *getuienis* continue to inspire and empower generations of believers in their ongoing quest for liberation and justice.

Notes

1 'Coloured' is a contested identity category that was part of the racial stratification system of Apartheid in South Africa. For a discussion of this term and its complexities, see, among others, Erasmus and Pieterse (1999); Erasmus (2001); Adhikari (2009); Mellet (2020); Dooms and Chutel (2023). The term 'Cape Flats' collectively refers to Black and Coloured townships in Cape Town, which is a result of apartheid-forced removals and spatial planning located on the outskirts of the city of Cape Town, far removed from the city centre.

2 Also see Resane (2022) for further discussion on the origins of the AOG in South Africa.

3 For an argument that suggests that *juiging* (or *koordans*) and *koortjies* trace back to ancestral Khoisan roots, see Engelbrecht (2023). Also see Adhikari (2005, pp. 9–23).

4 See the video clips of *koortjies* and *koordans* to illustrate what it is and to demonstrate its cultural idiosyncrasies: Selwin Romeo Production, 2023, 'Herlewing Tent Diens volk in wegstry', YouTube, 26 May, https://youtu.be/baFtr1Ocuo8 (accessed 3.3.2025); Kunjalo, 2020, 'KLFT Band – My hart Jubel (Dit Jubel, Jubel, Jubel)', YouTube, 30 July, https://www.youtube.com/watch?v=qOVZoWdht2E&t=15s&pp=ygUaa29vcmRhbnMgcGlua3NoZXIgZXZhbmdpbGU%3D (accessed 15.1.2025).

5 See these video clips that illustrate the movements of this dance: Johan Nelson, 2016, 'Graskoue trappers rieldans, Cederberg Kunstefees 2016', You Tube, 24 October, https://www.youtube.com/watch?v=uvUU9AUWetU&t=5s (accessed 15.1.2025); TygerBurgerWeb, 2014, 'Riëldans by Durbanville plaasfees', YouTube, 17 March, https://www.youtube.com/watch?v=qMpgv1wkt8U&t=88s (accessed 15.1.2025); Moja Multimedia, 2019, 'The ATKV 2018 Rieldans Finals', YouTube, 3 December, https://www.youtube.com/watch?v=YKswme7emEI&t=216s (accessed 15.1.2025).

References

Adhikari, Mohamed, 1994, 'Coloured Identity and the Politics of Coloured Education: The Origin of the Teachers' League of South Africa', *International Journal of African Historical Studies* 27(1), pp. 101–26.

Adhikari, Mohamed, 2005, *Not White Enough, Not Black Enough: Racial Identity in the South African Coloured Community*, Athens, OH: Ohio University Press.

Adhikari, Mohamed, 2009, 'From Narratives of Miscegenation to Post-modernist Re-imagining: Towards a Historiography of Coloured Identity in South Africa', in Mohamed Adhikari, ed., *Burdened by Race: Coloured Identities in Southern Africa*, pp. 1–22, Cape Town: UCT Press.

Alexander, Paul, 2009, *Signs and Wonders: Why Pentecostalism Is the World's Fastest Growing Faith*, San Francisco, CA: Jossey-Bass.

Arnolds, H., and A. De Jager, 2013, 'Lifeworld of the Karoo People Expressed in the Riel Dance – a Geographical Perspective', in Papers Presented at Confluences 7: Dance, Religion and Spirituality, School of Dance, University of Cape Town, 11–13 July, Cape Town: UCT School of Dance, pp. 1–21.

Bam, June, 2021, *Ausi Told Me: Why Cape Herstoriographies Matter*, Auckland Park: Jacana Media.

Crawley, Ashon, 2008, '"Let's Get It On!" Performance Theory and Black Pentecostalism', *Black Theology* 6(3), pp. 308–29.

Dooms, Tessa, and Lynsey Ebony Chutel, 2023, *Coloured: How Classification Became Culture*, Cape Town: Jonathan Ball Publishers.

Engelbrecht, Inge Alvine, 2023, 'Die Koortjie Undercommons', PhD thesis in Musicology, Stellenbosch University.

Erasmus, Zimitri, 2001, 'Re-Imagining Coloured Identities in Post-Apartheid South Africa', in Zimitri Erasmus, ed., *Coloured by History, Shaped by Place: New Perspectives on Coloured Identities in Cape Town*, Cape Town: Kwela Books.

Erasmus, Zimitri and Edgar Pieterse, 1999, 'Conceptualising Coloured Identities in the Western Cape Province of South Africa 10', *National Identity and Democracy in Africa* 95, pp. 167–87.

Jethro, Duane, 2021, 'Ash: Memorializing the 2021 University of Cape Town Library Fire', *Material Religion* 17(5), pp. 671–7.

Jodamus, Johnathan, 2022, 'The "Pinkster Kerk" As a Site of Indigenous Religious Expression within Black Pentecostal Theology', *Ecumenical Review* 74(4), pp. 600–16.

Jodamus, Johnathan, 2023, 'Why (Do) We Still Need Black Theology? A Pedagogical Case for Intersecting Intersectional Black Theology and Biblical Hermeneutics', in D. Solomons and E. Baron, eds, *Liberating Black Theology: Emerging South African Voices*, pp. 156–68, Stellenbosch: Sun Media Press.

Jorritsma, Marie, 2016, 'Hidden Histories of Religious Music in a South African Coloured Community', in S. Reily and J. Dueck, eds, *The Oxford Handbook of Music and World Christianities*, New York: Oxford University Press.

Kgatle, Mookgo S., 2019, 'Singing As a Therapeutic Agent in Pentecostal Worship', *Verbum et Ecclesia* 40(1), pp. 1–7.

Mellet, Patric Tariq, 2020, *The Lie of 1652: A Decolonised History of Land*, Cape Town: Tafelberg.

Nadar, Sarojini, and Demaine Solomons, 2022, 'Black Theologies of Liberation: How Should Black Lives Matter Theologically?' *The Ecumenical Review* 74(4), pp. 503–14.

Pinn, Anthony B., 2010, *Embodiment and the New Shape of Black Theological Thought*, New York: NYU Press.

Resane, Kelebogile T., 2022, 'From Small Country Churches to Explosion into Megachurches: A Modern Pentecostal Cultural Fit for the Assemblies of God in South Africa', *Verbum et Ecclesia* 43(1), p. 2460.

Scandrett-Leatherman, Craig, 2011, 'Rites of Lynching and Rights of Dance', in Yong, Amos and Estrelda Y. Alexander, eds, *Afro-Pentecostalism: Black Pentecostal and Charismatic Christianity in History and Culture*, vol. 16, pp. 95–115, New York: NYU Press.

Thompson, Robin, 2015, 'The Production of Gospel Music: An Ethnographic Study of Studio-Recorded Music in Bellville, Cape Town', thesis presented for the degree of Master of Arts in Anthropology, Cape Town: University of the Western Cape (UWC).

Van der Westhuizen, Marichen, and Gawulayo Sibulelo, 2021, 'Youths in Gangs on the Cape Flats: If not in Gangs, then What?' *Social Work* 57(1), pp. 118–32.

Van Wyk, Micheal M., 2013, '[Re]vitalize Khoisan Art and Culture via a Community Outreach Initiative', *Studies of Tribes and Tribals* 11(2), pp. 145–51.

Williams, Andrew, 2016, 'Spiritual Landscapes of Pentecostal Worship, Belief, and Embodiment in a Therapeutic Community: New Critical Perspectives', *Emotion, Space and Society* 19, pp. 45–55.

Williams, Quentin, 2021, 'Into Collabs: Public Applied Linguistics and Hip-Hop Language Technicians', *Applied Linguistics* 42(6), pp. 1125–37.

Williams, Quentin and Christopher Stroud, 2014, 'Battling the Race: Stylizing Language and Coproducing Whiteness and Colouredness in a Freestyle Rap Performance', *Journal of Linguistic Anthropology* 24(3), pp. 277–93.

6

Dancing, Drinking and Feasting: Rarámuri Worship During Holy Week as an Ecclesial Third Space

ÁNGEL F. MÉNDEZ MONTOYA

Introduction: Two Preliminary Concepts

In April of 2023, I attended the Holy Week celebrations with the Rarámuri community at the Jesuit missions of Samachique in the Tarahumara mountain range in the State of Chihuahua, northern Mexico. The Rarámuri culture and religion are mainly corporeal, having very few oral or written practices. Its religious sensitivity is expressed through dance and collectively sharing food and drink. The method used for this research is a thick description and autoethnography (Geertz, 1977), insofar as relying on my immersive experience of observing and being among the Rarámuri community in Samachique, highlighting the symbolic and interpreting aspects of their culture and religion. Based on this immersive experience, and after studying Pedro de Velasco's book, *Danzar o morir: Religión y resistencia a la dominación en la cultura Tarahumara* ('Dance or die: religion and resistance to domination in the Tarahumara culture') as a main bibliographical source, this chapter bears witness to the Christian-Rarámuri inculturation experienced by this indigenous community.[1]

Feet of a dancing Rarámuri

This chapter is also the result of several years of research into the relationship between food, dance, theology and religious studies. Earlier in my research, I carried out separate studies on food and theology (Mendez

Montoya, 2012) and, later, dance and theology (Mendez Montoya, 2023). I am currently intersecting both dance and food with religious studies, including anthropological studies that focus on embodiment or corporeal religious experiences, mainly in Mexico. These embodied religious experiences are also epistemic poetic expressions since they represent the wisdom and genius of indigenous traditions that enhance, rather than impoverish, Christian experience and insight. I am particularly fascinated by the multiplicity of Mexican cultures directly or indirectly intertwined with religious-related feasts (*fiestas*) that incorporate dancing and communal practices of eating and drinking or fasting. From birth to death, in liturgical, ritual or secular feasts, from Catholic to many other religious traditions, eating and drinking, as well as dancing, are culturally and socially co-implicated. As I have stated elsewhere, 'People dance and eat in religious celebrations such as baptisms, weddings, sweet fifteen presentations to society (*fiesta de quinceañera*), and locally important popular celebrations of saints and liturgical seasons' (Mendez Montoya, 2023, p. 25).

These expressions and practices intimate an in-between space beyond any dichotomies or antagonisms. As such, these intersected cultural practices evoke what Homi Bhabha, the postcolonial theorist, calls a hybrid 'third space' (1994). This interstitial space is an epistemic, social and anthropological concept that Bhabha propounds as an alternative to Western and colonial dichotomies, 'which leads to a reflection, not only on space, but also on discursive attitudes that reflect an in-betweenness that hybridizes cultures, epistemologies, traditions, and languages, and allows a third space of enunciation in post- and neo-colonial times' (Mendez Montoya, 2024, p. 54). I refer here in this chapter to the Rarámuri indigenous community in Samachique, in the Mexican North State of Durango. I argue that the Rarámuri cultures are paradigmatic of this first concept, the 'third space' – an entanglement of body and spirit; dancing, eating and drinking; Catholic and indigenous religious traditions; and ritual and social space.

The second concept I apply to this study is that of 'inculturation'. There is a fascinating sense of inculturation through which the Rarámuri indigenous communities express their religion within their own cultural and religious stance, rather than from a dominant Catholic colonial tradition. In agreement with Aylward Shorter, inculturation could be defined as 'the creative and dynamic relationship between the Christian message and a culture or cultures'. This category has been criticized because it has been constructed using a colonial perspective of Western Christianity that subordinates the religious traditions of the original people. However, the Rarámuri people and their rituals – specifically the religious rituals and feasts during Holy Week in Samachique, Chihuahua – shed light on a strong, prevalent Mesoamerican inheritance that interweaves intercultural religions with a diversity of Catholic traditions. The mutual cultural and religious engagement between Catholic traditions and pre-Hispanic Rarámuri religious inheritance enriches one another without endangering 'the nature and values of Christianity as a revealed religion, nor does it jeopardize human culture as an expression of society's life and aspirations. Christian worship should not be reduced to becoming a mere ingredient of local culture, nor should culture be reduced to an ancillary role. The interaction and mutual assimilation between Christian worship and local culture enhances both, rather than causing mutual extinction' (Chupungco, 1992, pp. 28–9). I concur with Laurenti Magesa that the deep individual and communal experience enhanced by inculturation forms part of the intertwining between the Catholic and Rarámuri religions: 'True inculturation is a deep experience in the life of the individual and the community that occurs when there is a constant search for identification between gospel and culture, and when there is mutual correction and adjustment between them' (2004, pp. 144–5).

Both concepts, 'third space' and 'inculturation', are important to this hermeneutical exercise and are applied here to more clearly appreciate both the genius of the religious wisdom characterizing the original peoples and a religious experience in which eating, drinking, dancing and worshipping interweave with one another. As I set forth here, the Rarámuri ritual practices enrich Christian spirituality and knowledge, as well as shedding light on the possibility of decolonizing Christianity.

Rarámuri

In the Rarámuri language, the word 'Rarámuri' means 'running feet'. This is appropriate since they are great athletes who run miles across the rocky lands of the Tarahumara mountain range (Sierra Tarahumara).

Compared to the vast number of interdisciplinary studies on different regions inhabited by Mesoamerican peoples in Mexico, there is insufficient information about the Rarámuri culture, since it dates back to pre-Hispanic times and is a culture without much written or oral tradition. For this reason, it is deeply important to gain access to their religious worldview from a mainly corporeal hermeneutics, considering that dancing, drinking and eating are so foundational to their religious experiences, expressions and practices.

The Rarámuri are exceptional people. They are survivors living in the heart of the Sierra Tarahumara, which reaches a height of 3,000 metres above sea level.

Sierra Tarahumara

Living conditions are extremely difficult given the harsh climate of the Sierra Tarahumara, particularly during the lengthy winter. Food is scarce and includes corn, beans and squash. Along with farming, the main activities are shepherding and handicraft making. Mining, too, is a main source of employment and income, while, at the same time, opening the door to exploitation:

> Since the arrival of the Spanish colonizers in the sixteenth century, the Tarahumara communities have been exploited by large-scale mining. Their mineral-rich lands bore the consequences of the early colonizers' predatory extractivism, a practice perpetuated by the neocolonial stakeholders who continue to exploit, abuse, and violently control the territories today. (Mendez Montoya, 2024, p. 29)

These conflicts with mining have prevailed throughout the history of colonial and neocolonial Mexico in general and the Tarahumara region in particular. The Rarámuri people have endured a long history of struggle and survival, not only because of the harsh climate and natural conditions, but also because of the extensive abuse and extractivism, which they have managed to resist.

Since the end of the nineteenth century to this day, forest exploitation has been on the rise, causing irreversible ecological damage, as well as increasing impoverishment of the Rarámuri. Their most current serious problem is resistance to organized crime and the drug cartel system. From the beginning of the Jesuit missions in the sixteenth century to this day, the Jesuits have strongly supported and even defended these communities. However, crime is so extreme that two Jesuit priests were recently murdered in the Rarámuri mission:

> The extreme level of violence inflicted by organized crime, as well as the domination and wars of the drug lords in the northern part of the country invaded and increasingly devastated the Tarahumara Mountain Range. On June 20, 2022, two Jesuit priests, Father Javier Campos Morales and Father Joaquín César Mora Salazar, were murdered in the Rarámuri mission of Cerocahui, Chihuahua. Alleged members of the Sinaloa cartel hit-squad entered the Jesuit church and shot a local tour guide who was seeking refuge in the church. When the priests intervened, they too were shot dead. The three bodies were not found until two days later. The Jesuit Province in Mexico issued a strong denunciation, expressing concern about the escalating violence and unrest that affected both the religious and the laity serving in the Jesuit missions. (Mendez Montoya, 2024, p. 32)

I include here a photo I took of the altar at a Jesuit Chapel in Samachique during Holy Week in April 2023, almost one year after the murder of Father Javier Campos Morales and Father Joaquín César Mora Salazar.

Altar with photos of Father Javier Campos Morales and Father Joaquín César Mora Salazar

Despite this climate of fear and violence, the Rarámuri are peaceful, very hospitable, community-minded, and share a deep sense of the sacred both in nature and in their bodies. For them, the sacred and the profane are not really separate. It is as if there were a third liminal space in which there is a mutual and dynamic interplay. Likewise, culture and religion are inseparable, for they are co-implicated, creating a mutually-constructed third space. Because the Rarámuri communities lived in such remote areas, they were not fully colonized with the arrival of the Spanish missionaries. This is also the reason why it is so fascinating to witness these Catholic-Rarámuri religious rituals and practices that have survived for so long, creating a third space even after more than five hundred years of colonial Christianity in these Tarahumaran missions.

The Rarámuri people are not churchgoers. Holy Week and other liturgical seasons like Advent, Christmas and Lent, are the only days when the Rarámuri visit the chapel. Unlike most indigenous Catholic communities throughout Mexico, Rarámuri temples are minimalist with few saints and religious images. It is also interesting that for them moral guilt does not really exist, and the sense of being a sinner is not prevalent. Murder, theft, lying and adultery are the only sins recognized. However, the greatest sin of all is to refrain from dancing.

Dancing is an essential part of the Rarámuri culture and religion. They believe that God dances with them and invites everyone to join this cosmic dance. In a few Rarámuri creation myths, there is a narrative about the earth being far too soft in the beginning. To strengthen the earth, God danced until it became firm. The earth is, therefore, created through God's dancing feet.

In the following photo, we see some of the clothes that the Rarámuri wear. Some clothing is more traditional, as in the case of most women, while men usually wear more everyday clothing.

Clothes that Rarámuri wear

They often wear shoes or sandals. They wear a headdress, sometimes with turkey feathers (in the following photo). Some men also carry wooden swords, which are distinctive of different ranks within the community.

Rarámuri garments

The younger generations also participate in the ritual dances. Many do not wear traditional garments, but rather urban youthful clothing such as sweatshirts, jeans, sneakers or ankle boots, and baseball caps. Most of the youth participate more intensely in playing the drums rather than the dancing rituals.

Younger generation of Rarámuri

The dances are often concentric or in a figure of eight. Although not everyone dances, the spectators become part of this ritual and do not consider themselves mere observers, for they can participate at any time. Even simply observing is considered a way of dancing. It is often men who dance, but women and even children also join in. Dancing is not just a performance, but a ritual practice and experience and a form of praying or worshipping with a dancing body. As aforementioned, their cultural traditions are not very oral or written. Instead, their worship is expressed through the body, whether through dancing, eating or drinking.

Sharing food and drink, drinking and eating together, are also of great importance in their religious celebrations. As you can see in the following photograph, their food is simple and they drink large amounts of *tesgüino*, which is an alcoholic drink made from fermented corn that is very thick, very rich in nutrients, and can be considered food because it helps counteract the extreme temperature and hunger, particularly during winter, when the temperature drops below zero, mostly at night or before dawn. Since most of their celebrations take place outdoors and last all night, drinking *tesgüino* truly helps to cope with the freezing weather. It is their understanding that God eats and drinks with them, and that is why they drink large amounts of *tesgüino*. This allows them to socialize and overcome inhibitions. Besides, *tesgüino* also has some medicinal qualities and is used in remedies.

Their principle of relationality is based on what they call '*kórima*', which is the virtue of sharing and redistributing wealth in a spirit of co-responsibility and interdependence. The Rarámuri is a culture that always shares food and drink. *Kórima* is central to them, and, unlike the white people or 'colonizers' – as the Rarámuri refer to them – they do not eat alone, but always in the company of others, because for them eating and drinking together and sharing from the same cauldron is a form of creating community. Their food is very simple.

Corn tortillas and stew

From the beginning of their mission, the Jesuits tried to punish the Rarámuri for those feasts and excessive drinking of *tesgüino*, but the Rarámuri persisted with their traditions. The Jesuits finally gave up and allowed them to celebrate following their traditions. Finally, the Jesuits recognized the enormous value of religion and the importance of culture, rituals and feasts. The Rarámuri regularly dance and drink all night long.

The Rarámuri experience religion in a very physical way. That is the way in which they understand and experience their relationship with God and religion. The individual body is always relational, i.e. related to other human beings, but also to the earth. Body and earth are always related, for the body forms part of the planets as well as the whole cosmos. The natural and supernatural are lived through their bodily experience in such a way that body and spirit are inseparably related.

To summarize this section, the Rarámuri religion creates the sense of a third space, a space in which body and spirit, God and humankind, humankind and the planet construct each other beyond any dichotomy. It is also important to emphasize the intersection between body, dancing, drinking and worshipping as also generating a third space of religion and culture.

Holy Week in Samachique, Chihuahua

After having carried out the research on the Rarámuri, especially concentrating on the book by the Mexican Jesuit Pedro de Velasco, *Danzar o morir* (2006), I took on the task of doing fieldwork at the Rarámuri mission in the Sierra Tarahumara. I was eager to become immersed in the Rarámuri culture beyond books and have the experience of being in the actual territory of the community. Reading a book and being in the location are definitely not the same.

Just a few days before leaving for Samachique, I suffered a serious knee injury, and it was still swollen and painful. However, I was determined to attend, even if I could not dance. Instead, I became a very discreet observer, trying not to disturb them, keeping the camera almost out of sight so as not to interrupt their ceremonies and rituals. My physical impediment, nonetheless, provided an opportunity to listen, observe and learn while I witnessed the ceremonies.

I flew to Chihuahua, a three-hour flight from Mexico City. Once in the capital city of this northern state, I took an eight-hour bus ride to the deepest and highest part of the Tarahumara mountain range. Its geography displays a fabulous landscape of high cliffs and rocky mountains with a great variety of pine trees, rivers and lakes. For most of the bus ride we drove on a very sinuous road, sometimes traversing dangerous cliffs. The weather was chilly, but springtime was starting, enjoyable sunshine during the day, unusual most of the year for Samachique and the rest of the Sierra.

I arrived in Samachique, a village of about one thousand people, on Holy Wednesday. People were still engaged in preparations for the following days of this very important liturgical season. The small and minimalist chapel was being ornamented with flowers and scented with incense, readying for the forthcoming days of intense dance worship until its culmination on Easter Sunday.

Jesuit chapel in Samachique

When I arrived at the chapel, I met Enrique Mireles SJ, the Jesuit Father, who was the only priest in charge of the mission during this liturgical season. He was very busy with baptisms during these dates. Many people came to be baptized. The vast majority were children from infancy to fifteen years of age. This Holy Week, around thirty people were baptized every day. Father Mireles welcomed me in a very kind and brotherly way. He assigned me a small room in a shack in front of the chapel where I could stay throughout Holy Week.

That Wednesday, I took a brief tour around the village and went back to the chapel where Father Mireles introduced me in the Rarámuri language, explaining the purpose of my visit. He mentioned that I was going to be a very discreet witness taking some photographs and videos. He also told people about my injury, explaining that I would be unable to follow them everywhere or join in the dancing.

After that, Father Mireles took me to a house slightly uphill, where a family offered us dinner: a vegetable stew with rice, beans and hand-made corn tortillas. People's houses in Samachique are very simple. They live very precariously. I admired their generosity not only towards us but also towards other people who came to eat, bringing food to share. This was the case every day I was there. The Rarámuri families would welcome and feed me. We talked and shared stories around the hearth and at the table. That was for me an experience of *kórima*, eucharistic conviviality.

Early that afternoon, I went back to my room and settled in, caring for my swollen knee. I went to bed early. In my sleep, I could hear drums playing all night long. Somehow the sound induced deep sleep and rest. The next day, Holy Thursday, was when the most intense ceremonies started to take place. From early morning, the beat of drums could be heard coming from different directions from the dwellings on the mountainside. Groups of about ten, mostly young men, went around playing in different places in the village. The aroma of food cooking on many small grills pervaded the village. Tamales, corn, beans and tortillas were being prepared to be shared upon request. Large pots containing *tesgüino* were placed throughout the village so that people could drink at any time. The chapel was in the middle of the village, and people could be seen coming back and forth. The chapel was always filled with the smoke and intense scent of copal incense.

Chapel filled with copal incense

For the Catholic Church, all around the world but particularly in Mexican Catholic churches, this is a day to celebrate a Mass in remembrance of the institution of the Eucharist, remembering the Last Supper and Jesus washing his disciples' feet. These Gospel narratives are performed in many ways around the world. It is also a day on which the seven temples are visited, so people walk and pray in street processions from one temple to another. Eucharistic Adoration is practised in most churches throughout Mexico.

However, in Samachique there are no prayers, no mass, no washing of the feet, no eucharistic institution, no visit to the seven temples, nor adoration of the Eucharist. All of that was replaced by embodied practices of dancing, eating and drinking with different groups in different houses around the village. Occasionally, groups arrived at the chapel entered dancing, and then left the chapel dancing to keep dancing throughout the village. This went on the entire night until about 6 o'clock in the morning.

Father Mireles continued to baptize almost the whole day long but made a few pauses for breakfast at around 8 o'clock in the morning, dinner at around 2 o'clock, and supper at 7. Different families invited us to their homes, where food, drink and stories were shared. Despite not being a 'customary' Catholic tradition as the eucharistic rituals held around the world, amidst the Rarámuri community in Samachique, Chihuahua, I experienced eucharistic sharing and the making of a celebratory community through sharing food, drink and dance. That night, when I retired, I heard the drum beat the whole night long. I fell asleep rejoicing in the feeling that I had had one of the most significant experiences in my life of the institution of the Eucharist, both corporeal and spiritual experience of the making of community and becoming eucharistic people.

In the Mexican Catholic church, the procession rite of the Stations of the Cross, the *Via Crucis*, is regularly performed on Good Friday. In the streets, people enact the Gospel narratives of the Passion of Christ, culminating in his crucifixion. The performance is usually an enactment of Jesus' imprisonment, torture and death in a very corporeal and sometimes rather extreme manner. The Rarámuri circumambulate the streets carrying a large and heavy cross. The procession includes songs and rosary prayers, chanting hymns grieving the drama of the death of Jesus on the cross. However, in Samachique, instead of the stations of the cross, a sculpture of the Virgin Mary covered with a veil was carried on the women's shoulders. People danced during the whole procession circling around the chapel.

The procession would stop at a few 'stations' to pray the Lord's Prayer and the Hail Mary, only to continue to the next station where

Stations of the Cross

the ritual was repeated. The procession concluded after closing the circle around the chapel and entering the chapel to dance and complete the rite. The dancing, drinking and eating continued until the next morning at around 6 o'clock. The dancing was not joyful, but neither was it dramatically sorrowful. It was very sober, evoking an inner and deep lamentation. Although people continued dancing, eating and drinking the whole day, it nevertheless expressed great communal sorrow, as when attending a funeral. Again, the experience of the Passion of Christ was very corporeal, as was the entire Holy Week.

Holy Saturday is the day the Catholic Church remembers the passage of Christ from death into resurrection. It is an in-between space of transit rather than the reaching of a destination. Christ both dies and resurrects. There is a belief that Holy Saturday represents the triumph of good over evil, of eternal life over death. The Rarámuri community of Samachique performs ritual dances enacting the fight between good and evil, represented by warrior dances in which Christians and Pharisees fight each other. The Pharisees have their faces painted white, a criticism of the whitening of colonization rather than a criticism of a particular religious group. It is a ritual dance symbolizing the power struggle and resistance to the colonizers and the victory of good over evil. Most of the day, the Rarámuri worshipped with this dance rite, playing music, eating and drinking *tesgüino*.

By the late afternoon, they all gathered in a huge circle in a massive open space. Many people arrived from other nearby villages. The circle was divided into two groups – one representing the Pharisees and the other the Christians. Then, the master of ceremonies called one person from each opposite team to enter the circle and 'fight' one another. The fight consists of holding each other's belts and pulling them until the opponent falls to the ground. The winner is the one who remains standing. The master of ceremonies makes sure that the fight is even. Each of the selected couples was the same gender, age, height and weight. Even women joined the fight. While the two opposites were fighting, people around the circle cheered their team and celebrated or booed according to whether the fight was won or lost. It was a highly spirited corporeal collective performance that animated everyone as it was a representation of their own personal struggle against the forces of evil and trust in the power of the goodness of Jesus who resurrects in triumph over death.

Child with face painted in white representing the Pharisees

Fight between Christians and Pharisees

At the end of the fight, the master of ceremonies gave the verdict and publicly declared that the Christian team had won. Everyone cheered and went back to the chapel, some dancing and some chanting.

Father Enrique Mireles was completely dedicated to baptisms because many people from the neighbouring villages came to celebrate and took advantage of the opportunity to be baptized. After the fight, people danced back to the chapel, where Father Mireles was awaiting. This dance was a corporeal rite of gratitude and celebration for the resurrection that overcame death. At one point of the dancing, some children approached the altar dancing with small boxes in their hands. When they reached the altar, they opened the boxes to free the enclosed birds. The birds started flying among the dancing bodies inside the chapel and then flew into the open sky. The children rushed out to see the birds flying away. This corporeal ritual represents the ultimate freedom of the resurrection and the earth joining God's eternal dance. The ritual ended with people leaving the church dancing. It was a very festive evening.

In the late evening, the feast continued outside the church with several groups of people gathered around grills set in different house yards. In every place they offered and shared food and *tesgüino*. I had to get back to my room around 9 o'clock since my knee was badly swollen and I was experiencing significant pain. As I fell asleep, again, I heard people chanting, drumming, dancing and celebrating all night long until about 6 o'clock the next morning.

Easter Sunday is when the Catholic Church around the world celebrates the glory of the resurrection, the victory of a good, loving and everlasting God. Easter mass was celebrated at around ten o'clock in a very simple but solemn way. I had to leave immediately after the mass, so I thanked everyone for their hospitality and the opportunity to learn so much by being among them during Holy Week. Father Mireles gave me a very fraternal farewell and made me feel welcome in the community.

A man in the community offered to take me in his pick-up truck to the main highway, where there was a bus stop about a 15-minute drive from the village. En route to the bus stop, we were chatting, and he mentioned that the night before, there had been a dispute between a white man belonging to a drug cartel and a young Rarámuri who was shot in his leg and had to be rushed to the nearest hospital, about two hours away from the village. Indeed, during my visit to Samachique, I noticed about ten armed men scouting the village all the time. People avoided them as much as possible. Father Mireles had told me about them and mentioned that the Jesuit priests had decided to avoid confrontation as much as possible in order to fend off any serious conflict.

Unfortunately, violence could be felt in the atmosphere amidst the community's celebratory spirit.

During the bus drive back to the airport in Chihuahua, I had a mixture of contrasting feelings. On the one hand, I truly experienced a spiritual renewal, as if something had cracked open inside me in a good way, revealing new horizons of divine and sacred radical embodiment. There was also a sense of sacred wisdom re-emerging from ancient Mesoamerican roots, a connection with the earth, a more cosmic awareness of God's eternal life and love, and a sense of the resurrection of the body. On the other hand, I sensed sadness for experiencing the crucified in the resurrected. The Samachique community experiences great scarcity, exploitation and violence, in addition to the extreme natural conditions of their land. They really are a 'crucified people' (Ellacuría, 1989). In retrospect, after the experience of being among the Rarámuri Catholic community of Samachique, I became more aware of the rich meaning of the content of the book by Pedro de Velasco SJ, the title of which translates as *Dance or Die: Religion and Resistance to Domination in the Tarahumara Culture*. The Rarámuri in Samachique dance in order to survive, to resist, to insurrect. Dancing enables them to keep going and live. They dance to live and live to dance.

Dance to live and live to dance: Rarámuri circle dancing

Conclusion

I would like to conclude by emphasizing the idea of an ecclesial 'third space'. The village of Samachique is an incredible example of a third space because culture and religious wisdom have not been as obliterated by colonial Christianity there as in other regions in Mesoamerica. For sure, throughout centuries, it has experienced important mutations, which is why it is also not 'pure' Rarámuri. Christian experience and symbolism have also penetrated the traditional Tarahumara religion, creating a hybrid. It is both Rarámuri and Catholic, a third ecclesial space completely unique to the Tarahumara experience of the sacred. Herein we encounter a concrete paradigm of inculturation but in an intensely corporeal sense. The Jesuits allowed the Rarámuri to celebrate in their own ways and with their own religious sensibility of embodied experiences of the sacred, of God who is both Mother and Father, is both in the earth and in the cosmos. God dances, eats and drinks with them, uniting body and spirit, the individual and society, society and the planet, uniting the whole of creation with God. Samachique represents a third ecclesial space, particularly during their sacred dancing rituals of the simultaneously crucified and resurrected body of Christ.

It is imperative that religious studies include a decolonial perspective that recognizes and reaffirms the sacred wisdom and genius of indigenous communities. The colonial perspective prevalent throughout centuries of colonial hegemony forbade the religious perspective of the indigenous communities. Sadly, the Rarámuri culture and religious practices are becoming increasingly extinct. That is why it is urgent to adopt another epistemic approach to our hermeneutics of religion and experiences of the sacred beyond Christianity. There is still a lot of work ahead of us to prevent the total extinction of our ancient traditions and the rich sacred wisdom of pre-Hispanic cultures.

Lastly, I would like to highlight the great importance of revisiting the concepts of incarnation and embodiment in sacred traditions within Christianity and beyond. Within colonial Christianity, the body became an instrument for domination, control and exploitation. Religious experience of embodiment was censured and banned, becoming a source of shame, sin and mortality. The Rarámuri ritual dances, practices of conviviality, and sharing of food and drink reveal the importance of epistemic poetic expressions integrating body and spirit in order to value and celebrate with our body the presence of God who dances, eats and drinks with us.

Note

1 This chapter springs from my participation in an anthology coordinated by Antonio Sison (2024). Orbis Books granted permission to republish the photos used in the chapter.

References

Bhabha, Homi K., 1994, *The Location of Culture*, London/New York: Routledge.
de Velasco Rivero, Pedro J., 2006, *Danzar o morir: Religión y resistencia a la dominación en la cultura tarahumara*, Guadalajara: ITESO-IBERO.
Ellacuría, Ignacio, 1989, 'El pueblo crucificado. Ensayo de soteriología histórica', http://www.redicces.org.sv/jspui/bitstream/10972/1101/1/RLT-1989-018-C.pdf (accessed 15.1.2025).
Geertz, Clifford, 1997, *The Interpretation of Cultures*, New York: Basic Books.
Magesa, Laurenti, 2004, *Anatomy of Inculuration: Transforming the Church in Africa*, Maryknoll, NY: Orbis Books.
Méndez Montoya, Ángel F., 2003, *Bodily Theopoetics: Dance, Philosophical Theology and Bodily Mediations*, Mexico City: Universidad Iberoamericana.
Méndez Montoya, Ángel F., 2009, *The Theology of Food: Eating and the Eucharist*, Oxford: Wiley-Blackwell.
Méndez Montoya, Ángel F., 2024, 'Dancing, Eating, Worshipping: Inculturated "Third Space" in Rarámuri Celebrations', in Antonio D. Sison, ed., *Deep Inculturation: Global Voices on Christian Faith and Indigenous Genius*, pp. 25-56, New York: Orbis Books.
Shorter, Aylward, 1988, *Toward a Theology of Inculturation*, Orbis Books, Maryknoll, NY.

PART 3

Trauma, Spectrality and Ritual

7

Rituals of the (Para)normal: Spectrality, Trauma and Liberation in Latin America

MIGUEL M. ALGRANTI

Introduction

Theology of the People (*Teología del Pueblo*) is based on the idea that people are the body of Christ and places the path to liberation in popular culture instead of class struggle. As a local current of liberation theology, this orientation should disrupt the modern Christian universalist idea of ritual as a symbolic (not instrumental) behaviour exclusive to religious systems and institutions and return it to popular culture where it regains its instrumental-affective embodied dimension.

In Latin America, due to the collaboration of parts of the Roman Catholic Church with dictatorships promoted in the region since the 1960s, the lack of rituals for the victims of state terror has resulted in the emergence of popular rituals as a spontaneous product of social grief. In the case of the victims of the Argentinian dictatorships of the 1970s, spectrality and ritual collide through the terror of *los desaparecidos* (the disappeared). This spectral presence of the more than 30,000 young activists who disappeared during the 'National Reorganisation Process' by the military regimes still haunts the country.

This chapter will analyse the case of *ANTIVISITA*, an artivist performance by Mariana Eva Perez and Laura Kalauz, both from families of the disappeared, which proposes a guided visit through the spectral dimensions of the clandestine centre of detention, torture and extermination (CCDTaE) known as Escuela Mecánica de la Armada (ESMA). My own participation as a performer and dramaturgical collaborator in the work gave me a privileged perspective to interrogate how to process this trauma through the spiritualist heritage of the authors' family and to analyse how spiritualist ritual and liberation meet where spectrality and trauma are embodied and healed.

This chapter embarks on a critical exploration of ritual and trauma through the lens of the Theology of the People 'spectres', a movement that reimagined the role of popular religion and rituals in the context of systemic oppression and dictatorship. At the heart of this investigation lies an inquiry into how marginalized communities in Argentina, after the harrowing period of military dictatorship, crafted spaces of resistance, healing and collective memory through the deployment of art, rituals and symbols.

The Theology of the People, with its deep roots in a preferential option for the poor, posits a radical re-evaluation of ritual's function within society. It argues for the recognition of popular religious practices not merely as expressions of faith but as potent forms of social and political transformation. This perspective is particularly resonant in contexts where official channels of dissent are suppressed, and the fabric of everyday life is imbued with fear and silencing. In such environments, the spontaneous emergence of popular rituals becomes a critical avenue for articulating grief, solidarity and hope.

One of the most striking examples of this dynamic is the *ANTIVISITA* artivist performance that engages directly with the spectral legacy of the ESMA, one of the most notorious clandestine detention centres of the dictatorship era. The *ANTIVISITA* performance, and others like it, illustrate how ritual, when infused with the collective energies of resistance and remembrance, transcends its traditional religious meanings. Instead, ritual becomes a transformative space where the living engage with the spectres of the past, weaving together narratives of loss, resilience and liberation.

The exploration of popular rituals as sites of spectral engagement and resistance also opens new avenues for understanding the dynamics of memory and trauma in post-dictatorship societies. It raises critical questions about how communities reconstruct their identities in the aftermath of violence, how they navigate the ongoing presence of the past in their daily lives, and how rituals can serve as bridges between the past and the present, between the dead and the living.

Finally, this chapter seeks to illuminate the complex interplay between spectrality, trauma and liberation in Latin America, with a particular focus on Argentina. Through an examination of an artivist performance authored by two of state terror's victims, this study aims to provide insights into the power of art and popular religiosity as a tool for social and spiritual emancipation. In doing so, it not only contributes to the understanding of Latin American liberation theology and politics but also offers a poignant reflection on the universal themes of memory, resistance and the quest for justice.

La Teología del Pueblo – The Theology of the People

José Manuel Perez Rojo was a seventeen-year-old high schooler when his best friend, Luis Frutos, encouraged him to join the Scout group *La Merced* at a Roman Catholic school in Caseros, in the province of Buenos Aires. The Boy Scouts were led by Father Mario Bertone, a Roman Catholic priest who was part of the Movement of Priests for the Third World. It was the end of the sixties when the Cuban Revolution was in every newspaper and conversation in the cafés. Bertone, heavily influenced by the Vatican II option for the poor, commended the Scouts to undertake social work in the poorest parts of the neighbourhood. The Scouts moved to a chapel in the Fiat district of Caseros, where the old car factory was located. They began to work on the construction of the Saint Francis of Assisi Chapel and began to engage in social work with the community, integrating the priests into the communities through social work rather than through a religious relationship.

The Movement of Priests for the Third World was the first priestly movement to embrace the reforms of Vatican II alongside a social and political commitment. This movement was born in Argentina and had a public presence for almost a decade between 1967 and 1976. In terms of its sociological characteristics, its organization was characterized by the absence of formalities for entry and membership. This gave its composition a certain flexibility, for there was no centralized and stable list of members but rather fluid regional lists. However, this lack of a formal register did not mean that it consisted of an uncoordinated mass of individuals. On the contrary, a first appreciation of the movement can be made from the list of priests who, between 1967 and 1968, signed the Manifesto of eighteen Bishops of the Third World.[1] The Manifesto appeared in the same year as the work of the Vatican II and the encyclical *Populorum Progressio*. The Manifesto demonstrated a commitment to act in the same spirit and direction as other reformist initiatives and acted as a marker of the desire that the Argentinian Bishops also express their approval and commitment to these wider movements. However, the typology of the Movement of Priests for the Third World cannot be reduced only to this first group of supporters of the Manifesto. Rather, the movement was redefined around a group of clerics who began to meet and then express themselves publicly through communiqués and public actions.

The Movement of Priests for the Third World's commitment to social justice, grounded in a preferential option for the poor, resonated deeply with the ethos of the incipient Theology of the People, which emphasizes the role of culture and popular piety in the process of liberation. By advocating for the rights and dignity of marginalized communities, the Movement of Priests for the Third World highlighted the importance of grassroots movements and the power of ritual in fostering a collective identity rooted in Christian faith and solidarity. This emphasis on the sacramental and communal aspects of faith helped shape Christian young people's approach to understanding how religious practice could inspire and sustain social transformation. Through their social work and community engagement, the Movement of Priests for the Third World illustrated the vital role of ritual in articulating a vision of hope and liberation, thus influencing the broader theological discourse on the intersection of faith and social action.

1967, Father Bertone and the Scouts, Saint Francis of Assis parish, 3 February 1967, Buenos Aires

In Argentina, Lucio Gera, Rafael Tello and Alberto Sily developed the Theology of the People. This theology sees the working people as an eschatological category, outside class struggle. The Theology of the People emerged with the political processes for democracy 1964–76, and from the meetings of the theologians of the Roman Catholic Episcopal Pastoral Commission (CEPAL). The Theology of Liberation influenced the Bishops' Conference of the Latin American Episcopate held in Medellín (1968). It famously made its 'preferential option for the poor' at the Bishops' Conference of the Latin American Episcopate held in Puebla in 1976. This was the year in which the Theology of the People was silenced by the military dictatorship that was installed in Argentina. Although the Argentinian Theology of the People followed the guidelines of CEPAL and assumed the see–judge–work method, linking cultural praxis with evangelical and sociological reflection, it differed from some liberation theology in its way of understanding 'the people'. While the liberation theology in the rest of the region privileged the socio-structural analysis and conceived of the people as a class, the Theology of the People privileged historical-cultural analysis and considered 'the people' only as a part of 'the working poor'. CEPAL theologians reinterpreted the category of the people as the popular part of the people in the philosophical sense of incarnated particularity that participates in what Roman Catholic theology called the 'universality of the People of God'. The Theology of the People viewed popular religion and symbols as essential pathways to liberation, emphasizing the power of grassroots religious practices to inspire resistance and community solidarity. This perspective celebrated the sacramental value of everyday faith expressions, seeing in them a profound source of hope and a vehicle for social and spiritual emancipation.

The impact of the disappearances during the military dictatorship in Argentina in 1976 has been profound on the development of the Theology of the People. This tragic period, marked by repression and the systematic violation of human rights, became a catalyst for the theologians of this movement to deepen their understanding of injustice and suffering as realities contrary to God's plan for humanity. However, the forced disappearance of thousands of people not only challenged the moral conscience of society but also led to irreconcilable differences within the Roman Catholic Church between those who sought to take a more active stance in defence of human rights and dignity and those who tacitly or explicitly collaborated with the regime. In this context, the Theology of the People began to emphasize the need for concrete solidarity with the marginalized and oppressed, recognizing in the faces of the disappeared the call for a more authentic Christian commitment to social justice. This decision cost the lives of many parishioners and leaders, such as Father Mujica and Father Angelelli.

Between 22 May 1976 and 10 September 1978, a group of 18 young men who were members of Father Bertone's Scout group were kidnapped and disappeared by an army task force operating in that area. The young men, who were between 17 and 27 years old at the time of their kidnapping, were later known as the 'ghost scouts' of Villa Bosch. One of them, José Manuel Perez Rojo, was taken with his pregnant wife Patricia Julia Roisinblit and her two-year-old daughter Mariana.

Argentina's Spectrality and the Geopolitics of Ghosts in Latin America

In the 1970s, various armed movements proliferated in the so-called 'Third World', many of them linked to the processes of decolonization. Even in 'First World' countries such as Germany, Italy and the United States, there were organizations that emphasized armed action as a means of creating so-called 'revolutionary conditions'. Numerous voices, including those of politicians, intellectuals and artists, were raised in defence of violence as a response to oppression, both inside and outside Argentina. To illuminate some of these aspects of violence, the notion of spectrality is useful. The spectral is presented in a double sense: firstly, as an attribute of the guerrilla; secondly, as re-appropriated by counter-insurgency in the ghostly figure of the disappeared. Alejandro Kaufman quotes documents from the Revolutionary Armed Forces, which refer to the 'ghostly condition of the guerrilla' and the need to use it tactically. The repression of the guerrillas in Argentina reversed the sign of this spectral condition and turned it into a negative feature. 'The figure of the disappeared turns chance and uncertainty against the guerrilla' (Kaufman, 2012, pp. 55–6). As Avery Gordon argues, to eliminate the threatening presence of subversion, which in the army's view was haunting the nation, the military attempted to replace one set of ghosts with another (Gordon, 2008, p. 125).

Similarly, I understand spectrality as a constitutive dimension of the phenomenon of enforced disappearance. Far from being just one of the modalities assumed by state repression, as in previous Argentinian dictatorships, the disappearance of people acquired a central place during the National Reorganisation Process, as the 1976–83 dictatorship called itself. The process can be thought of as a biopolitics of spectre production which, through the state's manufacture of ghosts, created the conditions of terror necessary to reconfigure Argentina's socio-economic structure in a regressive manner.

The word 'terror' refers to the sensation of dread and physical apprehension experienced at the possibility of extreme violence on the body and is often followed by horror, shock and revulsion at seeing the terrifying become reality. As an instinctive behaviour, terror is socialized at an astonishingly rapid rate through somatic markers and its biological-mimetic dispositions. The usual behavioural response to terror is to flee and escape from fear. The viral speed with which terror spreads among populations is the key factor that makes it a communicative prodigy. As Pilar Calveiro states, the enormity of the repressive resources available to the state apparatus makes state terrorism a privileged instrument of authoritarian powers, and it is even possible to affirm that the greatest number of victims of terrorism comes from its state modality (1998, p. 83). Thus, from a military perspective, terror is the use of extreme violence as a disciplinary and communicative device aimed at society.

In February 1975, a decree of the Argentinian executive ordered the extermination of the guerrillas and launched *Operativo Independencia* in the province of Tucumán in the northwest of the country, initiating a systematic policy of disappearances. Days later in March, another repressive operation, called *Operativo Serpiente Roja del Paraná*, was launched in the city of Villa Constitución (in the province of Santa Fe) and the surrounding area, combining the repressive deployment of all the security forces with paramilitary crimes committed clandestinely. After the *coup* of 24 March 1976, a fundamental change for the worse took place: disappearances and the concentration and extermination camps ceased to be just a tool of repression and became the privileged repressive modality of power (Calveiro, 1998).

Estela Schindel (2012) traces the history of the figure of the disappeared and finds an early antecedent in the 1941 Nazi decree known as 'Night and Fog' ('*Nacht und Nebel*'), aimed to repress resistance in the countries occupied by Germany. During the Cold War, the Counterinsurgency Doctrine provided the conceptual framework for the French military's application of enforced disappearance in Algeria and Indochina, while the National Security Doctrine did the same in Latin America, from Guatemala in the 1960s to almost the entire continent in the following decades. While there is evidence of the role of the French military in teaching torture (Robin, 2005), it is at the US Department of Defense's School of the Americas (now the Western Hemisphere Institute for Security Cooperation) that more than 85,000 Latin American military personnel were trained in counter-guerrilla tactics applied to the fight against communism and drug trafficking. One of the most chilling legacies of the School of the Americas' involvement in Latin American affairs is precisely the phenomenon of enforced disappearance.

The distinctive feature of how state terrorism operated in Argentina is linked to the centrality of forced disappearance. Disappearance reduces to spectrality the lives qualified as threatening to the whole. Through distinctions and hierarchies within the population, biopower inscribes racism in the mechanisms of the state, establishing a positive relationship between the death of the other, considered dangerous, and the proliferation of the species (Foucault, 2014, pp. 230–1). In Schindel's words, 'State terrorism was inscribed in a biopolitical project that establishes the need to kill in order [that] ... Those who represent a kind of "biological danger" to others are legitimately killed' (2012, pp. 301, 303). This other whose life represented a threat to society was, for the National Reorganisation Process, the 'subversive'. But in the framework of disappearing biopolitics, power modelled a new form of existence, a new state of being that is neither life nor death, but something in between the two, on the limit: the spectral (Derrida, 1994, p. 23). Biopower subtracted thousands of lives and hid their deaths, creating a population of ghosts. This is how the disappeared have remained ever since, suspended in this third state, materially absent but still central to the social and political life of the country, as demonstrated by the debates of the recent elections, in which the problematic legacy of the 1970s once again came to the fore.

Escuela Mecánica de la Armada – Enter the Spectral

According to Jacques Derrida, whose work opened the field of spectrality studies, mourning 'always consists of trying to ontologize remains, to make them present, firstly by identifying the debris and locating the dead' (1994, p. 23). Forced disappearance is aimed directly at preventing the mourning process for the victims by disappearing the remains. All the uncertainty surrounding the disappearance is concentrated on the question of location: where are the disappeared? Perhaps, for this reason, memory works in Argentina, repeatedly returning to spatiality as a privileged dimension. The different ways of thinking, designing and implementing the memory of state terrorism form a geography of places marked with graffiti, commemorative plaques, museums and memory sites in former clandestine detention centres.

In the spatial representations of the National Reorganisation Process, the Navy School of Mechanics, better known by its acronym 'ESMA', holds a prominent place. During the dictatorship, the Navy held about five thousand people in one of the buildings that make up the site of the Officers' Casino. In this concentration camp located in full view of passersby in the Buenos Aires neighbourhood of Núñez, political prisoners were tortured and subjected to inhumane living conditions for an indefinite period before finally being thrown, sedated, into the sea. At least thirty pregnant women, both kidnapped by the ESMA task group and coming from other clandestine detention centres, gave birth and their babies were stolen, generally by members or associates of the security forces, who raised them as their own children, hiding their origins. These births were attended by naval doctors and detainees who were later released and testified. The events that took place at the ESMA confer an important part of its emblematic character, as they illustrate not only the operation of the disappearing biopolitics but also this other modality of disappearance intended to perpetuate itself, the so-called appropriation of sons and daughters.

Patricia Julia Roisinblit was the young wife of José Manuel Perez Rojo. She was pregnant at the time of her detention and was sent to the ESMA. After months of captivity, she gave birth to a boy who was stolen and raised by a military officer. Then she disappeared. Mariana Eva Perez, daughter of José and Patricia Perez, was raised by her grandmothers, Argentina and Rosa, who were among the founders of Grandmothers of the Plaza de Mayo, a human rights organization that aims to locate and return to their rightful families all babies and children appropriated by the military dictatorship (1976–83), and to create the conditions to prevent the commission of this crime against humanity and to obtain corresponding punishment for all those responsible.

In 2004, because of sustained demands from the human rights movement, attended by a government that, significantly, made the demands its own and translated them into public policies, the entire ESMA site was allocated for the creation of a Space for Memory and Promotion of Human Rights. Shortly after, guided tours of the former Officers' Casino, the building where the clandestine centre itself was located and which was designated as a museum, began. In 2015, the permanent exhibition of the ESMA Memory Site Museum was inaugurated. In 2019, the exhibition Being Women at ESMA was inaugurated. In 2023, UNESCO declared the ESMA Memory Site Museum a World Heritage Site and included it among the monuments and spaces protected by the organization.

Alongside the consolidation of the former ESMA as an emblematic memorial site, the site has not ceased to generate narratives that, without competing with historical narratives, testify to the persistence of the spectral by inhabiting this paradoxical space. Schindel (2013) studied narratives about ghosts and supernatural phenomena in former horror spaces like the ESMA. Following the notion of narratives set out by Koschorke (2011), Schindel asserted that these places produce a form of anguish too overwhelming to be expressed narratively. If the haunting effect emanating from these ominous environments fails to organize itself discursively, it can instead be conceived as a 'form of thought' (Thrift, 2007) that, without competing with rationally structured narratives, would allow another way to recognize the traumas of the past (Schindel, 2013, p. 12).

MIGUEL M. ALGRANTI

Rituals as Sites of Resistance and Spectral Engagement

Throughout history, rituals have played a central role in structuring social life, mediating the passage between different phases of existence, and serving as instruments of collective cohesion. Rituals welcome newcomers and bid farewell to those no longer with us, transforming boys into men, students into professionals, and young lovers into families. The traditional conceptualization of ritual in social sciences recognizes two main dimensions of the phenomenon: the affective and the normative (Turner, 2005; Bell, 1992; Handelman, 2005). Rituals are conceived as formal collective behaviour, regulated and governed by belief in divinities or mythical beings. They function both as normalizing social devices that cohere the group and resolve conflicts, as well as embodied devices that disrupt ordinary experience and discipline the body. They actualize general symbols through particular bodies and sensibilities. In this sense, the tension between traditionalist and mystic forms of religious memory is expressed and negotiated through symbols as a basic unit of ritual behaviour. Moreover, both poles of the phenomenon, the normative and the affective, entail different and mutually supportive forms of agency and efficacy essential to the ritual's transformative function.

In Latin American liberation theology, particularly the Theology of the People, rituals are seen as pivotal not only for religious life but also for political and social transformation. This perspective asserts that ritual emerges organically from popular culture and offers a pathway to spiritual and political liberation. In a context where official state institutions failed to provide justice or closure for the victims of dictatorship, popular rituals became essential modes of processing grief and demanding recognition. Rituals in this context are not mere formalities; they are performative acts that allow communities to engage with the lingering spectres of the past, embodying memory and generating spaces for potential futures.

In contexts of profound social trauma, such as the aftermath of state terror and violence in Argentina, rituals become spaces not just for communal gathering but also for resistance and healing. The spectral presence of the *desaparecidos* – the disappeared – has created an enduring need to reconfigure traditional notions of ritual, particularly in response to the unresolvable grief that follows from enforced disappearances. Spectrality – the phenomenon where the past remains unresolved and haunts the present – permeates Argentina's post-dictatorship era, as the presence of over 30,000 disappeared persons leaves a void in the nation's social fabric (Schindel, 2013). This spectrality is manifest both in the public sphere, through commemorations, memory sites, and public performances, and in private, through familial rituals of remembrance and mourning. The presence of the dead, unresolved and unnamed, creates a unique need for rituals that engage directly with these absences, filling the void with symbolic action.

One of the most powerful examples of this ritualized engagement with the disappeared is seen in the symbolic use of the white handkerchiefs by the Mothers of the Plaza de Mayo. This simple act of donning a white handkerchief, symbolizing the diapers of their missing children, became a performative ritual that protested the erasure of their children by the state while also serving as an embodied reminder of the persistence of the disappeared in Argentina's social and political life (Taylor, 1997). This ritualized use of symbols not only fostered solidarity among the mothers but also marked public spaces with the presence of the disappeared, transforming these spaces into sites of resistance and memory.

These forms of ritual, however, differ from traditional religious rites, which often serve to resolve or transcend human suffering. Instead, rituals in the aftermath of state terrorism in Argentina work to sustain and hold the space for the disappeared, recognizing their ongoing absence and resisting closure. In this sense, rituals become not just instruments of healing but also acts of defiance, refusing to allow the state's attempt to erase lives to succeed. They hold open the question: Where are they? Where are the 'disappeared', and how can the living continue to engage with their unresolved presence?

The artivist performance *ANTIVISITA*, to be explored in the following section, engages directly with these ideas by transforming a former clandestine detention centre into a site of active ritual engagement. In post-dictatorship Argentina, where official channels of justice have been slow and inadequate, popular rituals have arisen as a means to confront this ongoing state of terror. These rituals do not aim to resolve or contain the trauma but instead offer spaces where the spectres of the past can be actively engaged. The spectrality of the disappeared is central to the fabric of these rituals. The dead, while no longer physically present, continue to exert influence, shaping the ways in which communities remember and resist.

In this context, ritual becomes a space where the living and the dead can interact – not in the traditional sense of religious transcendence, but in a political and affective engagement. This interaction is not necessarily about finding peace or resolution but about maintaining a connection with the unresolved, keeping alive the memory of those who were forcibly disappeared. Rituals, then, become a site of reparative work, where the community can collectively process the trauma, grieve the loss, and resist the erasure of the disappeared.

This type of ritual engagement is exemplified in the work of Argentinian performance artists like Mariana Eva Perez and Laura Kalauz, whose artivist performance *ANTIVISITA* situates the clandestine detention centre of ESMA as a space for both artistic experimentation and collective mourning. By inviting participants to engage in rituals of remembrance, the performance challenges the official historical narratives and opens a space for confronting the lingering spectral presences of those who were detained, tortured and disappeared within its walls (Algranti, 2021).

The performance specifically employs a spiritualist séance, not as a religious act but as a dramatic device through which the participants connect with the dead. This séance, described in detail in the following section, exemplifies how rituals can be reimagined as political acts of engagement with the unresolved spectrality of the disappeared. By participating in this séance, the audience becomes part of an emerging ritual that seeks not to resolve the trauma, but to sustain the presence of those who are missing, ensuring that their memory is not lost to history.

In this way, *ANTIVISITA* serves as both a performance and a ritual, embodying the principles of resistance, memory and liberation that are central to Argentina's ongoing confrontation with its past. It is through such rituals that the community continues to resist the finality of death and disappearance, keeping alive the demand for truth, justice and recognition.

ANTIVISITA – How to Get In and Out of the ESMA

ANTIVISITA: Formas de entrar y salir de la ESMA is a performance by Mariana Eva Perez and Laura Kalauz that is presented as an experimental guided tour of the (former) ESMA but takes place outside the space of the current ESMA Memory Site Museum. It takes the family history of the authors as cousins and child victims of state terrorism as a guiding thread, under the invocation of two absent female figures: Maria Maller (their great-grandmother, whose spiritist practices are traced in the work) and Patricia Julia Roisinblit (Perez's mother, one of the pregnant detained-disappeared women who gave birth in the ESMA). The subjective journey highlights the obstetric violence the state deployed in that concentration camp, but thanks to the intervention of a 'context witness' in the field of spiritism, the performance opens a non-testimonial instance of theoretical and phenomenological inquiry, involving all those present (and absent). Premiered in June 2022, over thirteen hundred people have participated to date in the collective mourning and liberation ritual proposed by *ANTIVISITA*. In the following, I will analyse in depth the scene of the session in which I have participated. I consider this scene the threshold between experimentation and ritual, from where *ANTIVISITA* proposes itself as a performative device to present radical absence. From the perspective of processual anthropology, I understand ritual as a genre of transformative performance, a complex sequence of symbolic acts, which reveals the main classifications, categories and contradictions of cultural processes.

The subsequent scene does not anchor itself in any specific area of the ESMA Memory Site Museum. Chairs surround a table. Perez introduces the figure of the context witness, who in a human rights trial is called upon to testify not from direct experience but to provide testimony based on specialized knowledge that will assist the court in interpreting and evaluating the rest of the evidence. In this role, he presents Miguel Algranti: 'Miguel is an anthropologist, he researched a spiritist school in the city of Buenos Aires for his doctoral thesis, and for this, he conducted his ethnography but also trained as a medium.' The 'witness', who until this moment has followed the visit from among the audience, places his badge with his name and that of the work, revealing himself as the third performer. Subsequently, the audience is invited to sit around a table, with Algranti at the head, and Kalauz and Perez by his sides. Some participants occupy the empty chairs, and the rest are arranged around the scene. In the form of an interview, Kalauz asks Algranti about the context of the emergence of spiritism. Expediently, the anthropologist talks about the history and main characteristics of spiritism. Then Kalauz asks about the mediums, about their ability to communicate with spirits. After another brief theoretical exposition, Algranti invites the audience to participate in an exercise of recognizing spirits in their own body. For this, he asks them to shake their hands while he explains the use of trance in spiritual communications. This discussion covers the dissociation of attention, the disruption of bodily experience, used in spiritism as a practice to perceive the spiritual world. Then, Algranti asks the participants to hold hands, forming an 'energetic circle' (rather, two: one around the table, the second around the first), to close their eyes and focus their attention on their hands, on the contact with the other. He reminds them that from then on, it is allowed, and encouraged, to utter any word that arises that is channelling spirits. Guiding the practice with a calm voice, Algranti proposes the exercise of alternating attention between two exclusive modalities of establishing physical contact: being the subject who touches or explores the hand of the other or being the body that is touched or explored. The silences extend, giving way to introspection. The theoretical exposition turned at this point into a guided meditation, in which the body is used as a surface of inscription. It is explained that in that state, the emergence of spontaneous thoughts or the presence of localized pains in the body are indicative of spiritual activity on the medium. Waiting and listening, the interventions of the public are thanked when they occur. The scene ends with the irruption of a metronome, a common pulse that will organize the movement to the next room. Kalauz carries the metronome and thus guides the participants who, 'waking up' from the trance, are invited to follow her down the stairs to the basement, where the transition between the experimental and the ritual will be fully realized.

Spiritism has a long tradition of spiritual performance both in Argentina and around the world. Historically, its practice assumes scepticism and operative intrigue and is constituted in exhibitions and spaces where the technologies of disenchantment and the tools of ritual critique are available or directly provided to observers. Combining technology, scientific methods and religious concerns, modern spiritism introduced spectrality as a business and space for religion and found new ways to inhabit its tensions. Spiritism as a biographical and performative vehicle for communicating with the dead has served in *ANTIVISITA* as a popular historical model that organizes the performative device for presenting spirits. The séance, the only scene that is not situated in a specifically dramatic space of the ESMA represented in the work, enables an undefined space that facilitates the emergence of spirits simultaneously as products and producers of each particular function. To this end, three axes of recursivity were worked on: 1) dissociation, 2) the pulse, and 3) identification or recognition. These three operations appear as recursive structures whose meaning is to give emergence and relative autonomy to the spectres of ESMA.

Israeli anthropologist Don Handelman links the emergence of autonomy of liminal entities in ritual contexts with the degree of recursivity in their performance. Recursivity is a mathematical term that refers to processes that develop and specify themselves based on their own definition (Handelman and Kapferer, 1980). The classic example of recursion is the snowflake of fractal geometry, the geometry that describes the natural world. Recursion is the ability to arrive at complex structures from the repetition of simple operations. The self-referential existence of cultural forms, as well as their degree of self-organization and self-integration, are intimately related to questions of recursion. To understand this, Gregory Bateson offers a simple physical example of recursion: a smoke ring, a torus, spinning on itself, giving itself a separable existence. 'After all', Bateson writes, 'it is made of nothing but air marked with a little smoke. It is of the same substance as its "environment". But it has duration and location and a certain degree of separateness by virtue of its own spinning motion' (1977, p. 246, quoted in Handelman and Kapferer, 1980). This torus is a curved form that contains the principle of elemental self-reference, the hallmark of integrity and thus of self-organization, which in turn exists through recursivity.

Thus, in *ANTIVISITA*, the relative autonomy of the spirits is proposed based on the repetition of three operations (dissociation, pulse, identification) at different levels and dimensions of the work. This means that the symbolic acts of the performance are not only references to an external social reality but also point towards the interior of the performance: they are self-referential. Like Bateson's torus, *ANTIVISITA* weaves in the sensibility of the participants in both directions, towards the inside of the performance itself and the surrounding reality.

This general characteristic of the work becomes corporeal and self-evident in the session through a double movement: bending inwards in introspection, twisting outwards through the form recognizing itself within itself (alternation), and, based on this self-integrity, moving outwards into the wider cosmic and social worlds. This double movement, inward and outward, is crucial for the existence of any social form that contains within itself the potential for self-organization, the tendency to form difference within itself and to exfoliate it, to twist it towards the wider socio-cultural environment. Through their self-curvature, the social forms of absence in the body, enclosing themselves as vectors of action, endow themselves with intentionality, organization, depth and direction, that is to say: form. This curvature, in the case of the séance, is inaugurated by the arm movement with which some strands of Argentinian spiritualism begin their trance. The involuntary movement is first an object separated from perception: I see my arms move, but I do not move them. This separation from the object thus proposes two lines of development: 1) the possibility of having experiences 'outside the body' and 2) the possibility of integrating, of perceiving, the body as an autonomous entity, alienated from the self. Both the separate 'I' and the separate 'body' can be the focus of attention. The use of trance to reach such an altered state of consciousness drives the first phenomenological recognition of the 'disrupted' body of spiritism.

Once arranged in the form of an 'energetic circle' concatenated by their hands, the participants are guided by Algranti towards the recognition of two mutually exclusive forms of subjective attention. These two modalities, active and passive, subjective and objective, that perception can acquire are also existential and dealt with by Merleau-Ponty (1964). Alternating between these two forms of attention, it is suggested to identify thoughts, sensations and pains that appear without the need for mental processing. This exercise is taken from the spiritual exercises for the development of mediumnity. As Bateson recalls (2006), one of the characteristics of the subjective visions of introspection and empathy is that they seem irresistibly true and self-evident; therefore, making a premise self-evident is the easiest way to make an act based on that premise seem natural. Here the kinaesthetic trance of the hand movement gives that first phenomenology of the spiritual world: the alienated body separated from attention functions as a model of the spirit separated from matter. Structural recursivity also begins to become evident: in *ANTIVISITA* this practice is simultaneous with the theoretical explanation of the effects of dissociation. That is to say, theory is dissociated from practice. Just as ESMA appears outside ESMA, the audience appears outside its body. The scene that follows will take this dissociation to the extreme of splitting Mariana's body by constructing an altar of her displaced voice, giving testimony. The recursive axis of dissociation is transversal to the work from the first moment when the audience is asked to dissociate what they see from what they hear, to recreate the dramatic space of the (former) ESMA in a different scenic space. The use of this resource is intensified at the end of the play, where Mariana dissociates her body and voice so that her body conveys the voice of the disappeared Luis Fruto, who functions as a synecdoche of all the absent victims.

Secondly, there is the idea of a pulse as an organizer and extension of both alternation and collective movement: the assembly of bodies and sensibilities. If *ANTIVISITA* uses spatial dissociation and marks its territory with photos and projections of family pictures in its first half, after the break, it is the pulse (first of the trance, then of the metronome, and finally of the song) that is the recursive axis that articulates and sustains the dissociation of time. The pulse, first from the spontaneous synchronization of people waving their hands and then from the metronome, works by organizing the movement and, therefore, the collective perception. The pulse, the most elementary form of socializing time, organizes group movement and sustains the 'disarranged' attention of the performance in its descent into the Basement. The alternation of silences and accents perpetuates the alternation of the performance's modes of attention and the automatic movement of the hands. It is the explicitly intersubjective dimension of the pulse that highlights the collective space of these spectres. The body and time are socialized in a single marker.

Finally, there is the axis of identity and restoration. Identifying and naming are not only performative actions in themselves, i.e. they produce an effect, but also one of the privileged actions of spiritism. Just as the exorcist must identify and classify within a pre-established order the anomaly represented by the possessing demon, the psychiatrist must identify and 'diagnose' the mental pathology; the spiritist must identify the spirit he channels. The spectral as a rejection of ontology, of being classified/identified in a particular time and space, proposes and indefinitely prolongs the search to restore this displaced identity. This axis is also transversal to the whole work. In the first half, in the problematization of space as evidence of crime: the identified, judged, marked space and its care and precautions. The identity of the space within a trial, its preservation as evidence, and its modifications as judicial strategies. The recognition of space also appears in the marked stairs and the identification of a priest by his cassock. In the Pañol, identification and restoration move into the family and historical-biographical sphere: relatives are named and identified in the photographs and the restoration of the figure of Maria is attempted; it is also pointed out that the identity of the stolen son has been restored, without going into further detail. During the session, this axis is transferred to the body in its possibility to identify the action of spirits in one's own experience, in one's flesh. The identification of spirits and the creation of a space for their expression is one of the central practices of spiritism. Identifying the imprint in prior perceptions, their place in my body.

The scene of the performance is a point of confluence of all these elements, shedding light on the deep structure of the work and allowing us to appreciate the resources from a first theoretical exposition that quickly involves the body. As a performative-ethnographic device, it attempts to (re)present radical absence from a popular epistemology, thus exchanging abstract theorizations for incarnated and effective methodologies. Although the practices of spiritism are more complex and sustained over time, dissociation, pulse and identification are central elements in its worldview and practices. As a performative model, spiritism also facilitates the transition between the scientific, the experiential and the ritual by making the ambiguous/dissociated/polysemic experience of its participants the very substance of the absence. The ritual character that sets the session in motion overturns the distinction between spirits and the audience by making its participants (and their bodies) the material manifestation and surface of inscription of spiritual agencies. Spirits as liminal figures, and cultural phenomena are 'internally consistent forms that are reified above the context but at the same time determined by it, in the sense that where they appear they tend to mould the context to their own internal consistency' (Handelman and Kapferer 1980, p. 41). In *ANTIVISITA*, spirits exist as ritual products and therefore exist in their own right, however fragile and transitory this existence may be.

Final Comments

The Theology of the People has played an important role in the religious and political thought of Latin America, especially in Argentina, by seeking to address the needs of marginalized communities through an emphasis on social justice and the role of the Catholic Church in public life. Based on a deep commitment to the struggles of the poor, it aims to build a collective identity centred on solidarity, community and national unity. However, despite its moral and ethical aspirations, the Theology of the People has struggled to create a ritual framework that addresses the deep and unresolved traumas left by state terrorism, particularly the spectres of the disappeared. One of the reasons for this failure lies in its rejection of more experiential and embodied rituals, such as those offered by spiritualism in the case discussed here, in favour of rationalist conceptualizations of ritual that focus on representation rather than direct and often irrational engagement with the spectral.

The rituals promoted by the Theology of the People tend to prioritize collective symbols, national narratives and moral discourse, often grounded in Christian iconography and teachings. These rituals focus on commemorating historical suffering, invoking the memory of past struggles through a lens of redemption and social justice. While these practices are effective in mobilizing collective memory and fostering solidarity, they fail to address the persistent and haunting presence of the spectres of state terrorism, particularly the disappeared during the Argentinian military dictatorship. The disappeared not only represent individual lives lost but also the deliberate erasure of their identities, leaving an open wound in the social fabric. The symbolic approach, which emphasizes meaning and representation, struggles to fully grasp the existential and persistent nature of this trauma, which is often experienced not as something abstract but as something deeply personal and embodied.

In contrast, the artistic/spiritualist device presented in *ANTIVISITA* offers a more experiential type of ritual that directly engages the emotional and bodily dimensions of loss, trauma and unresolved mourning. Spiritualist rituals, particularly those centred on communication with the dead, provide a space where the spectres of the past are not merely symbolized or commemorated, but actively engaged. In these rituals, it is believed that the spirits of the dead speak, offering messages that transcend time and space, directly influencing the present. By allowing these spirits to play an active role in the ritual, the performance provides a means to address the unresolved nature of loss that the symbolic-representational dimension of Catholic rituals fails to confront. The ritual is not merely representative but participatory; the past not only informs the present but intervenes in it, shaping the lived experience of those who participate in the ritual.

The rejection of these experiential practices, characterized as 'irrational' by the Theology of the People (and liberation theology), stems, in part, from its Catholic roots, which tend to emphasize hierarchical forms of worship and doctrinal adherence over personal mystical experiences of the divine. Although the Catholic Church is not unfamiliar with ritual, its rituals are usually structured in a way that maintains a clear distinction between the sacred and the profane, with a strong focus on symbolic representation (for example, the Eucharist as a symbolic recreation of the Last Supper). This symbolic structure may resonate with collective narratives of suffering and redemption, but it does not offer the same cathartic or healing potential as rituals that engage more directly with the spectral or the spiritual.

By not embracing more experiential forms of ritual, the Theology of the People misses the opportunity to provide a popular response to the specters produced by state terrorism. The affective nature of the sacred has a reach that transcends class differences and provides a common framework for social transformation. The unresolved trauma of the disappeared, whose presence continues to haunt the living, requires not only a symbolic device but also a ritual framework that acknowledges their ongoing influence and provides a means for both the living and the dead to find liberation.

Note

1 The manifesto emphasizes the Church's duty to stand with the marginalized and to act as a force for social change, urging Christians to work for a more just and humane world. Signatories include influential bishops from Latin America,

Africa and Asia, underlining the document's global perspective on the challenges facing the Third World.

References

Algranti, Miguel, 2021, 'Semantics of the Suffering: Torture Technologies and Mediumship in Buenos Aires', in D. E. Santo and J. Hunter, eds, *Mattering the Invisible: Technologies, Bodies, and the Realm of the Spectral*, pp. 46–66, Oxford, New York: Berghahn Books.
Asad, Talal, 1993, *Genealogies of Religion: Discipline and Reason of Power in Christianity and Islam*, Baltimore: Johns Hopkins University Press.
Bateson, Gregory, 1977, 'Afterword', in John Brockman, ed., *About Bateson*, pp. 235–47, New York: E. P. Dutton.
Bateson, Gregory, 2006, 'Algunos componentes de socialización para el trance', in *La Unidad Sagrada*, Barcelona, Gedisa, pp. 116–35.
Bell, Catherine, 1992, *Ritual Theory, Ritual Practice*, New York: Oxford University Press.
Derrida, Jacques, 1994, *Espectros de Marx: El Estado de la deuda, el trabajo del duelo y la neuva Internacional*, Madrid: Editorial Trotta.
Foucault, Michel, 2014, *Defender la sociedad*, Buenos Aires: Fondo de Cultura Económica.
Gordon, Avery, 2008, *Ghostly Matters: Haunting and the Sociological Imagination*, Minneapolis: University of Minnesota Press.
Handelman, Don, 2005, *Ritual in Its Own Right: Exploring the Dynamics of Transformation*, New York: Berghahn Books.
Handelman, Don, and Bruce Kapferer, 1980, 'Symbolic Types, Mediation and the Transformation of Ritual Context: Sinhalese Demons and Tewa Clowns', *Semiotica* 30 (1–2): pp. 41–71.
Kaufman, Alejandro, 2012, *La pregunta por lo acontecido. Ensayos de anamnesis en el presente argentino*, Lanús: Ediciones La Cebra.
Koschorke, Albrecht, 2011, 'In Praise of the Undefined: Toward a General Theory of Narrativity', Conferencia en el Wissenschaftskolleg de Berlín (Conference at the Berlin Institute for Advanced Study).
Merleau-Ponty, Maurice, 1964, *Fenomenología de la percepción*, Buenos Aires, Planeta-Agostini.
Robin, Marie-Monique, 2005, *Escuadrones de la muerte. La escuela francesa*, Buenos Aires: Editorial Sudamericana.
Schindel, Estela, 2012, *La desaparición a diario. Sociedad, prensa y dictadura (1975–1978)*, Villa María: Eduvim.
Schindel, Estela, 2013, 'Ghosts and Compañeros: Haunting Stories and the Quest for Justice around Argentina's Former Terror Sites', *Rethinking History: The Journal of Theory and Practice* 18(2), pp. 244–64.
Taylor, Diana, 1997, *Disappearing Acts: Spectacles of Gender and Nationalism in Argentina's "Dirty War"*, Durham, NC: Duke University Press.
Thrift, Nigel, 2007, *Non-Representational Theory: Space, Politics, Affect*, London: Routledge.

8

Conjure Freedom: A Womanist Perspective on Ritual

TERESA L. SMALLWOOD

The use of the term 'conjure' to describe the sacred ritual/religious practices of African-derived peoples in America has a fraught history. However, the concept is not abstract or foreign to many of the religious practices of African Americans currently. 'Conjure' enjoys a long and important history that must be reclaimed as sacred and holy. Womanism and feminism offer theoretical approaches and methodological impetus for the excavation of 'conjure' as a religious practice deserving of reclamation, revival and restoration.

In this chapter, I examine the socio-historical antecedents of 'conjure' as a heuristic tool. Then I explore the alignment of 'conjure' with Jacques Derrida's *hauntology* to demonstrate that the 'spectres' of 'conjure' are discernible in the current religious topography of African American religious practitioners of all kith and kin. Focused upon the work of Tracey Hucks, Dianne Stewart, Charles Long and Yvonne Chireau, I posit that 'conjure' is a normative, holy and discernible 'religious good' that offers insight, intrigue and paths into the mysteries of a revelatory God.

This is shown most particularly in the manifestation of African-derived peoples' ancestral yearnings for freedom *from* domination and oppression and freedom *to* express religious experience without limitation, which evolved in the middle passage as a continuation of their African spiritual practices as well as through the centuries since the legal abolition of enslavement in the Americas. Moreover, 'conjure' represents one of many spiritual border-crossings linking Ancient Spirituality with the miraculous, the aesthetic and the ghostly creating a synergy that instantiates 'Black girl magic' and gives rise to the full embodiment of the freedom yearned for and now being experienced.

Kinetra Brooks, Kameelah L. Martin and LaKisha Simmons pay homage to Black women's literary tradition as both a locus of intellectual prowess and a source of historical reclamation that dignifies ritual traditions that are often 'culturally disenfranchized'. Their claim is that Black women have been 'metaphorical conjure women' who summon the power to tell our stories, envision our futures and preserve our legacies (Brooks, Martin and Simmons, 2021, p. 453). Specifically, they aver:

> Indeed, Black women's fiction, in particular, has been a reckoning force through which sistas (real and imagined) have 'reclaimed their time' and carved out a specifically Black and feminist/womanist agenda. In hindsight, it is much easier to recognize the history of Black women's literature as an intellectual tradition worthy of study and preservation. Black women as metaphorical conjure women – whipping up tales of survival and sainthood; love and lasciviousness; redemption and ratchedness alike – have refocused our literary attention on 'connection rather than separation, transforming silence into speech, and [most important for our purposes] giving back power to the culturally disenfranchized'.

I am drawn to this scholarship because the writers offer concrete ways to identify this phenomenon and establish an epistemological genealogy that both honours the ancestors and embraces the futures that might be imagined. They give four basic tenets: 1) there are material, communal and spiritual consequences for one's actions; 2) death is not an ending but a transition; 3) one is beholden to the Ancestors as well as to future generations; and 4) spirit work is necessary for our physical, emotional and psychological health (Brooks, Martin and Simmons, 2021, p. 456). Each tenet represents an important epistemological move for the development of an ontological framework for the spirituality of conjure generally. Our material world forms the locus of our environment, our movement and our engagement. Our communal world connects us to the entire creation of an ecosystem that is interdependent. Our spiritual worldview or 'world sense' (Oyěwùmí, 1997) that acclimates us to the past, present and future is our conduit for nonrational experiences that transcend the material world. As a spiritual practice, then, I contend, conjure joins the 'pantheon' of spirit power expressed as transformations in the cosmos.

Brooks, Martin and Simmons rely upon Marjorie Pryse and Hortense Spillers, who claim that 'Black women writers, as conjurers, affirm the wholeness and endurance of a vision that, once articulated, can be shared – though its heritage, roots, survival and intimate possession *belong to Black women alone*' (Brooks, Martin and Simmons, 2021, p. 453, emphasis mine). (They rely upon the unknown root workers and conjurers as 'philosophical conjurers'). They posit, 'The philosophical implication is that novelists and thinkers such as Alice Walker, Toni Cade Bambara, Audre Lorde, Toni Morrison, Gloria Naylor and Zora Neal Hurston were privy to an intellectual and theoretical tradition that predates literacy and the written word altogether – Conjure Feminism' (Brooks, Martin and Simmons, 2021, p. 453). They go on to describe the place that Black women have occupied as a 'spiritual practice', which manoeuvred in the pantheon of forces that have broken attempts at annihilation of the whole race by acting as midwives in the service of Oshun or Mambo of Haitian Vodou traditions. In fact, they assert that

> women, in Haitian Vodou tradition, are believed to be the *poto mitan*, the central pole through which the *lwa*, divinity, and life itself descend from the invisible world. The feminine divine is not an abstract concept, but a living, breathing tradition in the form of Black women's bodies. Put another way, 'we ain't new to this'. (Brooks, Martin and Simmons, 2021, p. 454)

This is an important declaration considering the contested categories by which conjure has been described in theological communions over the centuries. There was a concerted effort, though fraught by the conflation of conjure with other practices that moved seamlessly between races, cultures and ethnicities, to distort conjure's spiritual value by characterizing it as a derogatory category.

'Conjure', according to Eddie S. Glaude, Jr, 'afforded the slave practitioner a way of making sense of evil and of controlling her immediate environment' (Glaude, 2014, p. 18). This assessment suggests a material, communal and spiritual functionality while concomitantly drawing from the wisdom of those believers who have gone before and protecting those who come after. Glaude contends that 'conjure expressed a religious worldview that enabled African American slaves to see themselves apart from white slaveholders. It is an African-derived spirituality that empowered its practitioners, through special knowledge, to garner some semblance of control over their environment' (Glaude, 2014, p. 18). It was necessary for enslaved Africans to see themselves differently as well as to develop spiritual practices that helped them cope with the brutality, greed and avarice of the slave system. The use of conjure helped to enflesh freedom.

In this chapter, I advance the positionality of Brooks, Martin and Simmons in their knowledge production around conjuring feminism by claiming that the work of conjure in Black woman imaginary, in

Black ontological beingness, and in Black philosophical aesthetics is more than metaphorical – it is spiritual. And in the province of Black women, conjure has been and continues to be a reckoning force without which our very lives would have been annihilated long ago. As many current practitioners proclaim, 'ancestral spirituality is foundational to community healing' (*Black Magic Matters*, 2021). I argue it is part of the *hauntology*, the very spectres, to borrow from philosopher Jacques Derrida (2006), of divine genius that make all sacred memory, sacred enfleshment, embodiment, spirituality and documentation come alive as truth declarations. Hauntology connotes a past that continues to show up despite bold, brutal efforts to erase its memory. Conjure is a central part of the logic of personhood that characterizes Black ontology. And it is a holy practice. I am calling what I will describe more forcefully Conjure Womanism. Womanist, as a methodological tool, seeks to excavate the wisdom of Black women and is defined as follows (Walker, 1983, p. xi):

1. From *womanish* (Opp. of 'girlish', i.e. frivolous, irresponsible, not serious). A black feminist or feminist of colour. From the black folk expression of mothers to female children, 'you acting womanish', i.e. like a woman. Usually referring to outrageous, audacious, courageous or wilful behaviour. Wanting to know more and in greater depth than is considered 'good' for one. Interested in grown-up doings. Acting grown up. Being grown up. Interchangeable with another black folk expression: 'You trying to be grown.' Responsible. In charge. Serious.
2. Also: A woman who loves other women, sexually and/or nonsexually. Appreciates and prefers women's culture, women's emotional flexibility (values tears as natural counterbalance of laughter), and women's strength. Sometimes loves individual men, sexually and/or nonsexually. Committed to survival and wholeness of entire people, male and female. Not a separatist, except periodically, for health. Traditionally a universalist, as in: 'Mama, why are we brown, pink and yellow, and our cousins are white, beige and black?' Answer: 'Well, you know the coloured race is just like a flower garden, with every colour flower represented.' Traditionally capable, as in: 'Mama, I'm walking to Canada and I'm taking you and a bunch of other slaves with me.' Reply: 'It wouldn't be the first time.'
3. Loves music. Loves dance. Loves the moon. Loves the Spirit. Loves love and food and roundness. Loves struggle. Loves the Folk. Loves herself. Regardless.
4. Womanist is to feminist as purple is to lavender.

By definition, Black women are steadily conjuring our way to freedom and moving the legacy of our ancestors forward. The definition of womanism authored by Walker suggests that, as a methodological lens, womanism gives credence to the lived experience that is commensurate with the lived theology of Black women. That theology issues from a panoply of influences both cultural and spiritual. Black women, in the sense of how they interact with social location, concepts of freedom, and intersubjective relationality – the participation in communal efficacity, which is integral to a womanist framework – distinguish themselves as womanist when the focus and intentionality of theories of change are radically inclusive. Womanist approaches to freedom consider the whole community and not just women. The fact that the definition references a Black feminist whose depth of persuasion and perception equates to a richness that shows up in everyday life ushers in the conjuration – a mix of everything imaginable and unimaginable in the quest for freedom. The use of symbols, rituals, prophetic utterances, meditation and the earth as soul force and progenitor are co-constitutive elements of this logic of personhood. This richness draws from conventional and unconventional theoretical, epistemological and paradigmatic streams.

Consequentially, in part, this move towards womanism is inspired by the descriptions and the gestures that Brooks, Martin and Simmons, as Black feminists, make towards 'working the land'. Womanism conjures a particularized notion of working the land that fundamentally appears in historical memory as root work. When we think of roots, we think initially of root-based plants but as we move deeper into meaning-making we can see that the use of roots also connotes a more nuanced tone and tenor, which accounts for a different colour and flavour – the kind of variations that one might perceive when comparing purple and lavender. As we think about the creation narratives, for instance, they describe how all of creation was formed from acts of our God concept encountering and working the land. The agricultural imagery relates the created order as witness to the acts of God. Building upon that metaphor, the human ecosystem supplies itself with a constant flow of witnesses from among those who die and rejoin the created order from the beginning and to this present moment as part of the great cloud of witnesses. It strikes me as ontological, this idea of the great cloud of witnesses, which we find in Hebrews 12.1–3 (NIV):

> Therefore, since we are surrounded by such a great cloud of witnesses, let us throw off everything that hinders and the sin that so easily entangles. And let us run with perseverance the race marked out for

us, fixing our eyes on Jesus, the pioneer and perfecter of faith. For the joy set before him he endured the cross, scorning its shame, and sat down at the right hand of the throne of God. Consider him who endured such opposition from sinners, so that you will not grow weary and lose heart.

Characterizing folks who have died as witnesses gestures towards proclaiming them a spiritual presence that is felt viscerally.

The function of witnesses in our popular imagination is to signify truth, to represent realities, and to confer veracity for the representations of a specified litigation. Particularly in our court systems, witnesses play the role of making or breaking the case before the court. 'A great *cloud* [emphasis mine] of witnesses' describes an overwhelming presence of affirmation for the truth claims proffered. Moreover, it speaks to the otherworldliness of the witnesses whose presence is felt/experienced. This realization offers a conduit to the esoteric beliefs of those who claim the truth of conjuration. Conjure, for those who believe, is a vehicle for the practice of powerful spiritual rituals that travelled with and were transformed by kidnapped Africans who made the treacherous journey through the African diaspora (Chireau, 1997, pp. 225–46). 'The sacred knowledge of Conjure, the enfleshed memories of the supernatural world and its denizens made present in the flesh and bones of its practitioners, was kept alive in hush harbours and in the dark recesses of resistance and survival, of healing and freedom throughout the U.S. American South' (Wood-House, 2021, pp. 131–51). The idea of 'enfleshed memories of the supernatural world' envisages a movement back and forth through the realms of existential realities – a manifestation of the super within the natural. Consequentially, there are provisions, exchanges, protections and powers conferred, which assist in the negotiation of the lived experience between the conjurers and the 'cloud' experience of the witnesses. In effect, the function of the cloud is that of the 'heavenly realm' (Eph. 1.3). For African Americans, that is also a place of transcendence, a space of alternative reality (Long, 1999, p. 166).

Our concept of freedom includes the symbolic noesis, an atemporal experience of the self in a construct of enfleshed freedom (Copeland, 2010). As with most symbols, we must ask how they fundamentally support our faith and ritual life in ways that connect us to the divine and to ourselves. One way that philosophy contributes an answer to this question is to examine the *cogito* or thinking that undergirds being. Apart from the 1637 Cartesian formula found in the *Discourse on the Method*, '*cogito, ergo sum*', translated 'I think, therefore I am' (Dika,

2023), sociologists of religions offer an explanation for this conception as well. Historian of religion Charles H. Long contended that 'every ontology of the self should begin with a comprehension of some particular aspect and expression of being before arriving at an ontological statement. It is only through the manifestations of being in the fullness of time and space that we come to know who we are' (Long, 1999, p. 53). For that, we need witnesses. Witnesses who transcend time and space.

Moreover, as Long posited,

> The historical *cogito* is a *cogito* whose horizon and intentionality may be defined as memory – a mode of perception that anchors our life in pre-reflective experience. It is this horizon and its intentionality which has been overlooked by those who portray the subject as an ego isolated in contemporaneity. (Long, 1999, p. 53)

On this authority rests a paradigmatic shift in perception that anchors conjure to a philosophical tradition emboldened by cultural schemata as is evidenced in the thought of Mircea Eliade and Paul Ricoeur. Eliade stresses not only *that* we know, but *how* we know. Long, by proffering the idea of a 'hermeneutic of the archaic', reorients the 'aim of historical knowledge to understand behaviour and objects as well as ideas', by suggesting that 'the interpreting subject must be pushed back to a level of consciousness commensurate with the forms that the subject wishes to understand' (Long, 1999, pp. 53–7) and suggests that it is in 'culture and history' that we can retrieve the 'great cultural symbols'. Ricoeur then proposes *le symbole donne à penser* (symbol invites thought) (Long, 1999, p. 55). For our purposes, the symbol of the 'cloud' invites thought on the cultural dynamic of witnesses and their role in the power brokerage of present-day ritual. Circling back to Eliade's work in *The Myth of the Eternal Return*, Long avers that 'death is not an absolute end or nothingness but an initiation which prepared the human being for a new life' (Long, 1999, p. 56). Herein lies the socio-religio-philosophical link to the 'great cloud of witnesses' that serves as a conduit for the workspace of conjure. It is in the already but not yet space where the connectivity to the living and the dead *conjures* the power to overcome evil with good. More importantly, Long writes, 'Eliade believes that religious symbols present us a spiritual universe' (Long, 1999, p. 56). I agree with Eliade. In fact, it is the symbol of naming that I wish to focus upon next.

What is in a name? Is a name a symbol for the person or thing it describes? Take the name Fani. Fani, from its Greek etymology, is short for Theofania, which means 'Manifestation of God' (greek-names. info). In its Latin etymology, it means 'free' (SheMedia, 2024). In our popular culture, the name Fani Willis is associated with the Black female prosecutor in Georgia who led the prosecution against Donald Trump. Could the ancestors be speaking? Could there be a connection through Fani Willis based upon the symbolism that her name inscribes to more powerful implications for what is happening in American politics? It would certainly help to explain her crucifixion in popular media (*Washington Post*, 2024). These are the questions that make conjure relevant to our current religio-political climate. They also stir up curiosity about the past and what was at work in the socio-political changes that were witnessed over centuries (Rucker, 2001). At the very least, a kind of symbiosis seems evident. My story is an example of this symbiosis.

I am 'Baptist born, I've been Baptist bred, and when I die, I will be Baptist dead'. But I was moved to a deeper understanding of my belief system when I read Tracey E. Hucks's *Yoruba Traditions and African American Religious Nationalism* (2012). Her chapter titled 'That's Right, I'm a … Yoruba Baptist: Negotiating Religious Plurality and "Theological Openness" in African American Yoruba Practice' (pp. 226–70) opened my eyes to something that was significant in my lived theological experience and my historical cultural memory. Since I was five or six years old, I distinctly remember the adults in my household describing what was done for a young teen who had been severely burned in a house fire. They spoke of 'calling in Mrs Florence', who was known for 'talking out the fire' (Chireau, 1997).[1] Talking out the fire. Mrs Florence could speak to fire and tell it to be gone from one's body. Fascinating. My first cousin, Mary Pugh Bailey, told me that her paternal grandmother, Mary Elizabeth Stewart Pugh, had an identical gift. Mary witnessed her father, Charles Bernard Pugh, who was badly burned on his hands, go to his mother who talked the fire out of his hands. When he healed there was no sign of the burn, inflammation, or skin erythema. My cousin witnessed a complete tissue regeneration of her father's skin.

Digging deep into the interstices of thick ancestral memory, most will recall stories of how people from the past used a talisman, stones, juju bags, charms, crystals, or any number of other 'occult-like' symbols in their quest for something – freedom *from* or freedom *to*. At the very least people may have applied oils, burned sage, or possibly even sacrificed some sentient being for the purpose of working in a world different from what they inhabited in time and space. Perhaps they did not drive down a street where a Black cat crossed to the right, or they habitually refrained from wearing red to a funeral, or they crossed their fingers when they made a wish, or they sat quietly during thunder and lightning. From our sacred historical memory, we can conjure many images and experiences that validate this spiritual practice. Hucks reminds us of how these stories imbibe a certain orientation towards a religious experience that occupies a place of liberty different from but instructive for our lived experience (Chireau, 1997). In effect, these memories are saved in the 'cloud'.

Historians of religion and Africana religious historians such as Yvonne P. Chireau, Tracey E. Hucks, Dianne Stewart and the late Charles H. Long helped me understand the relationality of certain phenomena in the formation of Africana religious sensibilities in service to my concept of conjuring freedom and moving the legacy of our ancestors forward. The history of Africans in America, following the African diaspora, is flowered with adventures where the practices of African indigenous rituals bleed through the memory of those who were captured. Those adventures took root in the culture that we know as Black.

Yvonne P. Chireau tells a story of the use of conjure in African American religious expression. One pastor explained his dilemma with church attendance. He consulted a conjurer for a 'hand'. Thereafter his attendance grew. The conjurer presented the minister with a 'talisman', which this minister attributed to his increased congregational presence. After four years, the minister destroyed the talisman, which he termed a 'luck ball', and his membership dwindled (Chireau, 1997). Chireau posits that the line between Christianity and conjure was often blurred as many practitioners of both exchanged practices for the fuller expression of their faith (Chireau, 2003, p. 27). As Chireau describes the scene in the movie *Daughters of the Dust* in which Nana Peazant conducts a sending forth of her children,

> she [Nana Peazant] clutches a leather pouch that is tightly wound with string and attached to a Bible. It contains personal keepsakes, such as a twist of her mother's hair and her own, some dried flowers, and various roots and herbs. Nana calls it a *'hand'*. Like herself, it embodies the spirits of the 'Old Souls', those enslaved Africans who touched down more than a century earlier on the backwater jetty known as Ibo landing. (Chireau, 2003, p. 1)

The commingling of Christianity and conjure worked in tandem because some practitioners believed in the mystical significance of dreams, prophecy and 'sleight of hand', because conjure, they believed, worked a spiritual function for their faith expression (Chireau, 2003, p. 1). In this description of Nana Peazant, one sees the interconnection between the material, the communal and the spiritual. Chireau ascribes to the proposition that 'Black Americans utilized conjuring traditions not only because they saw them as a valuable resource of resistance, but because they believed that the supernatural realm offered alternative possibilities for empowerment' (Chireau, 2003, p. 18). In essence, the power of conjure was just as effective in communicating meaning to enslavers whose belief in the powers may have substantiated its potency in their minds.

Tracey Hucks' chapter titled 'That's Alright ... I'm a Yoruba Baptist' expands the claim of the symbiosis between Christianity and conjure with her observation that 'for many African American Yoruba, the religious importation of other sacred philosophies such as Protestant Christianity into their lived Yoruba practice creates a multilayered and polysemous system of meaning that informs and enhances their religious identity in significant, valuable ways' (Hucks, 2012, p. 232). Reflecting upon the Black women's literary tradition and the multiple narrative storytelling episodes in both Hucks and Chireau of the lived experiences of many African diasporic peoples, Hucks' point validates the larger connection between my phenomenological claim and the broad landscape of religious meaning-making for Black women in the North American context. Its historical trajectory supports this claim.

African slaves carried their magical beliefs from Africa to the plantations of America. African and European magical traditions merged, creating new forms of magical practices by the late nineteenth century. Elements of conjure, voodoo, European American magic, and Christianity often intertwined. Although voodoo represented a complete religion with a pantheon of deities, conjure (also known as root-work or hoodoo) involved using substances such as roots, herbs, minerals, animal parts and other items to bring healing or harm to others. African Americans concerned with improving their relationships or financial situations and ensuring supernatural protection often turned to root-workers. The demand for the services of local hoodoo practitioners encouraged a thriving trade in spiritual products throughout the South and, with the Black Migration of the early twentieth century, in industrial cities throughout the United States (Rouse, 2017). Chireau (2003) documents the trajectory of this claim in the North American continent.

Tracey Hucks' first book had an indelible impact on me. Specifically, it was her reference to Orunmila, 'the Yoruba god of knowledge, wisdom, divination and destiny who consented to his children's practice of an auxiliary faith' that struck me (Hucks, 2012, p. 226). That was the evidence of the pluralist approach to faith, which figured prominently in my reconciling the stories of Mrs Florence from my childhood with my Baptist sensibilities. Hucks refers to 'this sense cognitive openness', which 'allows for multisourced notions of divine power to coexist in sustaining, fulfilling and beneficial ways for Yoruba practitioners' (Hucks, 2012, p. 227). It was not just Yoruba practitioners who benefitted from this open source. Recalling the work of Albert Raboteau, Hucks reminds us that he concluded,

> Conjure could, without contradiction, exist side by side with Christianity in the same individual and in the same community because, for the slaves, conjure answered purposes which Christianity did not and Christianity answered purposes which conjure did not. (Hucks, 2012, p. 229)

This phenomenon is what Hucks calls 'religiosity with traditions functioning not in direct tension or contradiction but in contemporaneous pragmatic coexistence' (Hucks, 2012, p. 229). These connections birthed 'anti-colonial resistance movements' towards freedom and against white domination and the imposed 'status of inferiority' (p. 230).

'Symbiotic religiosity', the phraseology Hucks uses to describe how several traditions might function together in the practice of one believer/practitioner, for me, presents a perfect container to express the need for spiritual ritual that operates within the configuration of traditional religious expression while simultaneously and perhaps clandestinely displaying tremendous, unseen power (p. 229). As Religion and African American Studies scholar Dianne M. Stewart tells the story of Black sacred imagination (2022, p. 47), it is quite obvious that 'invisible power' creates an advantage in overcoming evil. Writing about the religious identity of Trinidad's Yoruba-Orisa devotees, Stewart chronicles the ways their power confronted colonialist evil and survived. Hers is the second volume in a two-volume work, of which the first is by Tracey E. Hucks, detailing the story of Africans in the white colonial imagination (2022). This duo presents a fitting socio-historical backdrop for what many African Americans are facing in the present cultural ethos of America. Both spiritually and physically, a war is raging. The most effective weaponry is ritual. More specifically, one weapon is conjure.

I find this reference to ritual practice to be of significant import in this present moment with the uptick of rhetorical violence against Black women. It is evident in popular media, print media, news outlets, both broadcast and digital. The narratives of Claudine Gay, Fani Willis, Antoinette 'Bonnie' Candia-Bailey, Sandra Bland, Breonna Taylor and many others amplify the need for a strong, spiritual, ritual practice that taps into the supernatural powers of the 'Old Souls'. It is warranted for protection and for harm. There is a need to summon the great cloud of witnesses and to conduct court. Much of the systematic attack against Black women stems from what many spiritual practitioners would term 'demonic forces'. There is widespread biblical support for there being a war between the forces of good and the forces of evil. Some argue this war was animated by the mandates in Genesis when God declared to the devil, 'I will put enmity between you and the woman, and between your offspring and hers; he will strike your head, and you will strike his heel' (Gen. 3.15). The Apostle Paul described it this way: 'For our struggle is not against blood and flesh, but against the rulers, against the authorities, against the cosmic powers of this present darkness, *against the spiritual forces of evil* in the heavenly places' (Eph. 6.12, emphasis mine). If, in fact, spiritual forces of evil are at work, and I believe that they are, then what are the spiritual forces of good at work to counter them? Taken together, the theorists mentioned in this chapter point to conjure as one such spiritual tool. I contend that the ritual practices, symbols, thick memory and spiritual connection work together to protect and defend those who uphold the standard of good that advance human flourishing. These powers are seen in artful expressions, incantations, song and dance. They combine with the natural world such as burning sage, plant-based roots, soil and sacrificed animal parts to create powerful connections to the ancestors – that great cloud of witnesses.

So how does one invoke this power? Frederick Douglass tells of his experience with a conjurer (Douglass, 1881, pp. 166–77). Douglass had grown weary of his multiple beatings and wished to remove himself from his slaveowner's grip. In fear, he ran into the woods and hid after his last beating. Sandy, a familiar enslaved African, from another slaveowner, Mr William Groomes of Easton, stumbled upon Douglass while he was in the woods and invited him to his home. Douglass tells of his encounter this way:

> I found Sandy, an old adviser. He was not only a religious man, but he professed to believe in a system for which I have no name. He was a genuine African and had inherited some of the so-called magical powers said to be possessed by the eastern nations. He told me that he could help me; that in those very woods there was an herb which in

the morning might be found, possessing all the powers required for my protection (I put his words in my own language), and that if I would take his advice, he would procure me the root of the herb of which he spoke. He told me, further, that if I would take that root and wear it on my right side it would be impossible for Covey to strike me a blow; that with this root about my person no white man could whip me. He said he had carried it for years, and that he had fully tested its virtues. He had never received a blow from a slaveholder since he carried it, and he never expected to receive one, for he meant always to carry that root for protection.

Sandy introduced Douglass to conjuration, and it was his passport to freedom. Douglass had not theretofore believed in this practice, nor had he participated in it; however, his desperate circumstances made him test it. Douglass goes on to tell of his next encounter with his enslaver's brutality. This time Douglass records:

I was resolved to fight, and what was better still, I actually was hard at it. The fighting madness had come upon me, and I found my strong fingers firmly attached to the throat of the tyrant, as heedless of consequences, at the moment, as if we stood as equals before the law. The very colour of the man was forgotten. I felt supple as a cat and was ready for him at every turn. Every blow of his was parried, though I dealt no blows in return. I was strictly on the defensive, preventing him from injuring me, rather than trying to injure him, I flung him on the ground several times when he meant to have hurled me there. I held him so firmly by the throat that his blood followed my nails. He held me, and I held him.

This and many other stories validate the effects of conjuration when dealing with the spiritual forces of evil. Frederick Douglass went on to become one of the most prolific writers and abolitionists of his time. His work is celebrated all over the world (Blight, 2018). His mother, Harriet Bailey, died when he was approximately seven years old. Bailey, though a field hand, was the only Black person in her county who could read. Though she worked on a nearby plantation and could only visit Frederick a few times before her death, she was a part of his great cloud of witnesses (Douglass, 1881).

Conjuring our way to freedom must incorporate the spiritual forces of good to combat the spiritual forces of evil. The material world alone is simply not powerful enough to fight evil. Yes, I said it. Despite the power of atomic bombs, nuclear weapons and all other mastery of death-dealing material implements of destruction, nothing is more powerful than the spirit world. Engaging the spiritual forces of good is as simple as recalling the ways our ancestors dealt with the evil of their day and putting their practices to work for us.

What practices? This calls for the reconstitution of a typology known as the underground railroad through the practice of conjuring. This is the practice that acknowledges the power of the spiritual in perceiving danger, eradicating danger and ordering the elemental in service to the material for the purpose of protection from harm. Belief systems can work alongside these powers to reorder life for human flourishing. One important takeaway from the story of Frederick Douglass, as it pertains to the great cloud of witnesses, is that we are never truly alone.

Afia Atakora's novel *Conjure Women* (2020) joins the persuasive and deeply intellectual women's literary tradition as an exemplary installation of imaginative reclamation of ritual practice that makes conjuring our way to freedom lively and palatable through our fully enfleshed womanist sensibilities. Atakora, a master storyteller, weaves a story of intrigue and power as she develops the characters, mother, May Belle and her daughter Rue who are 'healing women' (Atakora, 2021, p. 20). Rue, who follows her mother's spiritual tradition, but who is also hesitant to follow her mother who serves as a midwife, is studied and clandestine. Written from the perspective, patterns and traditions of the Ante- and Postbellum American South, both Black women demonstrate prowess and acumen in negotiating freedom while constantly encountering their enslaver's white daughter, Varina. This story convincingly illumines the role of conjure in healing the ills of evil forces at work in the created world of two Black women. May Belle and Rue are central characters representing the delicate and intricate lives of the Black women with special powers – conjurers. The power to conjure freedom passes from generation to generation. Their stealth and worth cannot be discounted in this story because its evidence is undeniable. They illustrate the way Black women have always conjured our way to freedom. While many would try to ignore or even erase our presence, our capacities, our value, the fact remains unequivocally that the contribution of Black women in the quest for freedom has been steadfast, unmovable, and always abounding. How is that possible against the formidable forces of evil so constantly confronting us, particularly when, in the words of Angela Davis, 'freedom is a constant struggle' (Davis, 2016). Davis admonishes Black women: 'we must be willing to embrace that long walk to freedom' (Davis, 2016, p. 11). Alice Walker, author and literary genius who defined womanism, said of Angela Davis when *Freedom Is a Constant Struggle* was published,

> Here is someone worthy of the ancestors who delivered her. Angela Davis has stood her ground on every issue important to the health of our people and the planet. It is impossible to read her words or hear her voice and not be moved to comprehension and gratitude for our incredible luck in having her with us. (Davis, 2016, editorial review back cover)

Black women have always conjured our way to freedom with the help of the ancestors. The Spirit is still willing. Conjuring our way to freedom beckons us to a meaningful ritual that embraces the ancestors who delivered us and who are helping us on life's journey.

Note

1 Chireau references 'Wilhelm Johann Müller's Description of the Fetu Country, 1662–9', in Jones (1983, pp. 171–2). In this source there is mention of a priest who 'proposes to tell future things from the fire' dating back to the seventeenth century.

References

Atakora, Afia, 2021, *Conjure Women*, London: Fourth Estate.
Center for the Study of World Religions, 2021, 'Video: Black Magic Matters: Hoodoo as Ancestral Religion', Cambridge, MA: Harvard Divinity School, https://cswr.hds.harvard.edu/news/magic-matters/2021/11/10 (accessed 15.1.2025).
Blight, D. W., 2018, *Frederick Douglass: Prophet of Freedom*, New York: Simon & Schuster.
Brooks, K., K. L. Martin and L. Simmons, 2021, 'Conjure Feminism: Toward a Genealogy', *Hypatia* 36(3), pp. 452–61, https://doi.org/10.1017/hyp.2021.43 (accessed 15.1.2025).
Chireau, Y., 1997, 'Conjure and Christianity in the Nineteenth Century: Religious Elements in African American Magic', *Religion and American Culture: A Journal of Interpretation* 7 (Summer), pp. 225–46, http://www.jstor.org/stable/1123979?origin=JSTOR-pdf (accessed 15.1.2025).
Chireau, Y., 2003, *Black Magic: Religion and the African American Conjuring Tradition*, Berkeley: University of California Press.
Copeland, M. S., 2010, *Enfleshing Freedom: Body, Race and Being*, Minneapolis: Fortress.
Davis, A. Y., 2016, *Freedom Is a Constant Struggle: Ferguson, Palestine, and the Foundations of a Movement*, Chicago: Haymarket Book Publishers.

Derrida, J., 2006, *Specters of Marx: The State of the Debt, the Work of Mourning and the New International*, New York / London: Routledge.

Dika, T. R., 2023, 'Descartes' Method', in Zalta, E. N. and Nodelman, U., eds, *The Stanford Encyclopaedia of Philosophy*, Spring edition, https://plato.stanford.edu/archives/spr2023/entries/descartes-method/ (accessed 15.1.2025).

Douglass, F., 1881, *Life and Times of Frederick Douglass* (online), 'Documenting the American South', Hartford, CT: Park Publishing, https://www.docsouth.unc.edu/neh/douglasslife/douglass.html (accessed 15.3.2024).

Glaude, E. S., Jr, 2014, *African American Religion: A Very Short Introduction*, Oxford / New York: Oxford University Press.

greek-names.info, 2011, 'Fani' (online), https://www.greek-names.info/fani/ (accessed 15.1.2025).

Hucks, T. E., 2012, *Yoruba Traditions and African American Religious Nationalism*, Albuquerque: University of New Mexico Press.

Hucks, T. E., 2022, *Obeah, Orisa and Religion: Identity in Trinidad*, Vol. I, Duke University Press.

Jones, Adam, ed., 1983, *German Sources for West African History, 1599–1669*, Wiesbaden: Franz Steiner.

Long, C. H., 1999, *Significations: Signs, Symbols, and Images in the Interpretation of Religion*, Aurora, CO: Davis Group.

Oyěwùmí, O., 1997, *The Invention of Women: Making an African Sense of Western Gender Discourses*, Minnesota: University of Minnesota Press.

Rouse, W., 2017, 'Charmed Lives: Charms and Amulets in Urban America 1870–1940', *Journal of American Culture* 40 (March), pp. 21–33, https://doi.org/10.1111/jacc.12676 (accessed 15.1.25).

Rucker, W., 2001, 'Conjure, Magic, and Power: The Influence of Afro-Atlantic Religious Practices on Slave Resistance and Rebellion', *Journal of Black Studies* 32(1), pp. 84–103.

SheMedia, 2024, 'Fani', SheKnows baby names, https://www.sheknows.com/baby-names/name/fani/ (accessed 27.4.2025).

Stewart, D. M., 2022, *Orisa: Africana Nations and the Power of Black Sacred Imagination*, Vol. 2, Durham, NC: Duke University Press.

Walker, A., 1983, 'Definition of a Womanist', in *In Search of Our Mothers' Gardens: Womanist Prose*, Orlando: Harcourt Brace Jovanovich.

Washington Post, 2024, 'Read the Decision on Fani Willis and Her Conduct in the Trump Georgia Case' (15 March), https://www.washingtonpost.com/national-security/2024/03/15/fani-willis-pdf-judge-decision-trump (accessed 15.1.2025).

Wood-House, N. D., 2021, 'The Echoes of Conjure in African American Christianity as Enfleshed Memory', *Black Theology* (online) 19(2), pp. 135–51, https://doi.org/10.1080/14769948.2021.1955180 (accessed 15.1.2025).

PART 4

Ritual as a Site of Struggle and Transgression

9

Liberating Liturgy: Liturgy as a (Biblical) Site of Struggle

GERALD O. WEST

Introduction

When we as the Ujamaa Centre reflect on a particular Contextual Bible Study (CBS) that we have facilitated with a particular community-based group, we often recognize that while the CBS itself has enabled the collaborative articulation and planning of potentially transformative action, we often take an ideo-theological step backwards when we sing the final chorus. Liturgy, including the songs people of faith sing, tends to maintain dominant church ideo-theologies.

CBS is primarily an ideo-theological resource, contending with dominant-dominating ideologies and theologies for the purpose of community-based change for marginalized communities. We work within contexts where religion is a powerful and pervasive presence; often a constraining presence, but with the potential to be a liberating presence. CBS is invited into constrained ideo-theological domains with the hope that a CBS-facilitated re-reading of the Bible might invigorate the 'invited' space (Zwane, 2020, p. 215) that the Bible usually inhabits in (South) African (and other) contexts.

In this chapter, I conceptualize CBS as a ritual process that generates ideo-theological resources by which marginalized people of faith might resiliently subsist within their churches and perhaps even contribute reworkings of the liturgical infrastructure of their Christian tradition towards dissonant ideo-theologies of resistance.

CBS as Resisting Ritual

Church-based Bible study is a common ritual reality in most African churches, often located within church-based organizations like the women's *manyano* (women's prayer movement) groups or the men's *amadodano* (men's organization) groups, or part of a church's Sunday or mid-week routine. What is common to most of these ritualized forms of Bible study is that a religious leader within that theological tradition expounds a biblical passage *for* the participants. Such Bible studies are scaffolded by a particular theological tradition's liturgical practices. Such Bible studies and their attendant liturgies tend to sustain and maintain the dominant ideo-theological trajectories of that church.

The Ujamaa Centre's CBS work tends to cut across such Bible study groups, being invited by those who, while they may belong to such Bible study groups, are marginalized by their ideo-theological trajectories. For example, people living with HIV experience their own church's Bible studies as stigmatizing, discriminating, condemning and marginalizing (West and Zengele, 2006). They therefore forge their own 'invented' spaces (Zwane, 2020, pp. 216–17), establishing 'safe' and 'brave' spaces (West, Zwane and Carlos, 2023, p. 594) within which to affirm their agency, dignity and destiny (Zengele, 2023). It is into their invented space that the Ujamaa Centre is invited to facilitate an alternative form of Bible study, namely, Contextual Bible Study (CBS). Here CBS 'invigorates' traditional 'Bible study' space (Zwane, 2020, pp. 220–3), practising another form of Bible study *with* them. In many such cases the organized group, like the Siyaphila support group for people living with HIV, invites the Ujamaa Centre to work with them on a regular basis, constituting a ritualized practice of CBS, week by week, year by year (West, 2017b).

In our experience of more than thirty years of CBS work, organized groups with whom we work recognize that CBS is a very different kind of Bible study. Indeed, during another ritualized practice of CBS on land issues co-ordinated by the Church Land Programme, the Ujamaa Centre was explicitly asked not to refer to our CBS work as 'Bible study', precisely because CBS was not, in the opinion of the participants, an ideo-theologically constraining and controlling process (West and Ndlazi, 2010).

CBS reconstitutes the familiar 'Bible study' ritual and renders it as an unfamiliar participatory Bible re-reading ritual process for inclusion and social transformation. We have devoted considerable reflection to our understanding of CBS. For the purposes of this essay, a recent summary sentence offers a useful and concise formulation, with the terms in square brackets representing each of the six core commitments or values. Significantly, this formulation resonates with and has been endorsed by our sister (or, more appropriately, our mother) community-based Bible re-reading organization in Brazil, *Centro de Estudios Biblicos* (CEBI). Our sentence formulation is:

> CBS begins with the realities of particular local communities of the poor and marginalized [Community], working together in the organized structures and spaces they have established and control [Criticality], collaborating with each other and the socially engaged biblical scholars and theologians who are already working with them [Collaboration] for social transformation [Change] and whom they have invited to read the Bible with them [Collaboration], communally and critically making use of biblical studies resources [Criticality], within particular local contextual struggles [Context] for particular emancipatory outcomes [Change], recognizing that the Bible is both a community-building resource [Change] and itself a site of ideo-theological contestation [Contestation]. (West, 2015, pp. 235–42)

What this formulation indicates is how the various core commitments represent a coherent 'attitude' or 'posture' towards community-based Bible study. CBS is not a technique; it is a process, a ritualized process in the sense of ritual as a community-based 'art of resistance', to invoke James Scott's perceptive analysis of the forms of resistance embodied and practised by marginalized communities (Scott, 1990, pp. 184–7). Implicit in this sentence formulation is the See-Judge-Act process practised by the *Jeunes Ouvrières Chrétiennes* (Young Christian Workers) organization in Belgium in the 1920s (Sands, 2018, pp. 2–4), and taken up by liberation theologies around the Third World (Sands, 2018, pp. 4–6). We move from a particular local organized community's understanding of their lived reality (See), through a rereading of a Bible that is itself a site of contending ideo-theological voices (Judge), to a community-based series of planned actions for transformation (Act).

The Act phase of a CBS appropriates both already present local resources and the ideo-theological resources offered by the CBS for specific actions. We encourage participants to plan a series of actions, beginning with an immediate action, then an action that requires more detailed planning and resources, and finally a long-term plan of action that may involve years of work. We sometimes prompt participants to consider liturgical plans as the immediate action plan. We do this because liturgy is usually a site of contestation for them, incorporating as liturgy does the dominant ideo-theological trajectories of a particular church tradition. They often experience their church's liturgy as marginalizing. Furthermore, creating a liturgical resource is overtly ideo-theological in orientation, and so consolidates the ideo-theological resources produced by the CBS. Finally, doing work together as participants on liturgical change during the CBS is a practical option within the ritual time frame, while the other phases of the action plan require additional time in post-CBS planning meetings. We encourage participants who have done liturgical work as part of their action plan to find ways of incorporating their affirming, inclusive and resisting liturgies into the formal liturgies of their churches.

However, we recognize that liturgy is slow to change and that the process of liturgical change will be difficult. As with most action plans, the Ujamaa Centre does not monitor what the participants do, unless explicitly invited to do so or as part of an explicitly research-oriented project (see, for example, West et al., 2004). Increasingly, however, as our work takes on a more overtly community-based participatory development component (Zwane, forthcoming), we have constructed monitoring-and-evaluation processes to accompany the action plans of communities we work with. Following up on the liturgical resources constructed by CBS participants over the years would have been instructive, both to reflect on what they had appropriated from the CBS and how they had managed the process of having their liturgies included into their church's formal liturgical tradition.

My examples of potentially resisting liturgies in this essay are drawn from actual CBS work but do not reflect the actual liturgies constructed by various CBS participants over the years. Given my own experience with attempts at liturgical change, I suspect that the liturgies constructed by CBS participants were probably used on the margins of their churches, in youth groups, women's groups, HIV support groups, etc. Liturgical change within a church tradition is extremely slow in general and particularly difficult to initiate from a marginalized group within that church tradition. For example, returning to my example of HIV, notwithstanding the reality that 'around 8.45 million people in South Africa live with HIV – an estimated 13.9 per cent of the population', and that 'of South African women aged 15–49, approximately 24 per cent are HIV positive' (Bisnauth, 2023), and that women make up the vast majority of (South) African church membership (Zurlo, Johnson and Crossing, 2023, p. 15), yet there is almost no evidence of HIV realities in the liturgies of any contemporary African church.

Churches have not integrated the ideo-theological experiences of people living with HIV into their liturgies, and yet substantial and significant biblical and theological work has been done on HIV in the past 25 years (Denis, 2013; Haddad, 2011), including liturgical work (Dube, 2004). African churches have not taken heed of these resources, which makes it difficult for those living with HIV to introduce their liturgical resources into the life of their churches. Similarly in the world of work, specifically the realities of unemployment, despite decades of the Ujamaa Centre's Worker Sunday Campaign (collaborating with other organizations), have generated very little sustained liturgical change (Ujamaa, 2023).

Liturgy as Infrapolitical Rituals of Resilience

I return in this section to Scott's work, offering as it does remarkable resonances with the Ujamaa Centre's understanding of the social sectors we work among. I have already noted Scott's notion of subordinate groups' 'arts of resistance'. Here my focus is on a particular set of such arts, those Scott locates within the infrapolitical realm, with an emphasis on ritualized arts of resilience and resistance.

Scott's notion of 'infrapolitics' is useful in my analysis in two respects. First, he argues that the realm of infrapolitics 'lies strategically' between the safest and most public forms of subordinate discourse, where they make 'rhetorical concessions' to the dominant discourse within invited church space, and the discourse of the 'hidden transcript', 'off-stage, where subordinates may gather outside the intimidating gaze of power' in their own brave invented faith space (Scott, 1990, pp. 18–19). Second, Scott uses the term 'infrapolitics' in order to invoke the concept of 'infrastructure', suggesting that infrapolitics is a 'cultural and structural' system of 'mutually sustaining practices' of both 'material and symbolic resistance' (Scott, 1990, p. 184).

Implicit in Scott's understanding of 'resistance', the Ujamaa Centre argues, is Cindi Katz's understanding of 'resilience'. Indeed, Katz draws on Scott, but interrogates and reconceptualizes 'practices that are loosely considered 'resistance' to distinguish those whose primary effect is autonomous initiative, recuperation, or *resilience*; those that are attempts to *rework* oppressive and unequal circumstances; and those that are intended to *resist*, subvert, or disrupt these conditions of exploitation and oppression' (Katz, 2004, p. 242). Katz's distinctions and her continuum 'toward stronger forms of oppositional practice' that are 'interwoven and mutually sustaining' (Katz, 2004, p. 242) are extremely useful for understanding our CBS work. Matthew Sparke incisively summaries Katz's distinctions as follows: 'She contrasts resistance that involves oppositional consciousness and achieves emancipatory change, with forms of reworking that alter the organization but not the polarization of power relations, with forms of resilience that enable people to survive without really changing the circumstances that make such survival so hard' (Sparke, 2008, p. 424).

Katz begins with 'resilience', recognizing that in many contexts of oppression and marginalization, resistance and reworking are rooted in 'innumerable small acts of resilience' (Katz, 2004, p. 244). She conceptualizes 'resilience' as 'just getting by in the face of the oppressive and increasingly mean-spirited circumstances' (Katz, 2004, p. 244), which is not insignificant, as the 'survival' theologies of feminist theologians have argued (Haddad, 2004; Williams, 1993). But, she goes on to argue, 'If their acts of resilience sustained them, they also supported the general trajectory of the developments that necessitated these acts in the first place' (Katz, 2004, p. 246). This is crucial to Katz's differentiations, the recognition that resilience-as-resistance, while agentive is not transformative of the systems it inhabits. 'This double edge notwithstanding', she goes on to acknowledge that 'resilient acts are self-reinforcing, and inasmuch as they are fortifying, they offer the possibility of fostering something beyond recuperation', while acknowledging that 'in many historical geographies, recuperation itself is an achievement' (Katz, 2004, p. 246).

Our HIV-related work with the Siyaphila support network enabled us to understand how CBS developed forms of what we now refer to as 'interpretive resilience' (West, 2018, pp. 20–4). The Bible, which was previously far from them as women living with HIV, had come close to them; the Bible that had no place with them now had a place with them; the Bible that belonged to others now belonged to them; the Bible that had nothing relevant to say to them now spoke directly to their condition; the Bible that could not be touched or made to speak by them or for them was now in their hands, they could ask their questions of it, and they heard it speaking to them directly; the Bible that had brought judgement, stigma and discrimination now brought healing, hope and life (West, 2021, p. 152; West and Zengele, 2006, p. 58).

This understanding of our work has been supported through external evaluations of the Ujamaa Centre. In the 2010 external evaluation, the evaluators included the category of 'Unplanned Impacts', recording how CBS had contributed to capacity building in five related areas: understanding of God, self-confidence, integration of faith and life, reintegration and respect within their families, and an inclusive space within churches (West, 2021, pp. 152–5). Of particular relevance for this essay is the last.

In the 2015 external evaluation, some participants made a direct link between the dignity they experienced within CBS work and their yearning for a similar acknowledgement of their dignity within their churches: 'Many [women] participants spontaneously commented on the experience of being respected, when they are used to being judged, blamed and ridiculed for their different conditions. They spoke of feeling rejected by the church and finding it valuable to find acceptance from a church-based position [such as the Ujamaa Centre]. This led to a restored sense of dignity and self-worth as reported by participants' (Msunduzi, 2015, pp. 25–6). It is important to note that while some of these women still felt disrespected in their churches, they used the resources of CBS to build their capacities to re-turn to their churches. Specifically, CBS participants feel scripturally confident and equipped to re-turn to their churches (West, 2021, p. 154). They could talk back, whether privately or publicly, to the theologies proclaimed from the pulpit or ritualized in the liturgy. Our reflections on such participant understandings of our work have made it clear to us that CBS contributes towards forms of biblical interpretive resilience, enabling a deeper recognition that the Bible is not aligned against them but has inclusive and affirming ideo-theological voices and trajectories, confirming their understanding of a God of life in the midst of the idols of death, to invoke Pablo Richard's provocative formulation (Richard, 1983).

Biblical interpretive resilience in turn enables ideo-theological 're-working'. Katz explains that 'the practices of reworking are those that alter the conditions of people's existence to enable more workable lives and create more viable terrains of practice' (Katz, 2004, p. 247). Constructing and then using CBS-based liturgies would be a good example of Katz's notion of 'reworking'. 'Reworking', she explains, 'deploys a different kind of consciousness than the acts of resilience that sustain people facing difficult circumstances or the rituals that some authors suggest help to 'make and remake social facts and collective identities' (Comaroff and Comaroff, 1993, p. xvi). Projects of reworking tend to be driven by explicit recognition of problematic conditions and to offer focused, often pragmatic, responses to them' (Katz, 2004, p. 247). Offering alternative liturgies, forged within the realities of a particular marginalization through the ideo-theological work of CBS, would be a pragmatic response to the constraints of dominant church ideo-theologies, providing a provisional safe infrapolitical space within the very fabric of the church's tradition.

Katz is clear about the constraints that call for reworking rather than overt resistance. 'Projects of reworking', she explains, 'are enfolded into hegemonic social relations because rather than attempt to undo these relations or call them into question, they attempt to recalibrate power relations and/or redistribute resources' (Katz, 2004, p. 247). However, she insists, 'This is not to say that those engaged in the politics of reworking accept or support the hegemony of the ruling classes and dominant social groups, but that in undertaking such politics, their interests are not so much in challenging hegemonic power as in attempting to undermine its inequities on the very grounds on which they are cast' (Katz, 2004, p. 247). Offering alternative liturgies in an ecclesial context in which liturgy is used to maintain the dominant and marginalizing ideo-theological tradition would accomplish precisely this. As the external evaluation reports of the Ujamaa Centre's CBS work clearly demonstrate, but in Katz's terms, 'There are two interconnected aspects to the material social practices of reworking: one is associated with redirecting and in some cases reconstituting available resources, and the other is associated with people's retooling themselves as political subjects and social actors' (Katz, 2004, p. 247; see West, 2021, pp. 154–5). CBS contributes to both.

While CBS-related liturgy might not change church tradition, it would provide a discordant infrapolitical presence, destabilizing the dominant tradition and providing a regular ritualized reminder that the Bible can be interpreted differently. A contending ideo-theological voice within the dominant voice of a church's liturgy may even invoke others in the congregation, summoning them to collective action, leading perhaps to forms of 'resistance'. In Katz's analysis, 'If reworking reorders and sometimes undermines the structural constraints that affect everyday life both to make it more livable and to create viable terrains of practice, resistance takes up that terrain with the invocation of an oppositional consciousness' (Katz, 2004, p. 251). A shared recognition of the ideo-theological trajectory of an alternative CBS-generated liturgy may enable other practices of resistance. 'Practices of resistance draw on and produce a critical consciousness to confront and redress historically and geographically specific conditions of oppression and exploitation at various scales' (Katz, 2004, p. 251).

Both Katz and the Ujamaa Centre are clear about our theory: practices of resilience, reworking and resistance are overlapping. Katz helpfully distinguishes 'between them for practical reasons – not to create arbitrary categories of practice, but to better inform praxis' (Katz, 2004, p. 256). In the next section of my essay I offer particular examples of

CBS-related liturgical potential, some of which may already have been taken up by participants and used within their church contexts.

CBS-Based Liturgy

My first example comes from a CBS in which liturgical change is the primary focus of the CBS. I have always been troubled, as have others (Kittredge, 2006, p. 81), by what is known as 'The Prayer of Humble Access': 'We do not presume ...' This prayer has formed a component of the Anglican liturgy since 1548 (Dowden, 1908, p. 9), so it has a substantive Anglican theological pedigree. But as a biblical scholar, the question that hovers over this prayer every time I kneel to take the Eucharist is how Thomas Cranmer, who composed it, and the generations of Anglican theologians who have continued to include it in successive Prayer Books, have understood a constitutive Gospel text that has been used in its formulation, namely Mark 7.24–31 (and/or the parallel in Matthew 15.21–29).

In my own faith-based experience within a local Anglican church, I was conscious of the many kneeling around me who were constantly told by dominant theologies that they were not worthy because they were HIV-positive, or unemployed, or living with a disability, or queer. In our Anglican liturgy for 'The Holy Eucharist' (1989) we have the option, at the point of 'The Communion', to say what is generally known as the 'Prayer of Humble Access'. The prayer is commonly used in the Anglican Church of Southern Africa (ACSA, 1989, pp. 127–8), and goes as follows:

> We do not presume
> to come to this your table, merciful Lord
> trusting in our own righteousness
> but in your manifold and great mercies.
> We are not worthy so much as to gather up
> the crumbs under your table
> but you are the same Lord
> whose nature is always to have mercy.
> Grant us therefore, gracious Lord
> so to eat the flesh of your dear Son Jesus Christ
> and to drink his blood
> that we may evermore dwell in him and he in us.

The prayer clearly draws on Mark 7.24-31, among other texts. Cynthia Briggs Kittredge, a scholar of the New Testament and a scholar of Anglicanism, has written a comprehensive article in which she analyses many of this prayer's historical and theological developments (Kittredge, 2006), and Dorothy A. Lee, also a scholar of the New Testament and a scholar of Anglicanism, has written an essay in which she identifies four different interpretative approaches to this text (Lee, 2021).

Kittredge sums up succinctly the kinds of ideo-theological readings of the Markan text that are assumed in the prayer. 'Interpretations of the story as a statement of human unworthiness to receive the sacrament makes a number of related interpretive moves', argues Kittredge. She explains: 'They read the gentile woman as representative of all Christians who are identified with the gentiles in the text, and they universalize Jesus's apparent rejection of her supplication to mean the unworthiness of all to approach the table of God' (Kittredge, 2006, p. 89). Specifically, she continues, 'the phrase, "we are not worthy so much as to gather up the crumbs under thy table", takes the initial rejection evident in Jesus's remark to the woman, applies it to all Christian communicants, accepts and makes permanent the characterization of the woman and her daughter as dogs, and takes no account of the resolution of the story' (Kittredge, 2006, p. 90).

However, Kittredge argues, this text has undergone significant rereading in recent years, particularly from within feminist and 'Third World' biblical scholarship (see Hicks, 2003). That the protagonist is a woman and a foreigner resonates with the ideo-theological orientations of feminist and Third World interpreters. 'Interpretation of the story of the Syrophoenecian woman in its context in Mark's gospel has moved from a Jesus-centred reading that demeans the woman's role to a reading centred on the woman protagonist that recognizes Jesus's parochialism overcome by her insistent faith' (Kittredge, 2006, pp. 90–1). Kittredge confirms that such interpretations fit well within Mark's ideo-theological trajectory. 'Mark's gospel commends such exercise of faith as exemplified in the story of the friends who bring the paralyzed man to Jesus in Mark 2.1–12 and the woman with a flow of blood in Mark 5.25–34' (Kittredge, 2006, pp. 90–1). 'In the logic of Mark's gospel', she argues, 'those who are neither part of the inner circle of the disciples nor of the established scribes and Pharisees are the ones who recognize Jesus and exemplify faith. In the worldview constructed by Mark's gospel, the unaccompanied gentile woman [in Mark 7.24-30] with a demon-possessed, dependent daughter represents the extreme "outsider" who approaches Jesus in the house' (Kittredge, 2006, pp. 90–1).

Kittredge provides us here with a clear account of Mark's ideo-theological orientation in the gospel's own narrative world. Mark uses the disciples as characters who demonstrate a lack of understanding of the ideo-theological trajectory in which Jesus works, and the leadership of the Jerusalem temple (including chief priests, scribes, Pharisees, Herodians and Sadducees [11.27—13.2]) as characters who do not want to understand the ideo-theological trajectory Jesus represents, which Herman Waetjen refers to as 'a reordering of power' (Waetjen, 1989).

Dorothy Lee, too, recognizes that this text is constitutive of the 'Prayer of Humble Access', and like Kittredge she too acknowledges how feminist and Third World biblical scholarship have altered our understanding of this text. This Markan story, she says, 'makes its way into the Book of Common Prayer (1662), in the Prayer of Humble Access, in which the Syro-Phoenician woman serves as a model of humility and trust for men as well as women' (Lee, 2021, p. 77). 'Yet', she hastens to add, 'there is more than humility in the woman's spirituality' (Lee, 2021, p. 78). She too situates this story 'as cohering with the significant role that outsiders, particularly women, play in Mark's gospel' (Lee, 2021, p. 78), which 'establishes the woman as a model of faith and service, an example for the disciples with their misunderstanding and prejudice and for the implied readers of the gospel. The woman's story signifies the opening of doors, access to the table, and inclusion and belonging for those standing outside by reason of gender, ethnicity, or ritual impurity' (Lee, 2021, pp. 79–80).

Significantly, Lee recognizes that 'within the wider narrative framework of the gospel, the Syro-Phoenician woman's meeting with Jesus has notable *ecclesial* dimensions' (Lee, 2021, p. 79, emphasis mine), citing Ranjini Wickramaratne Rebera, who argues that the woman is 'an icon of power to women in today's [south Asian] church who are prevented from claiming the right to own their power and to use it for others' (cited in Lee, 2021, p. 80; Rebera, 2001, p. 106). In Lee's summation, 'the unnamed Syro-Phoenician woman and her daughter function not only as persons in their own right, with their own complex cultural identity, but also as representatives of the overturning of clean and unclean, with its far-reaching implications for women and outsiders, for femaleness and alterity' (Lee, 2021, p. 80). And yet this is not how this text is used in Southern African liturgy!

Provoked by biblical studies work on this text as I knelt in church during the Communion liturgy, refusing to recite the prayer, I wondered how many others around me were silently resisting this liturgical prayer. When the opportunity came via an invitation to the Ujamaa Centre to prepare a Lent series of CBS for the Anglican Church of Southern Africa (ACSA), we included a CBS explicitly on Mark 7.24–31 (Ujamaa, 2013). I workshopped each of the CBS as part of their production with my local Anglican congregation, collaborating with them to produce the series. The request for the series came because ACSA wanted to use CBS as a resource to revisit their vision and mission statements, among which was a commitment to 'liturgical renewal' (ACSA, 2021).

I have reflected on this CBS in detail (West, 2022), so here I will focus only on how the CBS invites participants to re-read the 'Prayer of Humble Access' alongside a rereading of Mark 7.24–31, and then encourages participants to become engaged in liturgical renewal by asking them: 'How would you edit the 'Prayer of Humble Access'. What would you retain and what would you delete?' The participants had no problem taking up this task, and various revisions of the prayer were shared as part of the CBS. Our consensus was that what was generally understood as a prayer of exclusion was based on a biblical text about radical inclusion (West, 2022, pp. 28–9). My hope was that this particular CBS might actually lead to a renewal of this particular liturgy in ACSA, but that has not yet happened.

This CBS is a good example of how doing biblical studies from the margins offers resources with which to deconstruct and reconstruct church liturgy. A CBS on Job 3 does something similar. Working with the Siyaphila network of people living with HIV, we contrasted Job 1.21, which is commonly used as part of our churches' funeral liturgy, with Job 3, which is an unfamiliar text to most. The accepting Job of 1.21 becomes a lamenting and protesting Job in 3.1–26. Again, we have reflected on this CBS at length (West, 2008, 2016; West and Zengele, 2004). As part of this CBS we invited participants each to produce their own version of Job 3, composing their own prayers of lament and protest. With their permission, which they were eager to give, hoping that their liturgical laments would become a resource to others, we have published their resilient liturgical laments (West, 2008, pp. 203–5). Their liturgical laments have become a resource to many, but as far as we can determine, they have not found their way into the liturgical life of the churches.

As with the Markan text, a slow and careful re-reading of Job 3 offers a completely different understanding of the book of Job, contending with the pious traditional-theology-affirming versions of the book so popular in the churches. A slow and careful CBS re-reading of a central liturgical prayer, 'The Lord's Prayer', supplemented with socio-economic resources about first-century Palestine, has had a similar effect (West, 2017a). This common liturgical prayer becomes uncomfortably unfamiliar, shifting its emphasis from personal sin to economic structural sin. Again, however, though the CBS encourages the use of Matthew's version of the prayer (Matt. 6.9–13), in which economic factors are evident, rather than the versions favoured by churches (West, 2017a, pp. 93–4), we have not witnessed liturgical change.

Each of the examples so far has engaged with existing liturgy, either directly or indirectly. CBS has also generated resources that could be used to construct new liturgy. For example, in a recent CBS on 1 Kings 12.1–16 and its (earlier) Septuagint version 3 Reigns 12.24p-t, we invite participants to construct a liturgical chant based on 3 Reigns 12.24t. We invite participants as follows: 'The people turn away from their king, rejecting both his leadership and his economic system. They respond with a chant (24t). Compose your own chant in your own language in response to state capture. What actions can you take in response to state capture?' (West, 2023, p. 13). There is widespread concern in African (and other) countries about corrupt political leadership, yet most churches that offer prayers for their political leaders use prayers which tend to take the form of prayers of support rather than revolt. This CBS, though very recent, has the potential to generate resisting liturgy. Similarly, our recent work on the poetic-liturgical response of Tamar to her rapist brother Amnon (West, 2024), has the potential for a liturgy of lament, sorely required in our context, crying out against patriarchy.

Finally, as our South African churches grapple with 'same-sex' (or queer) marriage, sanctioned by the South African Constitution, there are CBS resources to draw upon in reconstructing marriage liturgy. Our CBS work on Genesis 2 has the potential to re-read this 'normative' sexuality text (West, 2019), contending with textual detail for a more inclusive understanding of sexual partnership. Similarly, our current work on the book of Ruth (West, Zwane and Carlos, 2023), in which we prepare the way for CBS work on the intersections between sexuality and economics (among others), could generate queer 'marriage' resources on Ruth's impassioned response to Naomi in Ruth 1.16–17. Again, biblical scholarship offers both literary-narrative and socio-historical detail with which to disrupt traditional church-based understandings of this text. Significantly, this text is used in certain South African heterosexual marriage liturgies (for example, the Baptist Union of Southern Africa), but with no recognition of the queer resonances within this text. In our forthcoming CBS on this text, we might encourage participants to construct an inclusive marriage liturgy.

Conclusion: Liturgical Disruption

Though my CBS examples are taken from (South) African contexts, CBS is now widely used throughout the world (see, for example, Anglican Alliance and Ujamaa Centre, 2023; Cornwall and Nixon, 2011; Mainwaring, 2014). Reflections on our praxis come from each of the sites where CBS is used. One particular conversation, over many years, which haunts me has been with Cheryl Anderson, a colleague who has done extensive HIV-related CBS work within the African American church-based communities of the US. She has noted, like us, the significant impact a CBS has had on a particular group of participants, disrupting the settled theologies of their churches (Anderson, 2024, p. 98). However, her observation is that the disruption is not sustained, as the dominant theologies gradually reassert themselves. This is where CBS-based liturgy construction could make a difference, embedding within a church the disruptive ideo-theological contributions of CBS.

Such disruptive liturgical rituals would provide an invigorated space for a shift from resilience to reworking, in Katz's terms. My own experience of the 'Prayer of Humble Access', and the subsequent confirmation through a CBS that others shared my disquiet indicates that CBS-generated disruptive liturgy would create an invigorated brave space for church change.

References

ACSA, 1989, *An Anglican Prayer Book, 1989*, Cape Town: Collins.
ACSA, 2021, Mission Priorities. Retrieved from https://anglicanchurchsa.org/mission-priorities/ (accessed 15.05.2025).
Anderson, Cheryl B. 2024. 'Struggling with Culture: African American Biblical Hermeneutics in These Times of HIV and AIDS', in *Reading in These Times: Purposes and Practices of Minoritized Biblical Criticism*, ed. Benny Tat-siong Liew and Fernando F Segovia, pp. 93–104. Atlanta: SBL Press.
Anglican Alliance and Ujamaa Centre, 2023, *Re-Imagining Our World Together: Contextual Bible Studies on the Anglican Marks of Mission and the Sustainable Development Goals*. Retrieved from https://files.anglicanalliance.org/wp-content/uploads/2023/01/05100502/Re-imagining-our-World-Together-Contextual-Bible-Studies.pdf (accessed 15.1.2025).
Bisnauth, Melanie, 2023, 'HIV Care for Migrant Women in South Africa: The Gaps and 5 Steps Towards Offering Better Services', *The Conversation AFRICA* (12 June).
Comaroff, Jean and John, 1993, *Modernity and Its Malcontents: Ritual and Power in Postcolonial Africa*. Chicago: University of Chicago Press.

Cornwall, Susannah and Nixon, David, 2011, 'Readings from the Road: Contextual Bible Study with a Group of Homeless and Vulnerably-Housed People', *Expository Times* 123(1), pp. 12–19.

Denis, Philippe, 2013, 'HIV/AIDS and Religion in Sub-Saharan Africa: An Emerging Field of Enquiry', *Archives de sciences sociales des religions* 164, pp. 43–58.

Dowden, John, 1908, 'A Contribution Towards the Study of the Prayer of Humble Access', *Irish Church Quarterly* 1(1), pp. 8–24.

Dube, Musa W., 2004, *Africapraying: A Handbook on HIV/AIDS Sensitive Sermon Guidelines and Liturgy*, Geneva: World Council of Churches.

Haddad, Beverley G., 2004, 'The Manyano Movement in South Africa: Site of Struggle, Survival, and Resistance', *Agenda* 61, pp. 4–13.

Haddad, Beverley G., ed., 2011, *Religion and HIV and AIDS: Charting the Terrain*, Pietermaritzburg: University of KwaZulu-Natal Press.

Hicks, Jane E., 2003, 'Moral Agency at the Borders: Rereading the Story of the Syrophoenician Woman', *Word and World* 23(1), pp. 76–84.

Katz, Cindi, 2004, *Growing Up Global: Economic Restructuring and Children's Everyday Lives*, Minneapolis: University of Minnesota Press.

Kittredge, Cynthia Briggs, 2006, 'Not Worthy So Much as to Gather Up the Crumbs under Thy Table: Reflection on the Sources and History of the Prayer of Humble Access', *Sewanee Theological Review* 50(1), pp. 80–92.

Lee, Dorothy A., 2021, 'Clean and Unclean: Multiple Readings of Mark 7:24–30/31', in Monica Jyotsna Melanchthon and Robyn J. Whitaker, eds, *Terror in the Bible: Rhetoric, Gender, and Violence*, pp. 67–87, Altanta: SBL Press.

Mainwaring, Simon, 2014, *Mark, Mutuality, and Mental Health: Encounters with Jesus*, Atlanta: SBL Press.

Msunduzi, Evaluation Consortium, 2015, *Ujamaa Evaluation of the Theological Research and Community Development Programme*, retrieved from Pietermaritzburg.

Rebera, Ranjini Wickramaratne, 2001, 'The Syrophoenician Women: A South Asian Feminist Perspective', in Amy-Jill Levine and Marianne Blickenstaff, eds, *A Feminist Companion to Mark*, pp. 100–10, Sheffield: Sheffield Academic Press.

Richard, Pablo, ed., 1983, *The Idols of Death and the God of Life*, Maryknoll: Orbis Books.

Sands, Justin, 2018, 'Introducing Cardinal Cardijn's See–Judge–Act as an Interdisciplinary Method to Move Theory into Practice', *Religions* (4), 129, pp. 1–10.

Scott, James C., 1990, *Domination and the Arts of Resistance: Hidden Transcripts*, New Haven, CT / London: Yale University Press.

Sparke, Matthew, 2008, 'Political Geography – Political Geographies of Globalization III: Resistance', *Progress in Human Geography* 32(3), pp. 423–40.

Ujamaa, 2013, *A Vision and Mission for Our Church*, Retrieved from http://ujamaa.ukzn.ac.za/Libraries/manuals/A_Bible_Study_series_for_the_Anglican_Ch.sflb.ashx (no longer available).

Ujamaa, 2023, 'Worker Sunday Campaign', http://ujamaa.ukzn.ac.za/WhatUJAMAAdoes/campaigns.aspx#../Libraries/20150528_Worker_Sunday_Launch/15.sflb.ashx (no longer available).

Waetjen, Herman C., 1989, *A Reordering of Power: A Socio-Political Reading of Mark's Gospel*, Minneapolis: Fortress.

West, Gerald O., 2008, 'The Poetry of Job as a Resource for the Articulation of Embodied Lament in the Context of HIV and AIDS in South Africa', in Nancy C. Lee and Carleen Mandolfo, eds, *Lamentations in Ancient and Contemporary Cultural Contexts*, pp. 195–214, Atlanta: Society of Biblical Literature.

West, Gerald O., 2015, 'Reading the Bible with the Marginalised: The Values of Contextual Bible Reading', *Stellenbosch Theological Journal* 1(2), pp. 235–61.

West, Gerald O., 2016, 'Between Text and Trauma: Reading Job with People Living with HIV', in Elizabeth C. Boase and Frechette Christopher G., eds, *Bible through the Lens of Trauma*, pp. 209–30, Atlanta: SBL Press.

West, Gerald O., 2017a, 'The Lord's Prayer as Economic Renewal', in Anne Burkhardt and Simone Sinn, eds, *Global Perspectives on the Reformation: Interactions between Theology, Politics and Economics*, pp. 85–94, Leipzig: Evangelische Verlagsanstalt.

West, Gerald O., 2017b, 'Senzeni Na? Speaking of God 'What Is Right' and the 'Re-Turn' of the Stigmatising Community in the Context of HIV', *Scriptura* 116(2), pp. 260–77.

West, Gerald O., 2018, 'Facilitating Interpretive Resilience: The Joseph Story (Genesis 37–50) as a Site of Struggle', *Acta Theologica, Supplement* 26, pp. 17–37.

West, Gerald O., 2019, 'Deploying Indecent Literary and Socio-Historical Detail for Change: Genesis 2:18–24 as a Resource for Choice of Sexual Partner', in L. Juliana Claassens, Charlene van der Walt and Funlola O. Olojede, eds, *Teaching for Change: Essays on Pedagogy, Gender and Theology in Africa*, pp. 57–77, Stellenbosch: Sun Press.

West, Gerald O., 2021, 'Contextual Bible Study and/as Interpretive Resilience', in Ezra Chitando, Esther Mombo and Masiiwa Ragies Gunda, eds, *That All May Live: Essays in Honour of Nyambura J. Njoroge*, pp. 143–59, Bamberg: University of Bamberg Press.

West, Gerald O., 2022, 'Recovering Eucharistic Crumbs: Re-Reading Mark 7.24–30 for Liturgical Renewal', *Journal of Theology for Southern Africa* 172, pp. 16–29.

West, Gerald O., 2023, 'Textual Criticism, Literary Criticism, and State Capture: Returning 3 Reigns 12:24p–t to the Canon of Local African Communities', *Journal for Semitics* 32(2), pp. 1–18, https://doi.org/10.25159/2663-6573/13518.

West, Gerald O., 2024, 'The Poetics of Redacted Absence as Presence: Kin Eyes Hearing Tamar (2 Samuel 13)', in *Narrating Rape: Shifting Perspectives in Biblical Literature and Popular Culture*, ed. Rhiannon Graybill, L. Juliana Claassens and Christl M. Maier, London: SCM Press.

West, Gerald O. and Thulani Ndlazi, 2010, '"Leadership and Land": A Very Contextual Interpretation of Genesis 37–50 in Kwazulu-Natal, South Africa', in Athalya Brenner, Archie Chi Chung Lee and Gale A. Yee, eds, *Genesis*, Texts@ Contexts, pp. 175–90, Minneapolis: Fortress Press.

West, Gerald O. and Bongi Zengele, 2004, 'Reading Job "Positively" in the Context of HIV/AIDS in South Africa', *Concilium* 4, pp. 112–24.

West, Gerald O. and Bongi Zengele, 2006, 'The Medicine of God's Word: What People Living with HIV and AIDS Want (and Get) from the Bible', *Journal of Theology for Southern Africa* 125, pp. 51–63.

West, Gerald O., Phumzile Zondi-Mabizela, Khumalo Martin, Matsepe Happiness, P. Smadz and Mirolyn Naidoo, 2004, 'Rape in the House of David:

The Biblical Story of Tamar as a Resource for Transformation', *Agenda* 61, pp. 36–41.

West, Gerald O., Sithembiso Zwane and Helder L. Carlos, 2023, 'Contending for Invented Space in African Context and Biblical Text: Intersecting Gender, Sexuality, Ethnicity and Economics', *Old Testament Essays* 36(3), pp. 587–611.

Williams, Delores S., 1993, *Sisters in the Wilderness: The Challenge of Womanist God-Talk*, Maryknoll, New York: Orbis Books.

Zengele, Bongi P., 2023, *The Lived and Embodied Theologies of People Living with HIV and AIDS: A Phenomenological Study of Siyaphila Support Groups for PLHIV in Kwazulu Natal, South Africa*, PhD, Pietermaritzburg, University of KwaZulu-Natal.

Zurlo, Gina A., Johnson, Todd M. and Crossing, Peter F., 2023, 'World Christianity 2023: A Gendered Approach', *International Bulletin of Mission Research* 47(1), pp. 11–22.

Zwane, Sithembiso S., 2020, 'Invited, Invigorated and Invented Spaces: A Trans-Development Approach', in Jin Young Choi and Joerg Rieger, eds, *Faith, Class, and Labor: Intersectional Approaches in a Global Context*, pp. 212–33, Eugene, OR: Pickwick.

Zwane, Sithembiso S., forthcoming, 'Invited, Invigorated and Invented Spaces: An Analysis of the Ujamaa Centre's Ideotheological Conceptual Contribution to Participatory Community Development in South Africa and Beyond', PhD, Pietermaritzburg: University of KwaZulu-Natal.

10

Defiance and Democracy: Protests as Rites for Rights in Singapore

LYNNETTE XIANGLING LI

Singapore is a colonial project of the British Empire. It is a law-and-order society. It is known to be an authoritarian state and illiberal democracy where political dissent faces intimidation by the use of draconian legislation to annihilate defiant cries and critique of empire. Singapore's governance of its people is heavily dependent on the use of surveillance, disciplinary measures to conform to authority, and the willingness of the population to comply and submit to what have been called draconian measures. With 387.6 surveillance cameras per square mile on an island that has a landmass of only 281 square miles (Bischoff, 2023), Singapore is the utopia that Michel Foucault describes in *Discipline and Punish*. It presents itself as a 'perfectly governed city' with its use of disciplinary power (2012, p. 198). For Foucault, punishment is 'an exercise of "terror"' and public execution helps 'reactivate power' for the sovereign over their subjects (2012, p. 49). As such, punishment is a site of investigation that can contribute to exposing who controls power and social capital within the given society.

The use of punishment was an integral part of the colonial project to create a submissive, docile and domesticated population. Such methods were further refined by the postcolonial, newly independent Singapore governmental leadership that would intimidate political opponents with the use of imprisonment without trial, and publicly force social justice advocates into silence and compliance. This serves to forewarn citizens of the severity of punishment that the government leaders are willing to relentlessly unleash on whoever dares threaten their hegemonic rule. Additionally, it reminds citizens that everyone is conscripted into nation-building. Their obedience and compliance are imperative in contributing to the social, political and economic success of Singapore. Such social conditioning circumvents the diversity and plurality of multiple centres within society. In such a context, differing and diverse views are typecast as being disloyal and antagonistic, fragmenting national unity and thereby destabilizing the survival and resilience of the country. In such a context, civil and human rights are placed on the altar of nationalistic neo-capitalist interests.

In the case of rituals as resistance, I argue that they function as prophetic ways to dislocate, transgress and defiantly resist the powers of empire. Rituals are not isolated events. Neither are they mechanical or static. Rather, they are social and observable and some would see them as having a measure of performativity. In order for rituals to be performative, Molly Farneth suggests that 'the right people have to enact the right sequence of acts under the right conditions' and this is 'judged by multiple people with different points of view' (2023, p. 96). When empire demands its subjects to perform at its pleasure, rituals of resistance are rites of contestation that flip the script of conscripted obedience, loyalty and domestication of its subjects. They are rites of risk, transgression, defiance, subversion and dislocation, towards the conscientization of people towards a more just, equal and life-affirming world. In a culture of fear and intimidation, in an authoritarian place where people are heavily scrutinized and surveilled, who dares to raise their fists at empire when their livelihood, loved ones and lives are at stake?

When citizens are subjects of empire, socialized to comply and conform to the rules and regulations of law and order to serve the interests of the powerful political elites, social disruption leads to economic and political instability, which in turn goes against nation-building efforts. Survival is at the heart, particularly so during the first few decades of post-independence Singapore. Rituals of resistance contest empire's hegemonic ways that demand that all be in the posture of submission, subordination and servitude. Rituals of resistance offer dislocation of normative ways. They call forth an anticipated future. They lament for the dashed hope denied, unattainable, or diminished. Rituals of resistance are creative resistance and are transformative, using things that are seemingly insignificant to audaciously demand the attention of the political mighty and powerful to warrant penalty and retaliation. Rituals of resistance use props such as song, mirrors and a smiley face drawn on a piece of paper.

Creative Resistance

In *Ritual Process*, Victor Turner calls our attention to 'rituals of status reversal [which] make visible in their symbolic and behavioural patterns social categories and forms of grouping that are considered to be axiomatic and unchanging both in essence and in relationship' to each other (1977, p. 176). Turner considers 'rituals of status reversal' as a means of 'bringing social structure and communitas into right mutual relation' (1977, pp. 178, 183). As such, Turner implies that there is a need for both rituals of status for structure, and rituals of status reversal for the *communitas* to have an equilibrium in what he calls the 'effect of regenerating the principles of classification and ordering on which social structure rests' (1977, p. 180). In *Ritual Theory, Ritual Practice*, Catherine Bell reminds us that a rite 'affords a creative "anti-structure" that sets itself apart from the rigidity of compliance towards maintaining "social orders, hierarchies and traditional forms"' (2009, p. 21). This notion of transgressing boundaries of order and structure as creative 'anti-structure' that Bell posits resonates with the wrestling of the tensions between structural, systematic, ideological and pervasive intersectionality of oppression. This tension finds resonance with the early genesis of postcolonial thought that emerged from the margins and underbelly of empire. Postcolonial thought interrogates the formation of culture, particularly the mendacity of empire in how it dominates hegemonic modes of hermeneutical interpretation and the formations of identity and epistemology. Postcolonial sociologist Julian Go reminds us of how postcolonial thought 'recognizes that empire is everywhere' and is a 'silent shaper of our ways of seeing and knowing the world' (2016, p. 8).

The early leadership of independent Singapore inherited the colonial apparatus of governance. They used the colonial structure of its constitution and administrative governance to creatively form the national narrative of transition from a colony to an independent nation-state and thereby articulating a historical imagination of an ever-progressing national and cultural identity. In other words, they found ways to use existing structures to engineer the endeavour of nation-building, which fosters a sense of identity and belonging for an immigrant society. This strategy of establishing its sociocultural identity. Some might argue that this was an anti-structure experiment permissible by the ruling party leadership to establish and secure themselves in power. It was anti-structure to secure control over structure. Cherian George credits the careful and intentional 'calibrated coercion' of the people coupled with the 'rarity of open conflict and brutal repression' that gives the impression and sense of socio-political stability as a result of '"strong consensus" that bolsters socio-political pillars of PAP dominance' (2020, p. 42).

In such a context of politically manipulated fear, those who dare protest or engage in civil disobedience have to bear with risk-laden choices. Additionally, from a socio-legal position, the 'politics of rights' approach becomes an analytical point. According to jurisprudence law professor Lynette Chua at the National University of Singapore, 'rights are social practices' whereby their 'meanings and implications emerge' when they are 'put into action' (Chua, 2022, pp. 4–5). This is why mobilization as the rights of social practices, or 'politics of rights', is a social phenomenon as it 'emerges from the processes' that allow for 'rights claimants, their opponents and their supporters' to either 'contend, collaborate, or otherwise interact with one another' (Chua, 2022, p. 7). This connects to the idea of the Out-of-Bounds (OB) markers that is part of the 'lexicon of political repression' in Singapore (Barr, 2014, p. 34).

For Walid Jumblatt bin Abdullah, a political science professor, the challenge is how these boundaries of acceptable discourse have been both ambiguous and often redrawn. The ever-shifting boundaries, he adds, 'play a part in the psyches of both ordinary citizens and activists' (Jumblatt bin Abdullah, 2024, p. 72). As such, anti-structure is an essential part of creative resistance. The use of creative resistance as part of rituals of resistance is instrumental to communicating, engaging and empowering, offering outcomes that are emotional, thought-provoking, and system-challenging. It is through rituals of resistance that the boundaries can be redrawn and meanings are challenged.

I find Farneth's articulation of rituals helpful to unpack how rituals have agency for social and political transformation. Rituals 'give rise to communities, by creating and transforming and distributing goods within them, and it shows how rituals transform people within those communities, by shaping their habits and dispositions' (Farneth, 2023, p. 3). Another element that Farneth contributes to understanding rituals is its ability to regulate access to 'what forms of power, social capital and material groups' to 'place people (either) inside or outside of groups' (Farneth, 2023, p. 50). In other words, rituals are social constructs that help shape and influence boundaries. Boundaries, like OB markers, matter in demarcating and regulating what is acceptable or at best tolerable. Farneth contends that rituals can contribute to the formation of 'virtuous citizens as well as vicious ones' as they offer a habitus to either 'acquiescence or engagement' (Farneth, 2023, p. 147). Rituals of resistance through creative resistance use the tension and challenges of the boundary transgressing to evoke and provoke others to challenge systems of domination. Rituals of resistance are rites that redraw and transform social, private and personal boundaries. Those who read, watch and observe these rituals of resistance find themselves participants of observer-action, processing what they have witnessed as an experience that re-orients them away from the habitus they have been accustomed to. The following sections of the chapter explore ways rituals of resistance circumvent boundaries through 1) a song of lament; 2) indignity of civil disobedience; 3) calculated silence; and 4) the Pink Dot movement.

Song of Lament – Litany of Saints

In 1977, a young Singaporean lawyer, Francis Khoo Kah Siang, became a political exile because he had violated Singapore's Internal Security Act for alleged communist activities to destabilize the Singapore government. Khoo was a passionate public defender for the oppressed. Immediately after being admitted to the Singapore Bar, Khoo took on many civil rights cases. According to his widow, Dr Ang Swee Chai, 'his deep commitment to social justice was to him a Christian obligation. The first commandment is to love God; the second is to love your neighbour as yourself' (Ang, 2011). Khoo was one of several hundred Singaporeans arrested by Singapore's Internal Security and held without trial. With his desire for a more just and more democratic Singapore, Khoo paid dearly for his advocacy work that resulted in him having to live thirty-five years as a political exile never to return to Singapore.

As Khoo fled Singapore, he considered a quote by German playwright and poet Bertolt Brecht, who, like him, fled persecution. Brecht wrote the poem 'About the Dark Times' (first published in 1938), in which he asks whether there will be singing in the darkness, with the response: 'Yes, there will be singing.'[1]

Khoo, a poet and singer, penned the song 'And Bungaraya Blooms All Day' on the back of an old envelope as he was fleeing Singapore to seek political asylum:

> 'Twas the 15th of February
> At dead of the night
> They kept knocking
> And banging my door
> I slipped quietly away
> But the others could not

And I know that
I'd see them no more

They had taken so many
How many I know not
Well, there's Maha
And Mike and Samy
And there's Jing Quee
And others
The brave and the tall
And they're once more
Behind Changi wall

Then I packed
My small green bag,
Some clothes
And my toothbrush
Never knowing
What lies ahead
Though the darkness
Surrounds me
I'll hold my head high
And I know
I'm no longer afraid

O my dear bride,
My dearest
Just two weeks we're wed
Please remember
The vows that we made
I have left my homeland
For a place far away
But I know
I'll be back home someday

Oh my people,
My homeland
The ones that I love
I will never
See you again
Till the storm clouds gather

At the break of the dawn
And the bungaraya
Shall bloom in the rain[2]

It is a song of remembrance. It is a song that serves as a litany of saints for the justice advocates who were also being persecuted by the Singapore government in their involvement in fighting for democratic rights in Singapore. These were dark times. And indeed, there *will be* singing. Khoo's song was sung in a foreign land. Ironically, he sang it in the land of Singapore's former colonizer – the United Kingdom. His song was a different confession, it pierced forced silence and defied compromising his integrity. Such a different confession, different from what the Singapore Internal Security would have coerced out of Khoo.

Khoo sang this song in a BBC broadcast called *The Price of Freedom in Singapore*. Khoo's ritual of resistance was singing this song juxtaposed against the silence that the Singapore government had wanted out of him. Khoo's voice of lament was raised in his song as it tells the alternative narrative of violation, and immense personal sacrifice for the fight for democracy. It also demonstrates the creative intellect that the paternalistic parent-state that infantilizes its citizens does not celebrate. Khoo's song becomes a push back against such colonial attitudes. This song is disruptive as it humanizes the social deviants that the Singapore government made Khoo and his compatriots out to be. In the BBC television video recording (1978), Khoo spoke of his exile as the 'most traumatic experience' and that the alternative was to be coerced into making 'false confessions over television', and 'implicate my friends and endorse the government'. For Khoo, this would have been the utter betrayal of the cause. He was willing to live in exile as a sacrifice. In a sense, rituals of resistance are paid for at great cost and with great courage.

Indignity of Civil Disobedience

Protests in Singapore have been restricted to the Speakers' Corner. Freedom of speech is a constitutional right in Singapore. However, if one were to protest the government, one must request a permit from the Singapore Police Force. In the 1990s, Dr Chee Soon Juan, a leading member of an opposition party in Singapore, staged several acts of civil disobedience to deliberately violate the public assembly laws. In doing so, Dr Chee hoped his defiant actions would invite government repression. However, in an interesting turn of events, the Singapore government handled Dr Chee's civil disobedience in a very different manner. Cherian George recalls this by saying that 'Chee's lawbreaking events were usually handled on the ground not by riot police ... but by soft-spoken police officers, usually in plain clothes and with no visible weapons, not even megaphones' (George, 2020, p. 43). Such treatment of indignity is subversive. This is because the government's strategy was not to be conscripted into Dr Chee's narrative of how the government was brutal and oppressive. Nor did it want to satisfy Dr Chee's civil disobedience with dramatic photo ops and newsreels. Instead, as Cherian George reminds us, 'the government still uses authoritarian methods' just that it would rather 'settle scores later in courts' than 'on the streets' (George, 2020, p. 43).

In such a context, the critique of empire and its glaring injustices becomes suffocated. This is done with a strategy to preserve the dignified image and reputation of the nation-state. As such, calculated silence in the form of wordless protests becomes a ritual of resistance through creative resistance. Here, silence is met with silence. And this is something to consider as the silencing is not just done by the authoritarian government, but by members of society too. Silence is weaponized. So here, in this ritual of resistance, silence *is* met with silence as a way to flip the script. Hence, I consider this calculated silence because the interaction and engagement with power comes under scrutiny. Calculated silence particularly in a land where the *lingua franca* of the colonizer continues to be used. Such silence unbridles the tongue from such colonial melancholy. The wordless protest of Seelan Palay in 2018[3] and that of Jolovan Wham in 2020[4] are examples of this.

Calculated Silence: Wordless Protests

Seelan Palay, a visual artist had secured a permit from the police to perform. His act was to hold a mirror to commemorate Singapore's longest-held political prisoner, Chia Thye Poh. His performance was called, '32 Years: The Interrogation of a Mirror', bringing to remembrance Chia, who spent 23 years of detention and nine years of house arrest until his release in 1998 (Benner, 2018). The stipulation by the police permit confined Palay's act to be performed only within the Speakers' Corner. Instead, Palay processed with the mirror in his hands from the Speakers' Corner and ultimately made his way to the Parliament House and stood at the entrance of Singapore's Parliament House. When Palay was approached by the police, they said that he had committed an offence under the Public Order Act. He was asked to leave. Palay refused. His refusal led to his arrest. Palay was later found guilty of his procession from the Speakers' Corner to the Parliament House, done without securing the necessary permit. For his offence, the district court fined him SGD2,500, which he refused to pay. Instead, Palay chose to serve two weeks in jail. While it may seem that Seelan Palay's performance of holding up the mirror at the Speakers' Corner to the procession to the Parliament House to his two-week solitary prison confinement was a one-person show, it was not. Palay's solitude in performance mirrored the solitary confinement that Chia Thye Poh. His performance was not just the procession, it extended to his imprisonment. The similarity of solidarity shared between Palay and Chia is that both predicaments reflected the harsh treatment under authoritarianism.

Palay conscripts those who are part of the system that violates civil rights to become actors in his performance. The dynamic of this ritual is the distortion of the perception of who truly has power. The domination of powers here is destabilized. In *Asian City Crossings*, Danny Yung highlights how Palay's 'show' involved several 'co-performers' or 'facilitators' such as 'the police, prison wardens (and) judge' to 'carry out his act' (2021, pp. 136–7). This ritual of resistance calling out the injustice faced by a political prisoner, Chia Thye Poh, literally places a mirror in front of the very oppressing forces that justify such domination and subjugation. The transgression of Palay in his procession defies the literal boundaries set upon him – such is the role of rituals. Catherine Bell would consider Palay's performance as a ritual of embodied 'social dramas' where it has 'paradigmatic functions that make clear the deepest values of culture (2009, p. 41). Palay's defiant protest as a performance becomes a sophisticated demonstration of using the image of empire to demand redress. Palay's ritual of resistance glaringly draws attention to how pervasive systems of domination and oppression are relentless in suppressing disobedience and non-conformity. This is creative resistance flipping the script at empire.

Two years after Palay's act of resistance, on 28 March 2018, social justice activist Jolovan Wham held a cardboard with a hand-drawn smiley face to protest the treatment of two climate activists who had protested against Singapore's dependency on oil (Jha, 2020). While being held in police custody for questioning, their rights were violated. Like Palay's ritual of resistance that used creative resistance, Wham's hand-drawn smiley face on cardboard resists the silencing of social justice advocates in their efforts with silence – calculated silence. Wham held this sign for several seconds outside a police station, just enough time for a photo of himself to be taken. He then posted the photo on his social media as a sign of solidarity with the climate activists. Wham, who is a social worker, has been vocal about advocating for a variety of justice causes such as migrant workers' rights and the abolition of the death penalty had been on the government's radar. In 2022, the Singapore judicial courts fined and charged Wham for staging a one-person assembly without a permit. This was all for his hand-drawn smiley face cardboard protest. This is how the PAP-led government, in an attempt to eliminate political opposition, regulates and restrains the ability to protest in Singapore. The penalty Wham faced drew global attention as it showed the scrutiny of how a single person holding a smile face cardboard can be seen as social defiance and disruption. Clearly, this was politically manipulated fear to suppress further social justice activism that may stir renewed energy to demand greater democracy in Singapore.

Rituals of resistance as rites are not about the event or activity. Instead, as Bell argues, rites are to 'direct, inspire, or promote activity' (2009, p. 19). Both Palay and Wham's ritual of resistance could have gone unnoticed by the general public if not for the intolerance of the government being adamant in prosecuting them and thereby drawing further attention to their protests. As rituals of resistance, their acts of defiance resemble what feminist social critic bell hooks calls the 'oppositional gaze'. Palay and Wham's protests serve as the relentless, defiant 'gaze' that bell hooks considers 'a site of resistance for colonized black people globally' (hooks, 1992, p. 116). I would take the liberty to include those who occupy marginal spaces and whose backs are shoved against the wall. Palay and Wham were expected to be subordinate. Instead, they chose revolutionary resistance against fear as their way of gazing back at empire. Hence, they thwart the domination of being watched by looking back as a means to resist. This is their attempt to disentangle the webs of domination and psychological intimidation espoused by constant surveillance and police interrogation. Their wordless protest as rituals of resistance are rites demonstrating indestructible hope to secure the inalienable right to human dignity.

Pink Dot: Queer Rites as Transgressive

When it comes to media censorship in Singapore, the pro-family sentiments that the government wants to instil within its citizens mean that LGBTQIA+ people are never cast in a positive light. The Infocommunications Media Development Authority (IMDA) uses censorship to frame the narrative of LGBTQIA+ people as social degenerates and sexual deviants and their fate is often death through substance abuse, or in disparaging ways. It was only in November 2022 that the Singapore government voted in parliament to repeal Section 377A of the Penal Code that criminalizes male homosexual sex. Even with the movement towards LGBTQIA+ inclusivity, policies, regulations and laws continue to be centred around hetero-patriarchal normativity. In such a socio-political context, how do rituals of resistance employ creative resistance to invite and include voices that have been typecast as sexual deviants, social misfits and denigrated?

I feel that it is necessary to bring into conversation the Pink Dot movement that started in 2009 to support the social inclusion? of LGBTQIA+ people.[5]

I propose that the Pink Dot movement is a ritual of resistance – a queer ritual – to show subversive and transgressive compliance. It brings 'docility' into what Saba Mahmood considers strength. For 'docility' is not 'the abandonment of agency', instead it 'implies the malleability required of someone in order for her to be instructed in a particular skill or knowledge – a meaning that carries less a sense of passivity than one of struggle, effort, exertion and achievement' (Mahmood, 2005, p. 29). The Pink Dot movement flips the narrative, making that which has been devalued to be seen differently and made human – in itself a powerful and transformative movement.

The docility of the Pink Dot movement is found in its compliance with all the rules and regulations to secure their permit to gather at the Speakers' Corner. Again, what is seen as docility is malleability – transgressing by donning 'drag' and engaging in the performativity for both the government agencies that are scrutinizing and surveilling this movement, and also to give visibility to LGBTQIA+ people. In doing so, they are dislocating hetero-patriarchal normativity and presenting LGBTQIA+ people as worthy of intrinsic value and dignity. A site where 'free speech' is allowed or curtailed (depending on how one sees it) becomes a place where indignation disrupts and draws people into mobilization. The forming of a 'Pink Dot' at the end of the rally often ends with the forming of a word that brings on the theme of their annual gathering. In different years, the words were 'family', 'love' and 'repeal 377A'. At the 2022 gathering, the word formed at Pink Dot was *'majulah'*, which means 'progress' in the Malay language, the national language of Singapore. It is this very same word, *'majulah'*, that is part of Singapore's national anthem and used repeatedly by Singaporean politicians as a rallying cry calling for a future where all benefit from progress. Hence, for the Pink Dot organizers to use the same word, '*majulah*', draws attention to what progress can look like and can include.

For some, Pink Dot is Singapore's version of pride with its celebratory and affirming atmosphere. Like the original pride finding its genesis in Stonewall, Pink Dot is a protest for civil rights and a site of resistance against the denial of fullness of life. The audience for such a 'performance' is not the government. Instead, the goal for such radical rituals of resistance is to inspire, provoke and conscientize the people who have been domesticated and silenced for too long. In reflecting on the fifteen years of Pink Dot, Rachel Yeo puts it succinctly: 'Despite attempts by the state to regulate queer life and relegate it to the margins, we have found ways to be like water and find life in the cracks' (2024, p. 110).

Concluding Thoughts

I want to stress the importance and role of conscientization, which is the main thesis of Paulo Freire's *Pedagogy of the Oppressed*. Freire writes of how 'the "fear of freedom" which afflicts the oppressed, a fear which may equally well lead them to desire the role of the oppressor or bind them to the role of the oppressed, should be examined' (2000, p. 46). For Freire, conscientization is 'the deepening of the attitude of awareness' of one's social reality through reflection and action. Freire's emphasis on awareness of one's oppression becomes a source of engagement towards liberation. For the majority of Singaporeans whose habitus is meticulously manufactured by the government, their socialization positions them to be submissive, law-abiding citizens.[6]

As such, what are the ways to generate greater awareness among the people of Singapore in the areas of social, environmental, economic and gender injustices? What does the work of conscientization around such issues look like in Singapore? And how do people challenge subjugating power within such a climate of intimidation and hostility? One way to begin the groundswell towards conscientization is to create alternatives to the dominant narrative through the use of creative resistance. The acts of rituals as rites of resistance offer a pedagogy for and of the oppressed as it does the instrumental work of what Freire considers the 'critical discovery that both they and their oppressors are manifestations of dehumanization' (2000, p. 48).

Singapore is considered an authoritarian and illiberal democratic nation-state. Its state-controlled media censors and criminalizes anything that is considered detrimental to protecting the interests of the powerful elites. Those who dare challenge the status quo face political intimidation and psychological violence. As Cherian George succinctly puts it, 'the PAP's desire for "dominance" is not the issue', instead, the central problem is 'Singaporeans' weak rights and protections against the coercive powers of a domineering state armed with catch-all laws' (2020, p. 275).

In 2019, with the introduction of the Protection from Online Falsehoods and Manipulation Act (POFMA), Amnesty International and Human Rights Watch noted an increase in warnings issued to opposition politicians, social justice activists, free-lance journalists, and advocates for the abolition of the death penalty. Human Rights Watch (2021) reports that Singapore, through its 'overly restrictive criminal laws and civil defamation suits', penalizes peaceful expression and protest. What other approaches should the Singapore government embrace? Singapore's ambassador-at-large, Professor Tommy Koh (2019) calls for an embrace of those he calls 'loving critics', as Singapore does not need 'sycophants but loving critics and critical lovers'. Koh further says that 'the contestation of ideas is a necessary part of democracy' and that Singapore should 'welcome criticism as long as the critic loves Singapore and is not out to destroy Singapore'. Indeed, their voices should not be immediately deemed as anti-government. Rather, they should be welcomed and included to contribute to a robust and diverse social, political, economic and interreligious fabric of a democratic nation.

Rituals of resistance, with the use of creative resistance, are done to contest the subjugating and dehumanizing ways of empire. In rituals of resistance, it is not just Francis Khoo, Seelan Palay and Jolovan Wham as individuals who are involved. Their families, friends, priests and social networks are unseen participants. While it might seem that the sacrifice is on them to bear, it is not. There is a multiplier effect. For these are modern day prophets revealing the truth that the powerful elites want so desperately to conceal. Their sacrifices and tears are never for themselves but for the people. Additionally, their acts of creative resistance point us towards life-affirming ways in which all of creation is valued with dignity. Wordless as rituals of resistance because tongues can no longer be bridled and controlled by the colonized language. This is also where silence is met with silence. Silence then becomes a tool of power. In doing so, it amplifies the tension and contention that comes from the already oppressed margins who carry the heft of empire's insatiable demands. Empire can no longer command bodies to be contorted to serve its pleasure. Empire will no longer be entertained with performances at the indignity of the people. In rituals of resistance, song becomes disruptive; silence is met with silence – calculated silence; and queer docility is subversive, transgressive and transformative.

Notes

1 Brecht, Bertolt, 2019, *Collected Poems*, New York: Liveright Publishing Corporation, a division of W. W. Norton & Company.

2 Francis Khoo Kah Siang (1947–2011), published source unknown.
Bungaraya was the national flower of Singapore until 1981, when the Ministry of Culture selected and named the Vanda Miss Joaqium orchid to replace it.

3 Seelan Palay protested with a mirror in front of the Singapore Parliament House. No Solo Protests Allowed in Singapore: Singaporean Artist Seelan Palay has taken a one-man stand against the state's use of the Public Order Act to curb expression and dissent (Hans, 2018).

4 Jolovan Wham protested with a cardboard sign with a hand-drawn smiley face (Geddiein, 2020).

5 Pink Dot movement at Hong Lim Park, the Speakers' Corner. MC, Ali, 'Heterosexual Marriage Definition a Concern for Gay Singaporeans', *Aljazeera*, 6 September 2022, https://www.aljazeera.com/news/2022/9/6/marriage-definition-raises-new-concerns-for-lgbtq-singaporeans (accessed 15.1.2025).

6 The leaders of the People's Association Party of Singapore, including the Prime Minister and his cabinet leaders, at a political rally touting 'majulah'. Kelly Ng, 'Looking Ahead to 2018: Singapore's Political Succession to Pick Up Pace', *TodayOnline*, 26 December 2017, https://www.todayonline.com/singapore/year-ahead-spores-political-succession-pick-pace (accessed 15.1.2025).

References

Ang Swee Chai, 2011, 'Eulogy for Francis Khoo Kah Siang, October 23, 1947 to November 20, 2011', *Straits Times*, 25 November 2011, https://yoursdp.org/2011/11/26/eulogy_of_francis_khoo_by_his_wife_ang_swee_chai/ (no longer available).

Barr, Michael D., 2014, 'The Bonsai under the Banyan Tree: Democracy and Democratisation in Singapore', *Democratization* 21(1), pp. 29–48, https://doi.org/10.1080/13510347.2012.706606 (accessed 15.1.2025).

Bell, Catherine, 2009, *Ritual Theory, Ritual Practice*, New York: Oxford University Press.

Benner, T., 2018, 'Singaporean Artist Jailed After Peaceful Protest', *Aljazeera*, 12 October, https://www.aljazeera.com/news/2018/10/12/singaporean-artist-jailed-after-peaceful-protest (accessed 15.1.2025).

Bischoff, P., 2023, 'Surveillance Camera Statistics: Which Are the Most Surveilled Cities?' *Comparitech* 23 May, https://www.comparitech.com/vpn-privacy/the-worlds-most-surveilled-cities/ (accessed 15.1.2025).

Brecht, Bertolt, 2019, *Collected Poems*, New York: Liveright Publishing Corporation.

Chua, Lynnette J., 2022, *The Politics of Rights and Southeast Asia*, Cambridge: Cambridge University Press.
Farneth, Molly, 2023, *The Politics of Ritual*, Princeton: Princeton University Press.
Foucault, M., 2012, *Discipline and Punish: The Birth of the Prison*, Knopf Doubleday Publishing Group.
Freire, Paulo. 2000, *Pedagogy of the Oppressed. 30th Anniversary Edition*. New York: Continuum.
Geddiein, John, 2020, 'Singapore Activist Faces Fine Over One-Man Smiley Face Protest', *Reuters*, 20 November. https://www.reuters.com/article/idUSKBN2800DU/ (accessed 3.3.2025).
George, Cherian, 2020, *Air-Conditioned Nation Revisited: Essays On Singapore Politics*, Singapore: Ethos Books.
Go, Julian, 2016, *Postcolonial Thought and Social Theory*, New York: Oxford University Press.
Hans, Kristen, 2018, 'No Solo Protests Allowed in Singapore', *Asia Times*, 19 May, https://asiatimes.com/2018/05/no-solo-protests-allowed-in-singapore/ (accessed 21.1.2025).
hooks, bell, 1992, 'The Oppositional Gaze: Black Female Spectators', in *Black Looks: Race and Representation*, pp. 115–31, Boston: South End Press.
Human Rights Watch, 2021, 'Human Rights Watch: Singapore Events of 2021 Report', in *World Report 2022*, https://www.hrw.org/world-report/2022/country-chapters/singapore (accessed 15.1.2025).
Jha, Preeti, 2020, 'Singapore: Jolovan Wham Charged for Holding Up a Smiley Face Sign', *BBC News*, 26 November, https://www.bbc.com/news/world-asia-55068007 (accessed 15.1.2025).
Jumblatt bin Abdullah, Walid, 2024, 'The Tarik With Walid: Advocacy through Dialogue', in Constance Singam and Margaret Thomas, eds, *We Are Not The Enemy: The Practice of Advocacy in Singapore*, Singapore: Ethos Books, 2024.
Koh, Tommy, 2019, 'Singapore Does Not Need Sycophants. It Needs Loving Critics', *The Straits Times*, 3 October, https://www.straitstimes.com/opinion/singapore-does-not-need-sycophants-it-needs-loving-critics (accessed 15.1.2025).
Mahmood, Saba, 2005, *Politics of Piety: The Islamic Revival and the Feminist Subject*. Princeton, NJ: Princeton University Press.
'The Price of Freedom in Singapore with Francis Khoo Kah Siang from Singapore', 1978, *The Price of Freedom*, 25 September, London: BBC, available at: bamia285, 2012, 'The Price of Freedom in Singapore', *YouTube*, 19 February, https://www.youtube.com/watch?v=-yY5cHDVR2I (accessed 15.1.2025).
Thumboo, Edwin, 1976, *The Second Tongue: An Anthology of Poetry from Malaysia and Singapore*. Singapore: Heinemann Educational Books.
Turner, Victor, 1977, *The Ritual Process: Structure and Anti-Structure*, Ithaca, NY: Cornell University Press.
Yeo, Rachel 2024, 'Lessons from a 15-Year Journey to Repeal', in Constance Singam and Margaret Thomas, *We Are Not the Enemy: The Practice of Advocacy in Singapore*, Singapore: Ethos Books.
Yung, Danny, 2021, 'Culture of Exchange and Cultural Exchange', in Rossella Ferrari and Ashley Thorpe, eds, *Asian City Crossings: Pathways of Performance Through Hong Kong and Singapore*, London: Routledge.

PART 5

Rituals of Healing and Planetary Thriving

11

Bearing Grief and Breathing Liberation: Rituals after the Anthropocene

CLÁUDIO CARVALHAES

Prologue

The background to this chapter is the climate chaos we are now living, also called the Anthropocene. The starting point of our analysis is coloniality and its project of conquest and pillage. Within colonialism, the notion of coloniality is essential to understanding the destruction we live in under the modes of exchange developed within colonial capitalism. This capitalist process has created a spirit that orients our ways of being in a world marked by consumerism, competition and profit. According to Isabelle Stengers and Philippe Pignarre (2011), we are under the spell of this spirit of devastation, which creates many forms of death and loss. In the second part of the chapter, I call on all religions to help us with a multiplicity of rituals for the transnational dispossession of this capitalist capture. Then, I develop the notion of grief as a response to the colonial capitalist spirit and show how we must, through many forms of ritual, develop forms of healing and liberation. Finally, following Ronald Grimes (2024), I show how we need to first sense the world and understand what is happening so that rituals of healing and transformation can enact a different spirit from that of capitalism.

Introduction – Apocalypse

'It is like an apocalypse!' said one of the survivors in Hawaii after the fire that tore across Lahaina in Maui, a resort town reduced to ruins and turned to ashes. The deadliest US wildfire in 100 years with 93 people dead. An apocalypse indeed. Naomi Klein says:

> All over Maui, golf courses glisten emerald green, hotels manage to fill their pools and corporations stockpile water to sell to luxury estates. And yet, when it came time to fight the fires, some hoses ran dry ... Big corporations, golf courses and hotels have been taking water from locals for years. And there was no water left. Specifically, the water rights of Native Hawaiians, rights that a long parade of plantations, real estate developers, and luxury resorts have been stifling for nearly two centuries. As the flames approached, Tereari'i feared that, under cover of emergency, those large players might finally get their chance to grab west Maui's water for good. (Klein and Sproat, 2023)

This disaster was not 'mother nature'. It happened because of settler colonialism, capitalism and the arrival of the Anthropocene – the era in which the human element is the biggest factor in changing not only the earth's climate and crust but its core structure. Our human imprint is shifting the geological, biological and climatological patterns of the earth.

'It is like an apocalypse!' This phrase is resounding everywhere across our planet, and its utterance will increase exponentially if we don't do something. We are under a climate colonialism where capitalism is making profits out of environmental disasters and already going after local people and offering pennies on the dollar to buy their now-destroyed land that in turn will become luxury resorts and other forms of managerial profit. Doreen Martinez defines climate colonialism (2014, p. 63):

> Climate colonialism forces a re-embodiment and relocation of how, why, and who is at fault/responsible. The climate is failing to merely change. It is being colonized and forced to alter, modify, and – as catastrophes indicate – it is rebelling and resisting the assault upon it.

Climate colonialism is causing immense tragedies globally, and while the feeling of change is everywhere, it is the poorest countries that are paying the highest price. Who cares for Chad, Ethiopia, Sudan, Syria, Pakistan, Fiji, Somalia, the Sahel and the dry corridor in Central America? Only those who profit receive care.[1]

Sixty-one thousand people died of extreme heat in Europe in 2022, the year that set records for high temperatures across the planet, and fires everywhere. Over 1,000 active blazes are burning across Canada in its worst-ever wildfire season. Higher temperatures, along with reduced rainfall and relatively low humidity lead to more fires. Hot temperatures and fires continue to burn out of control around the Mediterranean, in

Algeria, Croatia, France, Greece, Italy, Portugal, Spain, Tunisia, Turkey, Peru and many places in the United States. Temperatures in some places went up 'by as much as four-and-a-half degrees Fahrenheit above pre-industrial levels' (*Democracy Now!*, 2023). The United Nations chief António Guterres (2023) said that 'the era of global warming has ended; the era of global boiling has arrived.' Perhaps he is just updating what Jesus said 2,000 years ago about a place 'where the fire never goes out' (Mark 9.43, NIV).

Recently, David Wallace-Wells (2023) welcomed us to 'the Age of the Urban Inferno'. Delhi in India has temperatures over 50°C, or exactly 52.3°C (126.1°F). 'More than 37 cities in the country recorded temperatures over 45°C' as I write this essay (Sebastian and Armstrong, 2024). Governmental decisions and organizations' work are limited; the real call should be to stop fossil fuel and its deadening consequences. However, the lobby for environmental deregulation has increased, and 2024 saw the largest investment ever in fossil fuels.[2]

Fossil fuel usage spreads disaster everywhere. A new study predicts that 'the system of ocean currents that currently distributes cold and heat between the North Atlantic region and tropics will completely stop if we continue to emit the same levels of greenhouse gases as we do today' (University of Copenhagen, 2023). And the 'Gulf Stream could collapse as early as 2025, study suggests' (Carrington, 2023). We are seeing the desertification of the soil with the potential collapse of food production due to weather instabilities and climate change. The complex issues with water give us two paradoxical results: the disappearance of freshwater and rivers, the overflowing of rivers, and the rise of oceans. The once-balanced system that kept the earth working is now being completely shattered.

We exploit every biome for profit, resulting in the disappearance of the animals, insects and plants that sustain us. New viruses and pandemics will appear. The earth, totally depleted, will no longer provide us with the most basic things to live. We are living in a new colonization period with countries like China, the United States, Canada and the European Union now pillaging entire nations under commercial contracts. But now the situation is much worse than in 1492 because we have the machinery to create massive destruction in a very short amount of time. Have you seen the machines that kill trees? They embrace the tree, and in a few seconds, they kill the tree.

The earth is hurt and in mourning. And we must realize as soon as possible that whatever happens to the land happens to us. Our bodies belong to the earth, and whatever happens to the body of the earth happens to our own bodies. In order to gain this consciousness, we must engage in new Anthropocene rituals of grief and liberation while attending to the ways our world is moving right now. To prepare ourselves for our rituals, we must take a deep and painful look at the causes of our deadening collective forms of living.

Colonialism/Coloniality

Colonialism is the historical process of violently uprooting people and the earth, exploiting, dominating and pillaging groups of people, animals and the land. Coloniality is the power that sustains colonialism. Colonialism and capitalism, which I will discuss in the following section, take away our freedom by individualizing our sense of freedom. We lose sight of the fact that freedom is only possible if it is a collective movement where everyone must be free. Philosopher Vladimir Safatle (2023) says that for the Greeks, freedom or liberty was based on three axes: 1) autonomy – the sense that we have our own *nomos* or law to live; 2) autarky – not being a slave to our passions; 3) autochthony – having a territory to oneself.[3] Colonialism is founded on the radical and violent loss of these three aspects: it replaces our own law with the law of somebody else; it radically transforms our desires and passions to that which the new law demands; and it takes away our territory, our home, our deepest belonging.

We could define colonialism with the words of Jesus in John 10.10 (NRSvue): 'The thief comes only to steal and kill and destroy.' In 1492, a thief came from Europe to steal the land, kill the indigenous people, and destroy everything. They wanted to own everything, use the local people as slaves, and live off the destruction of other people's lives and worlds. When colonialism came to the United States, the indigenous people were destroyed. Moving towards the West, natural landscapes were deeply affected; animals lost their habitat; the bison, for instance, were brutally murdered. Thus, colonialism is the destruction not only of people but also of the land and all the non-human species. The religious, economic, social and ecological landscapes were all shaped by one colonial project of domination. Forgetting the memories of our ancestors and how they used to live, we still live under the larger influence of white European colonialism, with its patriarchal rules, plantation projects, and capitalist economic and political systems.

Louis S. Warren writes: 'At least since the founding of Plymouth Plantation, English settlers had seen the colonization of North America as a sacred project commanded by God – the redemption of the garden from the wilderness' (2017, p. 49). Religious forms of coloniality still mark us. The discourse of capital, of profit, of development, of growth has become the new sacred form of the fullness of life. The theological idea of manifest destiny, whereby God promised a new land for the people, still rings loud in the religious battles of the US. The spread of Christian Zionism is everywhere, and the conquering of the West as a promise of God to the colonizers still holds true. What it seems we have not noticed yet is that every time God promises land to somebody, some other people who live in these promised lands will have to pay the price with their own lives.

Whereas colonialism puts us always in the wrong place, in a strange land, it has replaced the fact that we belong to the earth. We do not own the land; capitalism made us move from place to place without any connection to the land and its non-human living beings, with devastating results. Colonialism and capitalism produce brutality, devastation and melancholy, disasters and sadness, and create absences of all kinds. Melancholy is that continuous attachment to things we lost – lost objects, people, things, places – the lingering of unfinished process of loss that stays with us (Freud, 1966). The colonial process creates melancholia but does not allow us the processes of grief, for capitalism has taken away the presence of death. We do not have time to mourn or look death in the eyes; we do not have rituals for the dead. Sadness is the circulating emotion of capitalism, and the absence of deep thinking, wonder and awe, self-awareness and relationality are the main modes of being in our time.

Colonial Capitalism

Capitalism provides a monolithic ideal that leads to white supremacy, class struggle, heteronormativity, racial annihilation and human domination over other living beings. The result is that 1% of the global population has more money than more than half of the 8 billion people on earth. In every city in the United States, the empire of capitalism, we witness horrifying social inequalities and a growing population of unhoused people, hunger and malnourishment, job insecurity and lack of access to healthcare. Nancy Fraser argues that from the slave-based plantation capitalism of the seventeenth through nineteenth centuries to the Jim Crow industrialized capitalism of the twentieth century, 'capitalism has always been deeply entangled with racial oppression'

(2023, p. 27). Jails now are a multi-billion-dollar profit-making industry. By criminalizing people, one can build buildings to earn money from people's misery.

Capitalism creates monocultures of people, land and animals, excluding diversity in our societies and the fields. Out of thousands of grains and plants we have in the world, only a few major grains are considered by the market: rice, wheat and maize (corn). Out of a vast diversity of animals, only a few are exploited: chickens, cattle, pigs and sheep. The structures of slavery plantations continue through monocultures in our societies. People of colour, women, LGBTQIA+ communities, children, the elderly: all are targeted for either profit or destruction. Capitalism fosters emotional, social, cultural and sexual patterns that we, mostly unconsciously, introject and follow. Through capitalism we are suffused with competition, mistrust, destruction, predation, brutalism and cannibalism. Profit, abuse, privatization, exploration, devastation and endless progress, conquering and growth are all markers of this system.

Moreover, capitalism is not only an economic system, but also has emotional, spiritual and theological implications. Walter Benjamin showed us how capitalism is a religion that tries to solve afflictions, anxieties and problems that the system itself creates (Benjamin, 2004). The inner spirit of capitalism is based on the need to buy something. The worship space of the capital is the temples/stores of merchandize where people exude their souls by consuming things amidst priests and priestesses, managers of this religion. And the worship service of capitalism is endless and everywhere: in stores, on your computer 24/7, and in the notifications we receive from stores to buy new things.

The Spiritual Spell of Colonial Capitalism

Capitalism has kidnapped our spirits, implanting a spirit of anger, greed, division, fear and self-destruction. Capitalism creates a radical socio-economic rupture between people, extenuates the social conditions of living, and places people in very vulnerable situations, creating uncertainty regarding life itself. That is the perfect nest for fascism to show up and grow. Capitalism has taken over our metaphysics. We measure ourselves by what we have: the jobs we have, the houses we own, the places we live, and the money we have. The meaning of our lives rests in the ability to accumulate while it implants its own forms of anguish and release. We get depressed, bored, frustrated, exhausted. And we find relief by purchasing material things, by working more, by staying longer on the internet. However, all these forms of relief do not last because they are not related to our deepest desires but the simulacra of our desires. And when one does not know one's desire, one will always feel the anguish, the boredom, the emptiness, the frustration of life again. This is an endless cycle.

Capitalism as a religion is a totalizing system. The capitalist religion uses institutions, political speeches and religious leaders to destroy trust in each other. It focuses on the individual and not on the collective. The spirituality of capitalism is our own lonely survival. Pignarre and Stengers argue in a more speculative and spectral way that capitalism is, in fact,

> a system of sorcery without sorcerers (thinking of themselves as such), a system operating in a world in which judges that sorcery is only a simple 'belief', a superstition that therefore doesn't necessitate any adequate means of protection. (Pignarre and Stengers, 2011, p. 40)

Capitalism is a sorcery and divination that captures and possesses us all. Sorcery and divination are like cultural tentacles that enter our bodies through several forms of spells.

Capitalist sorcery works with a plethora of alchemies to 'capture' our bodies, minds and souls through a culture of 'spells'. These spells desensitize our connections with the land and reorient our lives endlessly towards our narcissistic wound, reshuffling our most fundamental beliefs and religions while freezing all forms of free and critical thinking. It makes us workers of the system as it disarticulates and even paralyses most forms of defiant social action. There is a feeling that there is no 'outside' of this system. Bodies, souls, minds, practices and desires – everything is captured. All we have left is personal achievements, individual liberty and self-happiness.

I further argue that capitalism has stolen God and God's many names such as Yahweh, the Holy Spirit, Olodumare, Allah, Buddha and every form of spirituality to offer false peace so that we will continue to buy. In my Christian tradition, we have huge social differences within our churches. Jesus Christ has become a fantasy, or better said, a fetish. We don't believe in Jesus, a peasant, social agitating revolutionary, but rather, a sort of divine someone whom we consume through bread and wine, Christian lollipops and glib music, while we continue to be under the spell of capitalism and colonialism extracting all the life of the earth, oppressing women, LGBTQIA+ people, and immigrants and smashing poor countries. There is no space for healing, for fixing mistakes, for offering forgiveness, for equality and justice.

For generations to come, the future is already completely compromised. That is why Greta Thunberg and other young leaders are demanding politicians change their ways, so their generation can have a future. There is a youth movement spreading everywhere. The United States witnessed what Generation Z did in Montana. Sixteen young activists argued that the US state of Montana was responsible for climate change impacting their lives. A Montana judge found that the state violated their right to a 'clean and healthful environment', which the state constitution guarantees (Brown, 2024). They are showing that it is possible to change this. Ecuador recently voted to decide whether they would allow oil exploration in their Amazon Forest, the Yasuní National Park. Ecuador is the only country that has given the status of 'rights' to the land in its own constitution. Imagine that! Yes, rivers, mountains, forests have the same rights as humans do. Ecuador's constitution (2008, revised in 2021) says in Article 71:

> Nature or Pacha Mama, where life is reproduced and fulfilled, has the right to full respect for its existence and the maintenance and regeneration of its vital cycles, structure, functions and evolutionary processes.

In a historical decision, 59 per cent of the population said no to this so-called 'progress of drilling'. Immediately the newspapers and corporate leaders proclaimed that this decision would impoverish already vulnerable communities. Liars! This type of progress never means money or support or development for poor communities.

If religion is to claim a fundamental place in our societies, our theologies and religious practices have to tackle capitalism and coloniality. When the apostle Paul appeals to his readers 'to present your bodies as a living sacrifice, holy and acceptable to God, which is your reasonable act of worship' (Rom. 12:1, NRSVue), offering bodies is not to find redemption by suffering. Instead, it is to understand our bodies as larger territories and consider our bodies as the bodies of other beings. It means offering ourselves to protect and care deeply for all the non-human beings near us. Their living bodies are my living body as well.

The earth is groaning for us to change our ways of thinking, feeling-thinking and engaging the world. To have our minds renewed (Rom. 12.2) means to have the earth as our main concern, to learn with the indigenous people that 'the struggle for the earth is the mother of all struggles' (Sonia Guajajara, 2019). If we gain this new mind, we will also need to have a new heart with new feelings. And we will need to have a new body for this new life, living in sync with the land which we inhabit. To renew our minds is to accept, engage and love the whole world as God's own body. To renew our minds is to renew our relationship with the animals, the waters, the insects, the mountains and the plants. It is a way to discern how God breathes in and from each leaf, each worm, each bird, each racoon, each tree, each plant, each living being around us.

We must put aside the centrality of human presence, agency, role and value. Even when we speak about racial, gender and sexual justice and intersectionality, we are not concerned with justice for non-humans. Our anthropocentric way of being is completely detached from the earth, and it engenders a disaster. When progress meets human centrism, we arrive at the place we are right now: impending death. We have become the people of death, sugar-coated with narcissistic stories, wrapped up in the ideology of manifest destiny and self-assured of our entitlements. Our situation is so dramatic that our imagination has been captured by the spells of colonial capitalism. As Frederic Jameson said, 'It's easier to imagine the end of the world than the end of capitalism' (cited in Fisher, 2022, p. 1.).

Rituals of Dispossession

I call on all religions to help us create a multiplicity of services for the transnational dispossession of capitalism capture. I call upon the magic of every religion to undo the spells of our time and help us cast out from our bodies these spirits who eat us alive without mercy. We need chants, songs, meditations, prayers, gestures, spells, anointments and body moves to wash us anew and cleanse our drive for money, accumulation, individual selves and anthropocentrism. We need to be transformed by the renewal of our collective minds.

Our crisis is not only moral but spiritual as well. We need to perceive forms of fugue and the hiddenness of bodies that survive. We need to learn the spiritualities and the gods and spirits of the land we inhabit, learn the law of the land with indigenous people, and see what movements such as the Landless Movement in Brazil or the Zapatistas in Mexico are doing to offer other possible worlds. As we cast out the demons from ourselves, perhaps we might consider casting out the demons of monotheism, to learn to live with the presence of other deities, spirits and gods. Antônio Bispo dos Santos from Brazil says that monotheisms create *cosmophobia*, which means the fear of living in other worlds, the worlds of people different from us, and the worlds of animals, vegetation and biomes. He says:

> At this moment, the Bible's colonial god – Euro-Christian, monotheistic – deterritorialized his people. When he cursed the land to colonialist people, he said that his people could not even touch the land. When he said that the land would offer them weeds and thorns, he said that the people could eat neither the fruits, nor the leaves, nor anything that this land offered. When he said that these people had to eat by the sweat of their brow, at that very moment he created work as an action of synthesizing nature. At the same time, he also created a disease that I call 'cosmophobia': the fear of the cosmos, the fear of god. The monotheist Euro-Christian subject feels hopeless. (Bispo dos Santos, 2023)

If there is to be love, fear must be cast away. No fear of other gods, no fear of other worlds filled with other spirits. This is how we can get dispossessed of our fears. Here I suggest some liturgical gestures to dispossess ourselves from the need to own the earth or anything in it.

- We rise and bless the skies, the light, the wind, the birds flying, the rain falling, the air we breathe, the planets, the stars, the galaxies, universes and black holes.
- We bow and honour every single being that inhabited that land, every spirit that lived in this land where we are standing.
- Bowing, we also mourn the death of every single person, animal, mountain, tree, field, river and ocean.
- We touch the ground and remember we are soil, humus, underground life, rock, fossil, seeds, worms and darkness.
- We breathe in with all of the living beings next to us, wishing them full life, joy, loving kindness and safety. We breathe out and we let go of what possess us with the rush to go buy things.

We do this to learn how to live within so many worlds around us. We do this not to consume, to own, to have, but to relate, to interconnect, to belong. We do this to dispossess ourselves of an economy of profit and exploitation and move towards an economy of reciprocity and gift.

In dispossessing myself of the fear and dreadlock of monotheisms, I honour polytheisms of many forms. I beg for local spiritualities, pantheisms of all kinds where the world of a bee would be as important as the life of my children, the flight of the hummingbird would be as important as the life of my mother and father; that the walk of the jaguar in the

Amazon forest would be more important than the oil companies who are destroying their homes; the presence of trees would be more important than my church buildings; and the course of a river would be more important than sacramental theology.

If we are to survive this colonial, capitalist world, we must think of an anti-racist, feminist, other-than-human, trans-environmental, anti-capitalist and anticolonial eco-politics. One that lets us mourn the loss of people, animals, plants, rivers and mountains with affection and mutual transformation. An eco-politics where our ancestors are not only humans but also the animals, territories, rivers and spirits of the land who came before us. I ask us to hear the prophecies of the earth. It is telling us to change our ways or else. It is telling us to pay attention to the land and to enter relationships with every being around us. The earth is telling us to consider every living being as a full being, with its honour and glory.

Bearing Grief and Breathing Liberation

Advocating many forms of ritual, forms of healing and liberation, I propose a ritual of mourning and breathing liberation. We have lost our ability to grieve, to mourn, to ponder our losses, to lick our wounds, to think about our lacerations, to wash our bodies with tears, to give time for our pain. Capitalism has normalized our sorrows, has taught us to brush off our hurt, and disregard our pain. We have gotten used to breathing many forms of death. By losing contact with our ancestors, our contemporary forms of religion have lost the power to relate, connect and heal. Our souls are piling up ashes of ancient worlds. While holding the prevalent notion of sin only attached to the individual spiritual mode of being in Christian theology, we push death aside. Anthony B. Pinn asks, 'What does it mean to mourn black death in a country that doesn't recognize black life?' (2023). I continue to argue that in a country marked by colonial capitalism where the annihilation of indigenous, Black, brown, red and yellow people has never been properly mourned we have to move beyond the melancholic places of stagnation. How can we find ways to mourn processes of death that had no tears? How can we shed tears for that which we never cried for? How can the spirits of the land help us shed some tears?

If we learn to be still and know, we will be able to see what is alive and what is dying within us and around us. Then, and only then can we learn to grieve and process our grief.

Safatle (2023) argues that:

> We should do our mourning as the elaboration of a loss as it throws us in front of an abyss, but also elaborate the loss as a function of transformation, as that which can reconstitute radically the field of experience. It does not mean the substitution of an object but a transformation of the mode of presence of the object. To be able to elaborate its presence not as we thought or wanted but open up other forms of presence. Other forms of presence. Not material physical.

In this way we expand the presence of the object beyond the totality of a present that vanishes without value, tribute or form of transformation. If we can extend some of our grief into past, present and future, we will see that the voices of our ancestors will come back fully. We will see that their stories are alive, that what they gave us can move us into the future. And we will see that our future is ancestral, that is, to cultivate ourselves and the land the way our grandparents did can help us foster a future for the new generations. In the words of Ailton Krenak we will have no future without learning from the sustainable cosmovisions of the past (2024, p. 7).

Expanding the totality of presence across time, we enter the process of bearing grief and breathing liberation by feeling ecological loss. Mick Smith defines the ecologist as 'someone who is touched by this loss in such a way as to mourn the toll of extinction instituted by human exemptionalism and exceptionalism. She is bereft and yet also understands that this feeling, her being touched by irrevocable loss, is itself a matter of realizing the existence of a sense of an ecological *and* ethical *and* political community with other species' (2013, p. 29). Ashlee Cunsolo who works with ecological disasters expresses the feeling of being bereft in a similar way:

> I felt adrift in waves of sadness, grief, loss, and pain, unanchored from my life, isolated from those around me, and unsure of how to process what I was experiencing. It was a sense of almost abyssal sorrow, without an idea of how to move forward, or how to see beyond the edges, the fringes of these feelings. It was a grief I did not expect or anticipate. Yet it was there waiting for me in the morning when I awoke, there at night as I drifted off, in my dreams and a constant companion throughout the day. And it was related to ecological loss. (Cunsolo and Landman, p. 137)

Since the land is all we are and all we have, the mourning of the land is deeply complex and difficult. Therefore, we need to learn to mourn as a constitutive element in the process of ecological restructuring. This means that we must continue to name the losses of the earth everywhere – name our alienation from the earth, our disconnection from the land, our arrogance as humans. Each name is a breath of liberation. Thus, we need to learn the names of the vegetation around us, the plants, trees, animals, mountains and rivers of our landscape so we can call them by name and once they die we say out loud: *PRESENTE!* Knowing our alienation and disconnection from the land is what will open the gates for healing, mutuality, and reciprocal restoration. To know what has brought us to this place of fire and destruction is to learn the processes of liberation. That is the work of a spirit free from the sources of capitalism.

I argue for breathing liberation in the midst of grieving by way of carrying the Holy Spirit, as well as learning with indigenous people that every place carries presences and spirits that care for the land. For example, when there is a mountaintop removal in the Appalachian Mountains, all of the spirits, gods and deities run and leave the land empty. If they leave, no life is possible in that place unless they are brought back. It is the Spirit who helps us pay attention to the land and renew our minds, which means expanding our subjectivity beyond our own sense of a discrete self. To change our subjectivity is to compose our very sense of being with other species, other beings and other landscapes. It is to suffer and rejoice fully with other beings as ourselves. This is why I argue for perceiving the presence of the Spirit within us, simultaneously opening ourselves to other forms of presence. Carrying the spirit of life is learning to be still and pay attention to what surrounds us, waiting for life around us to start manifesting itself to us. It is listening to all of the sounds beyond human sounds, feeling that there is a deeper relation between us and the ground we are standing on, the skies under which we wonder, and the rivers who give us the waters for our survival, the plants who give us the air to breathe, the bees and butterflies who pollinate all of the fields that prepare the food we eat. Carrying the spirit of life is to feel a new visitation of the spirit opening new forms of life within and before us.

Conclusion

I led a ritual with plants at Union Theological Seminary that was known as *Plantgate* (Carvalhaes, 2019). In that ritual, people were asked to consider plants as full beings and to be called 'he', 'she', 'they' and not 'it'. We were following the suggestions of indigenous and botanist thinker Robin Kimmerer (2015). During the ritual we were asked to talk to the plants and say how we felt about plants, and how we could change our relationship to plants. A student then said: 'I don't know how to relate to you in this subjective way. I am afraid that if I do, I might discover a level of pain that I don't know whether I can bear.'

In the process of grief and breathing liberation, something must happen: we have to learn to hold inner contradictions and opposite feelings together. Philosopher Julia Kristeva witnesses that pain was 'the hidden side of my philosophy; its mute sister' (1992, p. 4). We must hold our full despair and most radical hope, our knowing and our immense unknowing, our very distraught self and our longings for relation, our vulnerability and our small movements of change and transformation, our frailty and our power, our prayers and our curses, God's Spirit and the spirits of the land. But isn't this what we need to carry every day? As Timothy Morton says, 'now is a time for grief to persist, to ring throughout the world' (2007, p. 185). Milly Lacombe, a Brazilian queer writer states (2024): 'Unfortunately, one does not leave a legacy without this legacy also being the wreckage of oneself.' We offer ourselves, even our wreckage, as a living sacrifice to the land and other beings. This might be our legacy.

As Andrew Solomon says, 'To be creatures who love, we must be creatures who despair at what we lose' (Solomon, 2001, p. 17; Sandilands, 2017, p. 146). Deprived of the presence of the Spirit of God and deprived of a natural landscape of belonging, an economy of reciprocity, and deep forms of sleep and dreams, we have plunged into a social, existential, political and ecological abyss that seems to have no way out. When we despair, however, we do not grieve alone. We are a network of beings and collectives, and every process of mourning and liberation must also be collective. That in itself is a huge challenge since our economic system only allows individual processes of joy and grief. We must develop affection in order to learn to deal with our pain when we face disasters and calamities. One of the characters in a novel by Portuguese writer Valter Hugo Mãe said, 'Affection must be nurtured for a suffering that has helped us build happiness. Never cultivate the pain, but remember it with respect, for having been an inducer of improvement, for having made us be better' (Mãe 2013, p. 235). Ronald Grimes helps us understand rituals as ways of sensing the land and all its living beings around us. Through rituals we can sense the earthly death and life around us, and then we can create forms of mourning, healing, sustenance and transformation that can enact a spirit different from that of capitalism (Grimes, 2024).

I remember a time when my life felt like it was falling apart. I had to wait months for something to happen. I had no idea why it was happening but it had the potential to destroy my life. There was a friend of mine who lit a candle every single day for me at night. He would send me a picture of the candle every single night. It was the flickering of that flame that kept me going. To bear grief and breathe liberation might be lighting a candle when we have no idea what will happen. Perhaps we can start by lighting a candle for the trees ripped apart near our homes because of a new development in town. Perhaps we can light a candle with and for those who fight the companies that throw garbage and poison in our rivers, polluting our waters and destroying the future of our children. May every lit candle be a cry of sorrow and hope to the world. May we take care of the land we live in. Mourn the death of every animal killed on the road. If possible, offer them a burial. Yes, create rituals! Rituals that help you bear grief and breathe liberation. When you do your rituals, consider the following:

- Where are you? How much do you know/love this land?
- What is the condition of life that you envision for this place and all its people, animals, birds, plants, trees and rivers?
- In your imagination and discourse, are there other species among 'us'?
- What language do we need to speak to engage other people in this earth-loving movement, and what are the languages we need to learn in order to listen to the birds, to hear the trees, to listen to the waters, and to hear the cries of the raccoons?
- What practices of grief do you need to carry out in this place where you live? Who, among all beings, are dying or have died that need to be grieved?
- What forms of liberation/breathing/healing do we need to receive from the land, and what forms of liberation/breathing/healing do we need to breathe back?
- What kinds of emotions and desires do we foster and allow to circulate in these rituals?
- What kind of transformation does this ritual produce?

Rituals can help us reorganize our lives altogether. Bring back the future, the possibility of a future for the next generations, re-memorialize our past, renew our repetition, offer the circulation of social memory and the expansion of our subjectivity into other forms of belonging. The ritual space is a charged space where the political, social and ecological character of the work of mourning is done together. Doing ritual will carry the fullness of the Spirit of God as we continue to dispossess ourselves of the spirit of capitalism and enthuse ourselves with the spirit of the land. Can we bear grief and breathe liberation?

Notes

1 The new forms of colonialism are happening today with the destruction and stealing of the land, ethnic cleansing and genocide going on in Palestine.

2 Every year, the big monstrous oil companies like ExxonMobil, Chevron, Shell, ConocoPhillips, Valero Energy, BP, Phillips 66, EOG Resources, Cheniere, Pioneer Natural Resources, Occidental Petroleum, Diamondback Energy, Marathon Oil, Hess and others are profiting billions of dollars amidst record temperatures (Artis, 2024).

3 Vladimir Safatle (2023), speaking at the book launch of Christian Dunker, *Lutos Infinitos e Finitos*, São Paulo: Paidós.

References

Artis, Zanagee, 2024, 'Big Oil Made Billions Amidst the Hottest Year on Record, Natural Resources Defense Council (NRDC)', https://www.nrdc.org/bio/zanagee-artis/big-oil-made-billions-amidst-hottest-year-record (accessed 15.1.2025).

Benjamin, Walter, 2004, 'Capitalism as Religion', in Marcus Bullock and Michael W. Jennings, eds, *Selected Writings,* vol. 1: *1913–1926*, Cambridge, MA: Harvard University Press.

Bispo dos Santos, Antônio, 2023, 'We Belong to the Land. Insights from a Quilombola Thinker on Brazil's State-Sanctioned Violence and the Power of Oral Traditions', *Futuress*. April 12, https://futuress.org/stories/we-belong-to-the-land/ (accessed 15.1.2025).

Brown, David, 2024, 'Montana's Climate Change Lawsuit May See Sequels Across America, State Court Report', 9 July, https://statecourtreport.org/our-work/analysis-opinion/montanas-climate-change-lawsuit-may-see-sequels-across-america (accessed 15.1.2025).

Carrington, Damian, 2023, 'Gulf Stream Could Collapse as Early as 2025, Study Suggests', *The Guardian*, https://www.theguardian.com/environment/2023/jul/25/gulf-stream-could-collapse-as-early-as-2025-study-suggests (accessed 15.1.2025).

Carvalhaes, Cláudio, 2019, 'Why I Created a Chapel Service Where People Confess To Plants', *Sojourners*, 26 September, https://sojo.net/articles/why-i-created-chapel-service-where-people-confess-plants (accessed 15.1.2025).

Cunsolo, Ashlee, and Karen Landman, eds, 2017, *Mourning Nature: Hope at the Heart of Ecological Loss and Grief*, Montreal and Kingston: McGill-Queen's University Press.

Democracy Now!, 2023, 'Study Finds Human Activity Responsible for Record July Heat Waves', *Democracy Now!*, https://www.democracynow.org/2023/7/25/headlines/study_finds_human_activity_responsible_for_record_july_heat_waves (accessed 15.1.2025).

Ecuador Constitution, 2021, https://www.constituteproject.org/constitution/Ecuador_2021 (accessed 15.1.2025).

Fisher, Mark, 2022, *Capitalist Realism: Is There No Alternative?* Winchester, UK: Zer0 Books.

Fraser, Nancy, 2023, *Cannibal Capitalism*. New York: Verso Books.

Freud, Sigmund, 1966, 'Mourning and Melancholia', in James Strachey, trans, *The Standard Edition of the Complete Psychological Works of Sigmund Freud*, xiv: 1914–1916, trans. James Strachey, London: Hogarth Press, pp. 243–58. On the History of the Psycho-Analytic Movement, Papers on Metapsychology and Other Works.

Grimes, Ronald, 2024, 'A Sense for Ritual', Circling the Deep [blog], 27 February, https://circle.twohornedbull.ca/a-sense-for-ritual/ (accessed 15.1.2025).

Guajajara, Sonia, 2019, 'Sonia Guajajara na ONU: "A luta pela Mãe Terra é a mãe de todas as lutas"', September 27. *Mídia NINJA*, https://www.pressenza.com/pt-pt/2019/09/sonia-guajajara-na-onu-a-luta-pela-mae-terra-e-a-mae-de-todas-as-lutas/ (accessed 15.1.2025).

Guterres, António, 2023, 'Press Conference by Secretary-General António Guterres at United Nations Headquarters', United Nations, https://press.un.org/en/2023/sgsm21893.doc.htm (accessed 15.1.2025).

Kimmerer, Robin Wall, 2015, *Braiding Sweetgrass: Indigenous Wisdom, Scientific Knowledge and the Teachings of Plants*. Minneapolis: Milkweed Editions.

Klein, Naomi, and Kapua'ala Sproat, 2023, 'Why Was There no Water to Fight the Fire in Maui?' August 17, *The Guardian*, https://www.theguardian.com/commentisfree/2023/aug/17/hawaii-fires-maui-water-rights-disaster-capitalism (accessed 15.1.2025).

Krenak, Ailton, 2024, *Ancestral Future*, New York: Polity.

Kristeva, Julia, 1992, *Black Sun: Depression and Melancholia*, New York: Columbia University Press.

Lacombe, Milly, 2024, 'Infelizmente, Não Se Deixa Um Legado Sem Que Esse Legado Seja Também Um Destroço De Si Mesmo', *Universo On Line*, 25 March, https://www.uol.com.br/esporte/colunas/milly-lacombe/2024/03/25/vini-jr-e-um-legado-deixado-sobre-os-destrocos-de-si-mesmo.htm (accessed 15.1.2025).

Mãe, Walter Hugo, 2013, *O Filho de Mil Homens*, São Paulo: Cosac Naify.

Martinez, Doreen E., 2014, 'The Right to Be Free of Fear: Indigeneity and the United Nations', *Wicazo Sa Review* 29(2), pp. 63–87, https://doi.org/10.5749/wicazosareview.29.2.0063 (accessed 15.1.2025).

Morton, Timothy, 2007, *Ecology without Nature: Rethinking Environmental Aesthetics*, Cambridge, MA: Harvard University Press.

Pignarre, Philippe, and Isabelle Stengers, 2011, *Capitalist Sorcery: Breaking the Spell*, New York: Palgrave Macmillan.

Pinn, Anthony B., 2023, 'What Does It Mean to Mourn Black Death in a Country That Doesn't Recognize Black Life?', *April Online*, 3 January, https://www.aprilonline.org/what-does-it-mean-to-mourn-black-death-in-a-country-that-doesnt-recognize-black-life/ (accessed 15.1.2025).

Safatle, Vladimir, 2023, participant in Christian Dunker, 'Live de lançamento do livro Lutos Finitos e Infinitos (Christian Dunker)', *YouTube*, 12 August, https://www.youtube.com/watch?v=-5sROxMJQbU (accessed 15.1.2025).

Sandilands, Catriona, 2017, 'Losing My Place. Landscapes of Depression', in Ashlee Cunsolo, Karen Landman, eds, *Mourning Nature: Hope at the Heart of Ecological Loss and Grief*, Montreal: McGill-Queen's University Press.

Sebastian, Meryl, and Kathryn Armstrong, 2024, 'Delhi "unbearable" as temperatures near 50C', 29 May, *BBC News*, https://www.bbc.com/news/articles/c166xxd4y36o (accessed 15.1.2015).

Smith, Mick, 2013, 'Ecological Community, the Sense of the World, and Senseless Extinction', *Environmental Humanities* 2(1), pp. 21–41.

Solomon, Andrew, 2001, *The Noonday Demon: An Atlas of Depression*, New York: Scribner.

University of Copenhagen, 2023, 'Gloomy Climate Calculation: Scientists Predict a Collapse of the Atlantic Ocean Current to Happen Mid-Century', https://news.ku.dk/all_news/2023/07/gloomy-climate-calculation-scientists-predict-a-collapse-of-the-atlantic-ocean-current-to-happen-mid-century/ (accessed 15.1.2025).

Wallace-Wells, David, 2023, 'The Age of the Urban Inferno', *New York Times*, https://www.nytimes.com/2023/08/16/opinion/maui-fire-lahaina-hawaii.html (accessed 15.1.2025).

Warren, Louis S., 2017, *God's Red Son*, New York: Basic Books.

12

Release from the Tyranny of the Small Self: A Modern Subject's Initiation into the Power of Indigenous Ritual

S. LILY MENDOZA

Introduction

This chapter takes a big picture understanding of ritual not as – in its origins – a human-initiated endeavour intended primarily for human edification or succour, but as a response – one that takes from the earth's own requisite ethic of elegance, beauty, generosity, reciprocity, courtesy and subtlety. And at the core of this earth ethic is an honouring and respect of limits that beings (both human and otherwise) still intimately connected to earth's heartbeat continue to observe amid the assault (and insults) of our disenchanted modern culture. The narration here will be both analytical (drawing on insights from indigenous and native studies) and autobiographical (from the author's own first-hand encounter with indigenous ritual). I will argue that a return to a ritual way of living – far from serving merely as a kind of performative mimicry and surface fascination with the proliferating traditions of modern shamanic and other spiritual healing traditions outside Christianity in our time – is a deep probing into the bigger questions of the requisites for planetary thriving, our species' role (as only one among many) in keeping the grand symphony of life going, and what the recovery of a much bigger sense of self – engendered in ritual enactments – augurs for healing, renewal and transformation in our time.

A Ritual Initiation

It was the first morning of an organizing team retreat that I was part of at one of our members' homes in Espanola, New Mexico. Upon hearing of the site of our retreat, our resident shaman told us in no uncertain terms, 'Espanola is the home of the Pueblo people. The Pueblo people are a sun people. You must do a sun ceremony.'

The outfit that we were part of is a non-profit organization called the Center for Babaylan Studies (*babaylan* being one of the terms referencing the spiritual healing tradition shared by the Philippines' indigenous communities), one that has sparked a movement for decolonization and indigenous reclamation among diasporic Filipinos around the world. We have been learning about our respective ancestral lineages in the Philippines (and elsewhere – for those of us that are mixed) and at the same time learning what it means to live in a sacred relationship with the natural world from native and other indigenous traditions on Turtle Island that we understand is the heart of indigeneity.

On that first morning of our retreat, we made it a point to wake before dawn – without any real discussion of what we wanted to do; all we knew was that we were to 'do a sun ceremony' in honour of the Pueblo people on whose land we were holding the retreat. Rubbing the sleep from our eyes on our very first morning, the dark of night still blanketing the place, we don our *malongs* (long skirts), deck ourselves with beads and other native adornments from our ancestral homeland lineages, and, taking our native musical instruments with us, all twelve of us march out of the house to a small nearby clearing to prepare to greet Grandfather Sun as he rises from his abode on the horizon. The morning air is cool and crisp, not bitingly so, but gently, caressing our bare faces. Lining up facing east, we stand in breathless silence, awaiting the peeking of the first rays of sunlight. Then, at the manifest crowning of the magnificent orb slowly emerging out of the womb of night, as if to a person, we spontaneously break into joyful shouts and singing, dancing wildly in a circle while banging gongs, shaking rattles, and whatever other musical instruments we have with us. Before long, tears come streaming down our faces, simultaneously laughing and weeping, ecstatic with orgiastic joy as we give praise and gratitude to this wondrous Magnificence not just with our lungs, but with our animal bodies. How have I not seen how miraculous a sunrise could be until now? By now, Grandfather Sun has risen steadily above the horizon, as if aided by our joyous cheers to go on and do his holy work of shining light on all creation and making everything jump up and live again – at least for one more day.

I have since marked this ritual occasion as my baptism into a very different awareness of the meaning of the word 'sacred'. 'Animism' nowhere near captures the generative vitality of the kind of experience I went through in that moment of communal honouring and praising of this Mysterious Star Being we, modernized humans, so mundanely call 'the sun'. I had heard of native folk speak about each morning as a new day, that just because 'the sun' has been rising without fail for aeons does not mean it is obligated to continue doing so without the co-labouring of two-legged peoples like them – through their cheering praise, along with that of all other beings – in the wresting of a new sun each day out of the jaws of oblivion. They understand that this is what it means to be in a reciprocal and participatory relationship with the living world. As Don Trent Jacobs (Four Arrows) and Darcia Narvaez affirm, referencing Steve Langdon's writing on the Tlingit people's way of being: 'reciprocal sensations, not "seeing", are how Tlingit understand humanity's place in the universe' (2022, p. 3). In other words, to live among only sentient beings (be they a body of water, a tree, an animal, an insect, a whole forest, a cloud formation, a thunder being, etc.) is to carry awareness of this active, ongoing, reciprocal and participatory multi-species collaboration in a world of multiple (and multitudinous) subjectivities. Contrary to modern understanding, humans are not the exclusive seers and knowers (subject agents) of the world but equally 'objects' for other sentient beings' seeing and knowing, and the invitation is for us to enter into a participatory collaboration and mutually honouring relationship with our other kin as, together, we join in the ongoing remaking of the world each day.

Ritual in the Key of Colonial Subjection

I did not grow up with any of this sensibility, although I suspect it has always been present, simmering (and shimmering) just below the surface of my colonized spiritual formation. I grew up Methodist Protestant – an anomaly in a predominantly Roman Catholic country such as the Philippines. My father had been one of the early converts of the American missionaries who served as part of the US' civilian (and civilizing) 'army', along with the Thomasite educators and Peace Corps Volunteers, at the turn of the twentieth century when the Philippines was summarily seized and taken over as America's territorial possession just at the point of its declaration of independence from over 300 years of Spanish rule.

While some of my peers who grew up Roman Catholic recount their experience of church as one filled with sensate memories – the smell of incense, the tinkling of bells, the sunlight streaming through stained glass windows, the sung/chanted eucharistic performance, the visual surround of saintly statues and others – church ritual for me evoked no such nostalgia. Sunday worship, for the most part, was a chore – boring, to say the least. Stripped of all sensual evocations and ritual embellishments, our idolatry-averse local Methodist church had only an empty wooden cross adorning the front wall and a massive communion table for an altar with a vase of flowers at the centre and candles on either side. Such visual (as well as auditory) austerity gave church worship almost an ascetic quality with little to engage one's attention. So sitting out front in the choir loft each Sunday morning awaiting our turn in the programme to perform our choral number, I confess that my time was mostly spent scanning the pews for entertainment, such as catching the coiffured older women in the second or third row trying on each other's shoes, or those nodding off to sleep or otherwise having their eyes closed in seeming deep contemplation (never knowing which was which at any given moment). The congregational singing (of mostly Methodist English-language hymns) was not that much help either; only the pastoral prayer offered some reprieve and was my favourite moment in that it was my chance to sneak a little naptime unnoticed.

Becoming born-again in my first year in college did motivate me to try to put some heart into my worship attendance, believing that simply going through the motions was a disgrace and rude to the 'One' I purported to love and adore. But I quickly learned that disciplining the will, even when motivated, was tougher than I thought it would be. No matter my resolve, Sunday mornings remained dispiriting, failing to stir up either fervour or passion. Could it perhaps just have been the foreignness of the idiom, I wondered? Indeed, some of the nativizing churches in the city (experimenting with song compositions and sermons in colloquial Tagalog) did appear more enlivening (at least the ones I had the chance to visit on occasion), although I'm not sure now if 'enlivening' is the right word or whether they were, more accurately, (merely) 'entertaining'.

Breaking Free

Today, I count myself a decolonizing and indigenizing Filipina, reckoning with a history of having been raised as a pastor's kid (yes, my father became a Methodist minister later in life), having been run through the Inter-Varsity Christian Fellowship in college (where I had my born-again conversion experience), becoming an ardent evangelist to the intelligentsia in my post-graduate/university years, and, for the longest time, vocationally aspiring to become a full-time Christian missionary. That is, until my surprise hailing onto an altogether different path. That most unexpected detour came via my first-time encounter with the world of our Indigenous peoples – a story now part of all my autobiographical accounting of my subject positioning and spiritual journeying (cf. Mendoza, 2006). The truth is, indigenous difference did not really start out as an epistemological throwdown to my prior belief as a Christian, at least not initially, that is. If C. S. Lewis (1955) writes of his own Christian conversion as one of being 'surprised by joy', mine (this second time around) perhaps can be summed up pithily as 'stunned by beauty'.

The hailing first happened bodily, in a graduate seminar in the humanities taught by an esteemed ethnomusicology professor who brought into the classroom the diverse works of art of our ethnolinguistic communities and what such works expressed in terms of a different way of being in the world (e.g., their weaving designs, basketry, architecture, songs, dances, epic chants, mythic stories and so on). As I wrote elsewhere:

> I was stunned! Nothing prepared me for the power of that encounter with wild, untamed beauty: complex geometric designs that mathematicians noted could not have been wilfully conceived by the rational mind, mellifluous melodies able to call up grief out of all its hidden places, polyphonic sounds and rhythms coming from native instruments that not only sounded but looked utterly beautiful, dances as diverse as their ecologies of origination, intricate architectural structures that used not a single nail to bind parts together and so on, and all of these creations of beauty ritually sourced, many given in dreams, with materials taken from the wild only with the accompanying respect, honouring, and asking for permission, and, always, in service of beauty. (Mendoza, 2018, p. 90)

My response was visceral:

> Walking out of every class [session], I found myself bawling my heart out, not knowing what it was that hit me from all the innocent descriptions of our peoples' indigenous works of art (Mendoza, 2020).

It took me years to peel back the layers of meaning of that moment of encounter. Most consequentially, it facilitated in the most dramatic way a long hoped-for resolution of a long-standing psychic dis-ease, one that had been the bane of my existence for as far back as I could remember. That psychic dis-ease had to do with the feeling of being constantly surveilled, weighed and found wanting, one that puzzlingly persisted even through my years of ardent Christian missionizing (and preaching of God's unconditional love). It was not until much later that I began to understand that the neurotic self-judgement was not just my own, but part of a larger phenomenon suffered invariably by a people under conditions of colonial oppression. One theorization of the phenomenon uses the term 'epistemic violence' (Spivak, 2010) – the internalization of empire's surveilling gaze that I would note issues in the broader syndrome of colonial narcissism, the result, in Fanon's words, of colonialism's deracinating dynamic. To wit:

> Colonialism is not satisfied merely with holding a people in its grip and emptying the native's brain of all form and content. By a kind of perverted logic, it turns to the past of the oppressed people, and distorts, disfigures, and destroys it. (Fanon, 1963, p. 210)

We have a phrase in Tagalog, *ang Pilipinong nawawala sa sarili* ('the Filipino lost to herself'), that precisely names the condition – a psychic malaise particularly evident among the *akulturadong grupo*, the acculturated (educated) elite most keenly attuned to the imposed colonial idiom. Such inductees (to colonial culture) found themselves in thrall to a surveilling gaze unremittingly positioning them as 'other' – suspect in worth, less than human in bearing, and thereby condemned to labour ceaselessly to satisfy an elusive 'standard'. As W. E. B. Du Bois poignantly described the African American version of this kind of debilitating imposition half a world away, it is a 'peculiar sensation', a feeling, 'of always looking at one's self through the eyes of others, of measuring one's soul by the tape of a world that looks on in amused contempt and pity' (1961, p. 16).

In my case, the affliction took the form of morbid self-introspection – a feeling of never being enough. It did not matter that none of my teachers and mentors would have agreed with the self-deprecating assessment, the self-preoccupation persisted stubbornly. Given that my vibrant outward persona (capable, bright, curious, intelligent, etc.) gave no inkling whatsoever of the morass of failure roiling within, the jarring disconnect only added inauthenticity to the already interminable affliction. As articulated elsewhere, I would retrospectively describe the anatomy of that psychic malaise, thus:

> Given my Protestant upbringing, my journey began with a rationalistic moralism that effectively individualized the colonial malaise, reduced it to an inherent weakness of character, and encouraged a profound internalization of blame (as well as shame). The result was an inability to function unself-consciously, always feeling like one was constantly under surveillance. The self-preoccupation that followed became a mode of survival in a regime that perpetually called into question one's whole existence (I learned later that the syndrome had a name: *colonial narcissism*). (Mendoza, 2010, p. 101)

Stretched by Immensity

Before that classroom epiphany, none of the cognitive analysis uncovering much of the elided history of US colonization of my country could wrest me from the shackles of my ongoing psychic self-negation. Recruitment to the nationalist vision (offering a scathing critique of the attempted supplantation of an alien culture for our own) did foster righteous anger and indignation but stopped short of the needed psychic relief and release. Only that first-time encounter with that other world (of the indigenous) finally catalysed a breakthrough, with the accompanying heaves of emotion signalling homecoming relief after what seemed like a lifetime of wandering lostness.

How to make sense of the liberating power of that encounter with the world of our indigenous kin (now no longer just in the classroom but in many, many subsequent face-to-face encounters)? Probing more deeply, what I came to understand is that something else lay at the root of the colonial violation. This is the oft-unnamed civilizational imperative of domestication needing to tame all that is 'wild' – be it 'wild lands' ('jungles', uncultivated lands) or 'wild tribes' ('savage' peoples) – anything deemed standing in the way of the project of human conquest of the world otherwise referred to as 'progress'. As a most recent *New York Times* article (on Brazil finding the last survivors of an Amazon tribe) notes wryly, 'For centuries, Indigenous people were seen as obstacles to progress and slaughtered across the world' (Nicas and Andreoni, 2023). (Interestingly the term used for it is *'reducción'* – literally, to reduce the wildness in 'savage' peoples and places by subjecting them to the refining process of 'civilization'.) Topmost in the list of such 'obstacles to progress' then are 'uncivilized' folk that have yet to awaken to the 'benefits' of cultivation and permanent settlements, city-state governments, organized religion, standing armies, and the virtues of private ownership, pursuit of material wealth, prioritization of the rational (over feeling and intuition) and of the individual (over communal bonds). And most importantly, the subjugation and conquest of the natural world and its recasting from a most sacred relation to that of a (mere) minion, an object meant to serve exclusively human ends. For that civilizing project to be achieved, there had to be, first of all, a severing of native people's bond with the living earth and the abandonment of their land-based ways of living, given that living on the land was deemed no better than living like animals! This imperative, according to theologian Willie James Jennings, constitutes the deepest (epistemic) distortion of our time: the 'removal of the earth, the ground, spaces, and places' as 'living organizers of identity and as facilitators of identity' (2010, p. 39).

On the other hand, to get at the other end of the epiphanic configuration, what I realised I was encountering in those indigenous works of art is precisely the reverberations from the wild, channelled by untamed, unconquered peoples that still carried a measure of intactness despite the colonial assault (no surprise that these were also the farthest removed from the long reach of modern schooling and Christian missionization). This is what broke me open in such a visceral way – what hit my senses was not just human creative ingenuity but the vibrancy, potency and magnificence of the wild herself. The designs, colours and manner of execution were not just human-made, but the embodied response of a people still caught in the thrall of a magnificence whose fierceness and majesty they cannot help mirroring and honouring by becoming fierce and beautiful themselves, and this, not just in their ritual and artistic creations, but in their whole way of life.

And that magnificence is one that hails them in multiple and various ways – through trance, dreams, plant- and animal-speak, and other visionary seeing. When queried, they would say, 'The designs were given to us in dreams', in the case of the T'boli dream weavers, or 'We see a white louse moving over the cloth, guiding our needle and pointing to us where the next stitch should go', in the case of the Manobo master weavers in their tradition of ancient embroidery called *suyam*.

That – I realized – was what was showing up in those indigenous works of art: an aesthetic sensibility quite unlike more domesticated versions of 'creativity' (In one shamanic ritual ceremony I witnessed, one could tell the precise moment when human skill in dancing suddenly gave way to the stunning, stylized and mesmerizing movements of a body going into spirit trance. Such ritual performances channelled an ethos that prioritized the natural world as human beings' most important Other, and the care and honouring of Her, their most sacred obligation.) And when a people live in such an economy of a sacred relation with the Holy in Nature, it invariably shapes their psyche, their whole cultural way of being, as well as the specific forms of their ritual norms and ceremonial practices. Hailed daily by the wild array of species beings (both seen and unseen) and the rhythms of the seasons in their local ecologies, their bodily and psychic comportment invariably syncs up with and is shaped by such biodiverse and lavish vibrancies. Even just paying attention to colour preferences hints at the proclivity as explored by the renowned anthropologist Michael Taussig (2003). Partially quoting the German poet Goethe, who, exposed to reports from the colonial theatre in the nineteenth century, had himself become exercised by the awareness, Taussig remarks:

> 'Men [and I would add, women] in a state of nature ... uncivilized nations and children, have a great fondness for colours in their utmost brightness.' The same applied to 'uneducated people and southern Europeans, especially the women with their bright-colored bodices and ribbons'... On the other hand, people of refinement had a disinclination to colors, women wearing white, the men, black. And not only in dress. When it came to what Goethe called 'pathological colours', ... people of refinement avoid vivid colors in the objects around them and seem inclined to banish vivid colors from their presence altogether. (p. 3)

Likening the encounter to an uneasy encounter between two presences, Taussig adds:

> It is as if there are two presences glowering at each other, shifting uncomfortably from one foot to the other. It is as much a body thing, a presence thing ... One 'presence' is people of refinement. The other is vivid color. (2003, p. 3)

Second Initiation

It was the sixth morning of a ten-day session at a school my husband and I attend, taught by a beloved Tz'utujil Mayan-trained indigenous teacher. The day before, I had just received the final denial letter from my university provost rejecting my full professor promotion appeal following a contentious, racially configured battle focused on the matter of split student evaluations in my case (typical of classes covering politically charged and triggering subjects, especially those taught by faculty women of colour).[1] I had hoped that the university committee's near-unanimous vote endorsing my well-substantiated appeal (based, among others, on the vast literature naming the impact of race and gender on student perceptions and the very problematic nature of student evaluations in general, along with the countless meetings my faculty advocate and I had initiated to educate the administration on institutional racism) would have persuaded the provost, but receiving the provost's final decision via email felt like being shot by an enemy's arrow.

That evening, half of my head broke out in lesions (what would later be diagnosed as shingles at my doctor's office, my first time ever to experience such a disease). Sitting that next morning in front as hubby and I were wont to do in the big adobe hall where our sessions were held, we would see our teacher looking my way as he stepped onto the stage and energetically sense something going on with me. He inquires, 'What's wrong'? I say a bit about what has been going on with me physically, but hubby Jim also explains to him that I have been dealing with a racial battle in my institution. He then addresses both of us and says, 'You know I don't do personal healing – but if you want, I will give you a ritual to do. Know that whatever healing there is to be had comes only from the Wild'. Knowing we lived in Waawiyatanong (where the river bends, aka Detroit), he promises to send us instructions and implements for a ceremony to do – at the Detroit River.

A few days after we get home at the end of the ten-day school, sure enough, a package comes in through the mail from our teacher. Inside were some ritual paraphernalia, along with 15 pages of handwritten directions on a yellow pad and an assignment to procure the other required materials from the wild (which I will not detail here out of respect for the ritual's confidentiality). We follow the instructions faithfully, as best we understood them – going to the Detroit River to make the offering. We set up a little altar in our dining room corner where we committed to 'feeding' nightly the holy beings now in residence in our home with a little cornmeal and our prayers.

As we do this nightly ritual, something begins to happen. I notice my attention subtly shifting. No longer am I so preoccupied with the intensity of the fight I have been in – my anger at the provost's cowardice in not having the courage to do the right thing (even after his own commissioned Task Force for the Evaluation of Teaching Effectiveness came out with the exact same findings as I had argued for all along in regard to race and gender being salient factors), as well as my outrage at my white department colleagues' resistance to facing honestly the race question in their own evaluation of my case. Instead the ritual actions and words redirect my focus night by night towards a much bigger and more consequential co-sufferer of abuse: the Detroit River with all the decades of toxic dumping of sewage and pollutants her waters have endured, the endangerment of fish and wildlife habitat and destruction of her shoreline wetlands, along with the equally dire fate of the other nature beings (some of whom were ritually represented in tokens of their lives and now sat on our altar). No longer was my concern simply my own unjust situation. The quite real outrage and grief I was bearing now seemed minuscule and not so heavy compared to the much bigger grief and violation of all these magnificent nature beings at the hands of our kind.

That in itself would have been wonder enough, but even more miraculous and magical (I cannot think of better words) was what started happening in my face-to-face interactions with the white colleagues that had earlier voted me down (and thus provided fodder for the provost's later verdict) – at department meetings, at social functions and events, in the hallways. The truth is, anyone who has heard of my saga could not help asking how in the world I could continue to work in such a hostile environment. Yet, it did not take long – after beginning this little nightly ceremony – before I began to feel I was no longer this oppressed, invalidated minority faculty who had fought the good fight but lost. Instead, walking into those spaces, I now felt both very human but also very 'big' – a 'self' now buoyed by this entourage of wild presences, who, though silent and invisible, were very much present and animate in my own bearing and spirit. It was like having a secret potion or an unseen friend on my arm. I suddenly understood an epic figure we had encountered in one of the readings with our teacher of the epic poem 'Sunjata', which tells the story of the hero Sundiata Keita, the founder of the Mali Empire. The poem is an oral tradition of the Malinke people, going back to the thirteenth century, and of which there is no single or authoritative version. The epic figure in the poem is the medicine man Fakoli, who, though very short in stature, would suddenly inflate into a huge and invincible presence unaccountably filling up an entire room whenever he was decked out in his special amulet-hat. What was that funny talisman composed of?

> With skulls of birds
> Three hundred three and thirty
> Hanging from his helmet ...
> With the skulls of lions
> Three hundred three and thirty
> (Karp and Bird, 1980, p. 19)

My hubby, intimately alongside, witnesses the transformation and marvels and cries. We cry together – in deep gratitude and joy. Later, invited by the dean and provost to reapply, I do so, albeit no longer as invested in the outcome. The summer before my reapplication, I receive an unexpected public letter of apology from a senior colleague confessing (in so many words) his error in voting me down the first time and submitting the letter for inclusion in my dossier. I could only imagine him championing me during the repeat deliberations. The dean had also issued a directive to all departments to abide by and implement the findings of the provost task force around race and gender in all tenure and promotion deliberations. Tellingly, the department verdict this time around was *unanimously* in favour, ironically voting the exact opposite as their first vote on the *exact same record* I had before.

In the end, the promotion itself was just icing on the cake. The real deal is far more magnificent and consequential. And it is the awareness that life is not about me – about this small self, hankering after what it thinks is its due – but about this bigger, much grander reality whose immense generosity has rarely, in more modern understanding, been met with commensurate response (of gratitude, respect and honouring) from my kind. The entire process of being ritually initiated into this other way of seeing had been a profound gift to me, a remarkable exercise in being able to set aside my own 'little self' (focus) in deference to this big suffering – and its big wisdom and ancient resilience that is elder and teacher for us all.

Epilogue/Reflections

I have not always understood why indigenous peoples everywhere are big on ritual, ritual of all kinds – praising, grieving, celebration, asking for permission and, most ubiquitous of all, rituals of 'feeding' – actually *feeding* the holy wild. The language is that of courtship and utmost courtesy – eloquent, grandiose, replete with metaphor, excessive and exuberant. It doesn't matter how simple the material wherewithal is, no effort is spared in making the ritual offering (to the gods and deities and 'spirit personas' of the holy wild), unstinting in ornateness, lavishness, elegance, beauty and care. The understanding is that such is the only response worthy of the grand mystery we call by various names, singular or plural or summary (Creator, God, Mother Earth, Divine Beings, Wild Holies, the Universe, etc.). In the words of our teacher, Martín Prechtel (1998), speaking of how it was among the Tzutujil Mayans before their village got decimated during the Guatemalan civil war:

> Our very ability to carve, bend, and shape [the earth] should be used to feed and give gifts to what fed us from the other world. After all, they could kill us in a flash – why didn't they? Because the Gods were addicted to our beauty like an alcoholic to a delicious wine. They loved our poetry, our offering shrines, our beautiful clothing, the complex chirping banter of our village streets, and especially the expansive combination of all our abilities into ritual offerings and ceremonies. The Gods perceived us as delicious fruit. They loved our excesses as long as they were beautiful and the Gods got to eat a lot of them. (pp. 199–200)

The ritual lavishness, however, besides serving as the conduit for an ongoing honouring relationship with the natural world, also serves an important ecological function, namely, the setting of limits to human taking and hubris. Among our indigenous communities in the Philippines, for instance, I have witnessed healers not simply harvesting willy-nilly from identified medicinal plants, but singing and courting the mother plant, requesting her to lower her medicine (e.g. 'Mother Sambong [or whatever the name of the plant is], if you please, there is this sick child whose distraught mother has been sitting in despair back in the village ...'). Among the Manobo marshland community in the South, the visit of an outsider does not proceed without a divinatory ritual asking for permission, the lavish ceremonial offerings to the Crocodile gods (deemed to be the guardians of the waters) meant to signal good intention and a promise of courtesy and respect to all the water beings in the place. Similarly, at one Philippine conference on the relevance of indigenous values in a time of globalization many years ago, I had an opportunity to watch a documentary presentation on a similar indigenous practice in northern Japan – in this case, an ancient Ainu bear ceremony where the taking of a bear to feed the village was accompanied by a carefully orchestrated ceremony, one requiring an arduous snowy dawn trek outside the village in the dead of winter, the building of a beautifully crafted ceremonial house for the bear-king about to be sacrificed, the ceremonial placing of the severed head on a pole and its decking out with all manner of ornamentation, and, finally, the heaping of praise and gratitude upon the bear-god now sent to the spirit world to keep watch over the people. I recall exclaiming even then, before I had the sort of understanding I have today, 'No wonder they can only do this (i.e., kill a bear) on occasion! It is so costly ceremonially!' And while we may balk at what we might deem as a 'cruel animal sacrifice', should we not balk even more at the terror of our modern habits of killing – for sport, or in factory farming, without any thought of honouring the lives of our sentient kin before they are turned into fodder for the industrial food machine?

There is nothing efficient or simply utilitarian in this indigenous way of living. Why not simply take when the 'resource' is there simply for the taking? Among the Tzutujil Mayans, Martín Prechtel (2001) speaks of the concept of 'original debt' owed by each of us to the natural world for bringing us to existence given that it takes the life of other beings to bring us to life and to keep us alive (i.e., we literally live off the substance of other living beings whose lives we take and consume in the very act of eating). And our sacred obligation then is to do all we can to give back in commensurate measure. But we owe not only for the food we eat, but for everything else we take out of the earth's body for our inventions. Prechtel (2001) explains in this regard:

> A knife, for instance, is a very minimal, almost primitive tool to people in a modern industrial society. But for the Mayan people, the spiritual debt that must be paid for the creation of such a tool is great. To start with, the person who is going to make the knife has to build a fire hot enough to produce coals. To pay for that, he's got to give a sacrificial gift to the fuel, to the fire ...
>
> Once the fire is hot enough, the knife maker must smelt the iron ore out of the rock ... A ritual gift equal to the amount that was removed

from the other world has to be put back to make up for the wound caused to the divine.

... So, just to get the iron, the shaman has to pay for the ore, the fire, the wind, and so on – not in dollars and cents, but in ritual activity equal to what's been given ... There is a deity to be fed for each part of the procedure. When the knife is finished, it is called the 'tooth of earth'. It will cut wood, meat, and plants. But if the necessary sacrifices have been ignored in the name of rationalism, literalism, and human superiority, it will cut humans instead.

This, Prechtel concludes (2001), makes something (seemingly) as simple as a knife 'enormously "expensive"' ritually, which is why intact indigenous cultures deliberately refrain from inventions requiring heavy material extraction (such as backhoes and shopping malls), not because they cannot but to avoid unnecessary indebtedness. It is also why, I would surmise, that those that have gone that route, such as the imperialised cultures of the Aztecs, Incas and the Mayans, but who still retained memory of the original covenant with the earth (of not taking anything without giving something back of commensurate value) typically end up resorting to human sacrifice (a practice modern civilization has exponentially increased in initiatives such as recurrent genocides, enslavements, and now ecocide, absent any ritual recognition).

What would it mean to make our way back to this sacred relationship with the earth? To enact in ritual (both grandiose and in mundane everyday life) the understanding that we are inextricably tangled in a web of interdependent relationships from which there is no separate 'I' apart from the undulating, interweaving dance of bodies, large and small, wondrous and ordinary, that make up the living world? Today, in our collapsing crisis-driven world, I see no other silver lining but this – the return to this other way of being in the world. To fall in love and bow the head once more before this terrible magnificence that is not just benignly benevolent but perfectly capable of taking us out – artificial intelligence and other engineering boasts notwithstanding. The self-centring that has been the glory and legacy of the Enlightenment ideal of the sovereign, autonomous 'self' (now ratcheted into a culture of narcissism through social media's addictive algorithms) cannot be overcome despite having now reached its end-logic without a vision far grander, more wondrous and compelling than the illusory beast (of the imperial 'I') that has claimed dominion over all our seeing until now, at least for us modernized humans. But that alternative vision has always been here, has not been snuffed out, is speaking now, summoning us.

And its witnesses – from the Kogi of the Sierra Nevada mountains to the Aytas of Luzon, from the Sami of the Arctic Circle to the Mapuche of Chile – are eagerly calling us home. Will we heed them?

Note

1 As these two following quotes attest:

The bad news is that teachers who present minority history and literature – or similar topics – almost uniformly face varying degrees of hostility, anger, and rejection: reactions unlike anything they have faced before (Trzyna and Abbott, 1991, p. 1).

Hostility is to be expected in race-related courses. Behind each student's evaluation of such courses is the unacknowledged emotional turmoil that he or she has undergone (TuSmith, 2002, p. 113).

References

Du Bois, W. E. B., 1961, *The Souls of Black Folk*, New York: Fawcett.
Fanon, Frantz, 1963, *The Wretched of the Earth*, New York: Grove Press.
Jennings, W. J., 2010, *The Christian Imagination: Theology and the Origins of Race*. New Haven, CT, and London: Yale University Press.
Karp, Ivan and Charles S. Bird, eds, 1980, *Explorations in African Systems of Thought*, Bloomington: Indiana University Press.
Lewis, C. S., 1955, *Surprised by Joy: The Shape of My Early Life*, UK: Geoffrey Bles.
Mendoza, S. L., 2006, 'Tears in the Archive: Creating Memory to Survive and Contest Empire', in R. Lustig and J. Koester, eds, *Among US: Essays on Identity, Belonging, and Intercultural Competence*, pp. 233–45, Boston: Pearson.
Mendoza, S. L., 2020, 'On Filipinos and the Question of the Indigenous', *OneDown Media*, https://onedown.media/read/on-filipinos-and-the-question-of-the-indigenous (accessed 15.1.2025).
Mendoza, S. L., forthcoming 2024, 'Liberation at the Cusp of Apocalypse: A Small Move from Making More to Making Beauty', in *Stirring Up Liberation Theologies: A Call for Release*, ed. J. Havea, London: SCM Press.
Mendoza, S. L., 2010, 'Reflections on "Bridging Paradigms: How Not to Throw out the Baby of Collective Representation with the Functionalist Bathwater in Critical Intercultural Communication', in *The Handbook of Critical Intercultural Communication*, ed. T. K. Nakayama & R. T. Halualani, pp. 98–111, Oxford: Blackwell Publishing.
Mendoza, S. L., 2018, 'Babaylan Healing and Indigenous "Religion" at the Postcolonial Crossroads: Learning from Our Deep History as the Planet Grows Apocalyptic', in *Just Faith: Glocal Responses to Planetary Urbanization*, ed. S. Debeer, pp. 72–102, Durbanville, Cape Town: South Africa: AOSIS Publishing.

Nicas, J., and M. Andreoni, 2023, 'Brazil Found the Last Survivors of an Amazon Tribe. Now What?' https://www.nytimes.com/2023/08/19/world/americas/brazil-amazon-tribe-piripkura.html?campaign_id=9&emc=edit_nn_20230820&instance_id=100470&nl=the-morning&regi_id=46511526&segment_id=142462&te=1&user_id=1493f9e61d140e1b3ba3ef81ab9c45a3 (accessed 15.1.2025).

Prechtel, Martín, 1998, *Secrets of the Talking Jaguar: Memoirs from the Living Heart of a Mayan Village*, New York: Jeremy P. Tarcher.

Prechtel, Martín, 2001, 'Saving the Indigenous Soul', *The Sun*, https://www.thesunmagazine.org/articles/23617-saving-the-indigenous-soul (accessed 15.1.2025).

Spivak, Gayatri Chakravorty, 2010, '"Can the Subaltern Speak?" Revised Edition, from the "History" Chapter of Critique of Postcolonial Reason', in R. C. Morris, ed., *Can the Subaltern Speak?: Reflections on the History of an Idea*, pp. 21–78, New York: Columbia University Press.

Taussig, Michael, 2009, *What Color Is the Sacred?* Chicago: University of Chicago Press.

Topa, Wahinkpe and Narvaez, Darcia, 2022, *Restoring the Kinship Worldview: Indigenous Voices Introduce 28 Precepts for Rebalancing Life on Planet Earth*, Berkeley: North Atlantic Books.

Trzyna, Thomas, and Martin Abbott, 1991, 'Grieving in the Ethnic Literature Classroom', *College Literature* 18(3), pp. 1–14, http://www.jstor.org/stable/25111914 (accessed 15.1.2025).

TuSmith, Bonnie, 2002, 'Out on a Limb: Race and the Evaluation of Frontline Teaching', in B. TuSmith and M. T. Reddy, eds, *Race in the College Classroom: Pedagogy and Politics*, pp. 112–25, New Brunswick: Rutgers University Press.

Index of Names and Subjects

African spiritualities 59–77, 144–5
Afrofuturism 75n11
agency 60–1
agricultural festivals 42–3
Althusser, Louis 5
ancestral rituals 59–77
animism 62
Antivisita 11, 115–33
apartheid 84, 86–7, 92n1
Asad, Talal 3
Assemblies of God 80–1
Atakora, Afia 148

beauty 209
Bell, Catherine 4, 5, 172, 178, 179
Benjamin, Walter 192
Bhabha, Homi 10, 96
Bispos dos Santos, Antônio 195–6
Black feminism 135–9
Black theology 83–5
bricolage 62, 72n6
Brussels, African spiritualities in 59–77
bwiti religion 62

Camissa spirituality 80–1, 83, 85
candles 201
capitalism 187, 191–5
caste 46–8

celibacy 27
censorship 179–82
Chee Soon Juan 176–7
Chia Thye Poh 177–8
choruses 84–5
civil disobedience 176–7
climate chaos 187–202
colonial narcissism 211
colonialism 8–10, 187–202, 207, 210
conjuration 11–12, 135–49
conscientization 181
Contextual Bible Study 153–66
Cunsolo, Ashlee 198

dance 82, 85, 86–90, 212–13
  among Rarámuri in Mexico 95–6, 100–2, 104, 109–10
Davis, Angela 148–9
Derrida, Jacques 11
disappearance, in Latin America 119–33
Douglass, Frederick 146–8
dreams 212
dress codes 32–3, 48–9, 55n2, n3
Du Bois, W. E. G. 210
Dulucq, Sophie 59
Dupin, Claude-Marie 65

Earth, relationship with 14–17, 212, 217, 219

Easter 109
  see also Holy Week
eco-politics 196–7
Eliade, Mircea 141
embodiment 111
empire, and ritual 1, 171–2, 178–9, 182
Engelbrecht, Inge 84, 87

Fanon, Franz 210
Farneth, Molly 171, 173
feasting 102–3
feminist theology 33–4
food code 46–7
fossil fuels 189
Foucault, Michel 67, 170
Freire, Paulo 181

gender identity 5
George, Cherian 172–3, 177, 182
ghosts 120–1
Glaude, Eddie S. Jr 137
global warming 188–9
grief
  and colonialism 191, 197–9
  over ecological loss 200–1
Gutiérrez, Gustavo 1

harvest festivals 55n1
Hawaii 187–8
healing 14, 148, 187, 193, 205–6, 214
Hnuni, R. L. 33–4
Holy Week 103–9
Hucks, Tracey 144–5

inculturation 96–7
India 39–55
indigenous peoples 205–20

intersectionality 40, 53–4

Jennings, Willie James 212
Jézégou, Annie 71, 74n5
joy, in song and dance 87, 88–9

Kaaps language 82
Kairos Document 12
Katz, Cindi 59–60
Kemitism 62, 64–5, 69–70
Khoo Kah Siang, Francis 174–6
Kittredge, Cynthia Briggs 161–3
Klein, Naomi 188
Koh, Tommy 182
Kristeva, Julia 200
Kwanzaa 72

land 195–201, 212
Latin America 115–33
Lee, Dorothy 163
LGBTQIA+ people 179–81
liberation 1, 50, 197–9
liberation theology 1–2, 115–19, 124
liturgy 153–66
Long, Charles H. 141
Lord's Prayer 164–5

Maisonneuve, Jean 65–6
Martinez, Doreen 188
Maui 187–8
Mbog, Kirafiky 60, 65-8, 71-2, 75n9
M'Buzé, Momi 63–4, 66, 72, 74, 75n9
menstruation 23–9
Mexico 95–111
mourning 197–9
Mwamba, Djehouty 63–5, 69–70, 71, 75n9

Nagaland 43–5
names 66
New Mexico 206–20
ngoma faith 85
normalization 67–8
Northeast India 39–55

orisha religion 62–3

Palay, Seelan 177–8
patriarchy 31–2, 45, 50
Paul
  on bodies 194
  on role of women 30
Pentecostalism 80–92
Philippines 206–8
pilgrimage, to the Sabarimala temple 22
Pink Dot 179–81
Pinn, Anthony B. 197
plants 200
pollution, personal 26–36
post-transplantation festivals 42–3
Prayer of Humble Access 161–4
Prechtel, Martin 217, 218–19
public theology 12
punishment, by government 170
purification rituals 27
purity, personal 26–36

racism 46, 48
Rarámuri people 96–111
reconciliation 43–5
religious virtuosos 63–5
resistance
  against government policies 178–9
  by the marginalized 155–6
  in Pentecostalism 86–92

Ricoeur, Paul 141
rights 173, 194
ritual 1–16
  of dispossession 195–202
  and identity 65–8
  indigenous 205–20
  product of grief 115–16, 133
  as resistance 13, 124–6, 171–4
  as response 205
  womanist perspective 135–49
Ruether, Rosemary Radford 33

Sabarimala temple 21–3
Safatle, Vladimir 198
Singapore 13, 170–83
singing 48, 84–5, 88
Smith, Mick 198
solidarity, through song and dance 87–92
South Africa, Pentecostals in 80–92
spectrality 11, 115–33
Steart, Dianne M. 145
sun ceremony 206–7

taboos 41–2, 52
Taussig, Michael 213
testimony 90–1
Theology of the People 115–19
third space 96
transnationality 68–70
Turner, Victor 172

Uganda 43
Ujamaa Centre 153–66

Vatican II 117
violence, against oppression 120
Vodou religion 62, 137, 144

Walker, Alice 148–9
Walker, Bridget 33–4
Weber, Max 63–4, 75n10
Wham, Jolovan 178–9
witnesses 139–41
womanism 139, 148

women
 discrimination against 21–37, 45–6, 50–4
 leadership roles 30–1, 36–7
 role in rituals 50–1
 sexuality 26–7, 32